S0-BNE-835

Karoliina
Finland

Franzi
Germany

Kate
Russia

Wanning
China

Dasha
Ukraine

Tatiana
Kazakhstan

Natsupho
Japan

Miska
Slovakia

Angela
China

Hadil
Egypt

Naz
Turkey

Lavanya
India

Dieu
Vietnam

Shani
Israel

Meera
United Arab
Emerites

Priscilla
Kenya

Philomena
Kenya

Kiely
New Zealand

HYLAS
PUBLISHING

Publisher: Sean Moore

Creative Director and
Queen of Canada: Karen Prince

Art Director: Gus Yoo

Editorial Director: Gail Greiner

Designer: Rachel Maloney

Designer: Sarah Postle

Designer: Shamona Stokes

Assistant Editor: Hannah Choi

Assistant Editor: Angda Goel

Proofreader: Ginger Skinner

not pictured: Proofreader Andrea Johnson

Hylas Publishing

First Published in 2004 by Hylas Publishing
129 Main Street, Irvington, New York, 10533

www.hylaspublishing.com

Copyright © Hylas Publishing 2004
 e author has been asserted.

 published in 2004
     5 4 3 2 1

All rights reserved under International and pan-American
Copyright Conventions. No part of this publication may be
reproduced, stored in a retrieval system, or transmitted in
any form or by any means, electronic, mechanical, photo-
copying, recording or otherwise, without the prior written
permission of the copyright owner.

Set in Insignia, Frutiger, Bembo, and Adobe Garamond

Printed at MILANOSTAMPA/AGG
Distributed by National Book Network

Girl, 13
by Starla Griffin

To Natalie,
Enjoy!
Best,
Starla Griffin

PORTER COUNTY LIBRARY

Valparaiso Public Library
103 Jefferson Street
Valparaiso, IN 46383

YA NF 305.2352 GRI   VAL
Griffin, Starla.
Girl, 13 : Global snapshot of
33410011153949

HYLAS
PUBLISHING

Contents

Introduction

Have you ever wondered what your life would be like if you had been born in another country? Things would certainly be different. You might speak a different language, have a different religion, wear different clothes, and eat different food. You might celebrate different holidays, or live in a different kind of house. You might even learn different subjects in school. But deep down inside, would any of this change who you are now? Would you still have the same personality, the same interests, and the same dreams?

If you sat down in a room with 40 other girls your age, all born in different countries, and (using your imagination just a little more) if you could talk to one another in one common language, what would happen in the room? Would you have anything to talk about? Would you like the same books, the same foods, the same movies and celebrities? Could you compare dreams and trade funny stories? Would you be able to relate to all the other girls or would some of them be just too different from you?

Well, you may be surprised to know that for the first time ever, a combination of technological innovations and political changes have made it possible for you to connect and communicate with people from all over the world. Just think: you are the first generation to grow up after the Cold War—when your parents grew up with half of the world being off-limits to the other half! You are the first to grow up with the Internet, e-mail, and cellular phones (After all, these technologies only have become widely available during your lifetime!). And you are the first to grow up with Girl, 13! Quite simply, it would have been impossible to create this book if these amazing changes had not occurred.

As you turn the pages of this book, you will have the unique opportunity to see for yourself just how different or similar you are to girls your age growing up in places like China, Russia, Spain, Egypt, or Saudi Arabia. And you don't have to worry about being unable to read Chinese, Russian, Spanish, or Arabic because we have translated everything into English for you. So you are free from the language barriers that you would normally face if you met any one of these girls in person. What better way to understand the world and to learn about your unique generation!

You will meet girls like Katia from Bulgaria, Kiely from New Zealand, Philomena from Kenya, and many others eager to share their lives with you! Compare your life with theirs, and see if there are any similarities. But don't worry; this is not a classroom! This is a book full of 13-year-old girls!

The best part of Girl, 13 is that at the back of this book (go ahead, you can flip to the back), you too can become a Girl, 13 participant! You have a chance to answer the same questions each of the girls in this book answered and to include photographs of yourself, your family, and your home. This way you can create your

About Me

translated from Bulgarian

My name is Ekaterina Tsvetanova. I was born in our capital, Sofia, on the 10th of November. I live in a big family house, which belongs to my grandmother and great-grandmother. My father, Tsvetan, my mother, Vania, and I live together with my grandmothers in Belovo, a small town situated in the Plovdiv region of the little, but ancient country Bulgaria, which is on one of the oldest continents, Europe.

For my 13 years of age I am too short, as I dislike eating. I have a pretty face, a little nose, brown expressive eyes, and the most attractive smile, according to my mother's words. My hair is brown and is long to my lower back, which I find very irritating, especially in the morning when I am in a hurry to go to school. However, my mother does not want me to cut it due to my concerts and television appearances.

This year I am in year seven in school. I will need a lot more time to prepare my school lessons because at the end of this academic year there will be tests. Aside from my school tests, I must also take other tests for special schools in the country, which I hope to attend in order to further my professional development.

Katia and her cat, Decomo.

My after-class activities are: on Mondays and Thursdays I attend music lessons where I prepare myself for my individual performances—concerts and competitions—and I prepare for my tests for the musical schools. On Wednesdays I attend modern ballet classes. This is my third year and I love to dance. On Fridays I attend a club called "Little Journalist," where every month we prepare an issue of the children's journal *The Merry Bell*.

At home I help my mother only if I have spare time, after which I prepare my homework. I like computer and television games and sometimes I play with friends on the Net. The Internet offers a lot of information and this is one of the reasons I dream of having my own computer.

But now this is only in the sphere of promises. In my spare time I read books and collect comics. I sometimes go for bike rides or skate with my friends.

Sometimes I attend rehearsals with a Sofia rock band,

Katia with her father, great-grandmother, grandmother, and mother.

which is called "Fa-Diez." I also sing at all the local concerts in my school and in my town. I visit concerts and sing when I am invited and also participate in a lot of TV shows and interviews. I have met all of our greatest Bulgarian singers and performers and have sung on the biggest and most prestigious stage in Bulgaria, Stage No. 1 in the National Palace of Culture.

Up to now I have taken part in 148 concerts. I have plenty of top prizes in national competitions and received the third place prize during an interregional competition this year. For the next one I will try harder and prepare better. I think I have the strength and the potential to strive for the grand prize.

Not long ago, one of our famous poets, Mikhail Belchev, wrote the text of a song for me to sing, and the composer, George Denkov,

"I have been singing since I can remember."

SCHOOL DAYS

Katia attends the local school for children living in Belovo and the surrounding villages. To get there, she walks past the goats and chickens to catch the 7:30 bus from the center of Belovo every morning. There are 17 students in Katia's class. Her classes are Mathematics, Geography, French, English, Art, Music, Gym, and Industrial Skills. Her favorite subjects are Geography and Biology. She has a 5-minute break in between each class and a 15-minute break after the fourth lesson. The children don't have lunch until they are home. Katia usually has one or two hours of homework.

will write the music to go with it. After that, when I have recorded it in the studio, the song will be released on all the radio and television stations and media in Bulgaria to hear and enjoy. I hope it will be a hit song and a lot of people will like it. That was, in short, about my successes and me.

I did not write anything about the climate of my country, about the amazing countryside that surrounds us, about the four seasons, every one of which has its own beauty. I have forgotten to let you know that my home-town is situated at the beginning of the Trakia Fields and around it are three of our biggest mountains—Rila, Pirin, and Rodopite, which spread their sleeves around our village. I am telling you all this as I would like you to know where I come from, and so that you can understand why I like to visit the countryside so much.

On Saturdays and Sundays, if I have not booked rehearsals with the rock band, and I have not booked an hour to record in the studio, I go for picnics with my father and mother, and then I am the happiest child in the world.

Starla's note: Katia wants you to know that she finally got her longed-for computer!

My Best Day

translated from Bulgarian

For me personally, the best day in these last couple of years was my participation in the First International Sofia Festival of Children's Popular Songs, which took place in the town of Bankya. The contest was held in the Water World swimming pool complex. The stage was the sprawling, floodlit area between the two large kidney-shaped swimming pools, dotted with small islands with palm trees on them.

One of the pools was artificially warmed and you can easily imagine where I spent my time before and after my performance. Of course, I was busy coming to terms with my stage jitters and just couldn't relax, but it was definitely fun, with swarms of kids from different countries all speaking different languages. Still I was finding it hard to take my mind off my upcoming performance, as this was not a concert where I'd be cheered on by the audience, but a tough competition where every single fault of mine would be watched and recorded. I had been to similar contests previously, and I knew that the song I was going to perform usually had a strong impact on both the jury and the audience. What was bothering me was the unhappy possibility of my performing badly, because the song has some tricky parts. I was convinced there was not much use rehearsing immediately before the contest started, as finding faults is about all that can be achieved, especially when you have those pre-contest jitters—and finding those faults could prove fatal right before the contest's start.

Still, I decided to do what I considered normal—pray to God. I knew that perseverance alone was not enough. I

"...I sang in the winners' concert and felt extremely happy."

just prayed that He would give me the necessary strength to perform that song as I had on previous occasions. Nothing more. I was ready now; all dressed up, self-assured … and it was finally time.

Our hotel was not far from the complex, so my mom and I were quickly there. We sat at a table behind the stage and waited. They played the contest's title theme and then I heard the presenter announce, "And now let's start with a performance by Ekaterina, 12 years old, who will compete in the Under 18 category. She is going to perform for us a song by Cyndi Lauper, "I'm Gonna Be Strong."

I came out on stage and felt I could hardly stand on my legs. I wasn't able to see a single face in the crowd because one of the lights was in my face. It took a while before my eyes got used to the strong light and I could see my mom in the audience. I knew she was even more nervous than I was, but I was glad she found it possible to smile at me—she always does.

Suddenly calm and composed, I listened for the sounds of the violin at the start of my act, and waited for the moment when I would have to start. By the middle of the song I had that same light in my face, and I had no feeling of being on the stage in front of so many people. After the song ended, I didn't even wait out the applause, but ran straight toward my mother to find out what she thought of it all.

She waited for me off-stage. "How did I do?" I asked straight off. "Well … good," came her reply. I didn't find that satisfactory, as I expected more; I then got into tears and said, "No chance of making the rostrum then, if I didn't do a good job." Mom calmed me down at once. She told me she had heard people shouting "Bravo!"—something the jury had probably heard as well.

BULGARIAN FOLK SONG IN OUTER SPACE

One of Katia's favorite singers is Valia Balkansca. Balkansca's recording of a Bulgarian folk song, "Izlel je Delyo Hagdutin," was one of 22 musical works, including a Beethoven symphony, that were sent to outer space in the Voyager 1 and 2 spaceships along with scientific information about the planet Earth: a message from mankind to other civilizations. These unmanned spaceships were launched in 1977 to explore the outer reaches of our galaxy and beyond!

We sat down and watched the remaining 80 children in my category. The contest wasn't over before midnight. The organizers of the event had arranged for a disco party with a prominent DJ, but everybody felt so fatigued that they chose the hotel instead. Mom then told me that even if I didn't win, it really was worth it to take part, just to gain experience. Poor Mom, I knew if she started talking to me like that, it meant that either I had not been up to the job or had been outperformed. Soon, though, I stopped tormenting myself and quickly went to sleep.

The next morning we went out to have breakfast together. We had no specific plans, so we went to the park. There were children's seesaws, slides, merry-go-rounds, and stands. What I liked best were the ponies that stood tethered in one corner of the park and which my mom let me ride.

In the afternoon, I learned I had actually made it into third place according to both the expert and the children's jury. That was disappointing news, but mom reminded me of my prayer prior to the my performance, and told me that a girl from the country of Georgia had been declared the winner, and the second place had gone to Russia. Both of those girls had really deserved it; they were good performers. That sounded comforting.

That same evening I sang in the winners' concert and felt extremely happy I was representing my country. Also, my father, my two grandmothers, and my grandfather had come for the concert. I was really glad to sing for them, and for everybody else who was supportive. I had enjoyed receiving the prize, but was even happier to see them happy for me. To me, that meant I had been up to the job.

If I Could Be...

translated from Bulgarian

I have always wondered what would happen if I had the opportunity to investigate outer space. Now I will try to imagine that and will describe it for all of you.

At first I would need a team for such a complicated task. For this I would gather all of my best and most clever friends, as each and every one of them would need to carry out a certain task. After that, I would have to get some kind of a rocket or another form of transportation that could cover such a long distance. Let us imagine that we have started our journey already.

I know that our galaxy is called the "Milky Way," and that it consists of nine planets. But what about other galaxies and planets, do they exist? Together with my team we have traveled so far that we cannot see our planet any more. We are passing by other planets and all of a sudden we are at the end of the Milky Way. We are afraid of the unknown, but as we are explorers, we rush forward bravely into the new galaxy. Here we have discovered only one planet by itself. We have found a comfortable place and we have landed.

What an unbelievable beauty! This is like the Paradise described to us in the Bible, the same Paradise that we, the people, have destroyed beyond repair. This is just one beautiful world. How different it is from the cold and gray planet Earth, which we have left a little earlier. Here it is warm, spacious, and comfortable. It has clear lakes, rivers, and seas in which colorful fish are swimming, and a green and beautiful countryside where a great many different types of animals are living. Nobody is bothering anybody, from which I conclude that everybody is happy. Everywhere there are different colored flowers, which have the most wonderful smells.

We find all these beautiful things but there are no people to be pleased to see them. We ask ourselves, "What is the point of all this beauty if there is no one to admire it?" We take off our protective equipment and we are glad to discover that there is oxygen here as well, which is essential for our survival.

We have had fun all day: we climbed some trees, we had some of the different and delicious fruit, we drank some water from the clean springs, we made flower hair bands from the bright colored flowers, we sang and danced on the green fields until we dropped of tiredness. Pleased and happy from the day that has just passed, we get back on our rocket. We are deeply impressed by the beauty that we found on the new planet and on the way back home we talk only about that.

We ask ourselves why we have polluted our Earth, which most probably had once been just the same as this new planet. We want to know why we built all these industrial plants, cars, trains, and airplanes, the nuclear stations and bombs that are destroying our planet beyond repair. We know very well that they were made to make our life more comfortable, but is there another way? We give our word that when we get back on Earth, we will tell everybody about our new discovery and take care of this planet so it can begin to look a little bit like that paradise that I have just told you about. I am sure that we will succeed. All we need is just to want it badly enough.

Did You Know?

- Sofia, which means "wisdom" in Greek, is the capital city of Bulgaria. The name is well deserved since there are several universities, libraries, and other learning institutes that dominate the city center.

- When Katia's parents were born, Bulgaria was a Communist country and close ally of the Soviet Union. During Katia's lifetime, the Communist legacy in Bulgaria ended and it is even considering joining the European Union.

- Bulgarian, a Slavic language written in Cyrillic script, is the official language.

- Bulgaria is one of the oldest countries in Europe. The Bulgars were an ancient Turkic people that divided in the seventh century. One group assimilated with the Slavic people there and adopted Christianity. The other group eventually converted to Islam.

Bulgarian Flag

Bulgarian Currency

A view of Belovo. Katia's house is circled.

Bulgaria

Romania

Sofia

Belovo

Black Sea

Greece

Where Katia will study music

Katia's hometown

Some words in Bulgarian:
Hello = Zdravei/Zdrasti
Thank you = Blagodarya
Goodbye = Dovijdane, Sbogom

Good morning = Dobrutro
Good night = Leka nosht
Friend = Priatel
Nice to meet you = Priatno mi e

Miska Bratislava, Slovakia

Michaela ("Miska")

Nationality: Slovak

Religion: None

Languages: Slovak is my first language, and I am learning Spanish and English.

Brothers and Sisters: None

Pets: None

Hobbies: Sports; reading books; learning about plants and animals; and traveling. I also collect postage stamps and badges.

Talents: Sports

Favorite Sport: Volleyball and tennis

Favorite Books: The *Sisi* books by Marie Luisevan Ingenheim; *Now and Forever* by Danielle Steel; and *Uplynul*

_as Detsk_ch Hier (roughly translated to mean *When I Was Little*) by Sonjá Peterova

Favorite Food: Spaghetti with cream and mushroom sauce

Least Favorite Food: Brussels sprouts prepared in any manner

Whom do you most admire? Terry Fox. He had cancer, but still succeeded in running a marathon.

Favorite Possession: My tennis racket

Do you help with chores at home? Yes, I vacuum, clean the bathroom, and wash the dishes.

Do you have your own telephone or computer? I have my own cell phone and a computer.

Do you use the Internet? Yes, my favorite website is www.markiza.sk.

Overlooking the Danube River, the New Bridge, as it is called in Bratislava, even includes a UFO-shaped cafeteria.

Where would you most want to travel? France and Australia

What comes to mind when you think of the United States? The Statue of Liberty; skyscrapers

...and France? The Eiffel Tower; Versailles; The Louvre

...and China? The Great Wall of China and bicycles

...and Kenya? Safari and hot weather

What do you talk about with friends? Clothes; sports; and funny stories

What do you want to know about other girls your age? Their interests; the way they live; and their opinions on drugs

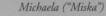

Miska with her favorite books.

About Me
translated from Slovak

I was born in a beautiful country in the middle of the mountains crossed by beautifully flowing rivers—in Slovakia. I live in its capital city called Bratislava. The city is located at the bottom of the Small Carpathian Mountains on the banks of one of the biggest rivers in Europe, the Danube.

I live here with my parents and am in my fourth year of the eight-year, bilingual school called F.G. Lorca, which specializes in the teaching of Spanish.

There are 30 students in my class. We have an excellent homeroom teacher, who teaches Mathematics and Physics. Every day we have Spanish lessons and two days a week we also have English lessons. I like going to school and seeing many friends and sharing lots of interesting and often funny stories. Every day I learn new skills and new things. That is why I like school and I like to study. When I am grown up, I would like to help other people or animals, as a doctor or veterinarian. Or I would like to dedicate my life to the preservation of nature. I have not made a final decision yet.

I also like sports and regularly attend volleyball and tennis classes. In my sports club, I have a lot of friends as well. I find sports so relaxing. And it is also a means for me to train and develop other important skills, such as perseverance and concentration.

My grandmother lives in a small village called Fačkov, which is at the bottom of the Malà Fatra Mountains. We visit her regularly. Her village is the most picturesque

Above: Miska with her parents. Below: Miska's granny's house in the Slovak Mountains.

place on Earth. When I am there, I hike and collect mushrooms and berries. The village is surrounded by beautiful mountains and bubbly brooks full of fish, where sometimes you can even find a crayfish. It is also not unusual to come across a deer, a fox, or even a bear in the woods.

I have other friends who live abroad, who enjoy staying in our house and spending their leisure time with us. I wish that many people would get to know my country, the people living here, and, obviously, my family and me. That is why I started exchanging letters with a pen pal in Spain (whom I met through my uncle, who lives in Spain). I would love to welcome her here in Slovakia in the future, so that she can experience for herself the true beauty of my homeland. I like Slovakia, and I am happy living here in a peaceful family with my parents. I also have many cousins, whom we meet quite often, mainly during holidays.

I think that people abroad do not know many things about us. We are a very young country, established only in 1993 when the former Czechoslovakia split into two independent countries—the Czech Republic and the Slovak Republic.

I would be happy if everybody else in the world realized that Slovakia is a civilized country in the middle of Europe, that all children go to school, that highways, houses, and tunnels are built here, that normal people live here with their ordinary sorrows and joys, and that we can smile like people in any other country of the world.

Meeting Miska
by Starla

My husband, my friend Alena, and I drive into the parking lot of a large apartment complex on a bleak and rainy winter morning. Like most people in Bratislava, Miska and her family live in a large apartment block. We dart from the parking lot through the rain to the entryway, and a pretty, petite Slovak girl with dark, curly hair is just getting out of the elevator. It is Michaela, better known as Miska (pronounced Meesh-ka) to her friends and family. She greets us with kisses on both cheeks.

I say, "Ahoy Michaela!" ("Ahoy" is an informal greeting in Slovak similar to "Ciao.")

Miska giggles and responds with "Ahoy."

She walks toward us, very natural, graceful, and beaming with a smile, dressed in flared blue jeans, a red sweater, and black, chunky boots. Then, very casually, as she takes my arm and guides me onto the elevator, she adds in nearly perfect English, "It's so nice to meet you, please come in. I am very sorry, but my English is not very good." Hmm, it sounds pretty good to me.

We huddle together in the small elevator and alight in front of the warm, welcoming home of Miska's family. Her parents, Gabriela and Marián, standing in the doorway to welcome us, promptly unburden us of our wet winter gear.

The previous evening, Alena drove my husband and I southeast to Bratislava, Slovakia from Prague in the Czech Republic. We passed through dense forests, rolling hills, and the passport control, which marks the border between the two young countries ever since the breakup of Czechoslvakia in 1993.

My first glimpse of Bratislava was from one of the many hillsides surrounding the city. We stepped out of the car onto the frosty street to take in the view of the town below, twinkling in the winter night. The wide and fast-flowing Danube River, the second longest in Europe, looked like black ink in the distance. The whole scene was like a drawing in a fairy tale. But it was freezing cold, so we climbed back into the heated car and wound our way down the hillside to the banks of the Danube.

Now, as we step into Miska's cozy apartment, I think about how the cold climate and the cold exteriors of these buildings don't prepare you for the warmth and homeyness found inside.

"Ahoy!" Miska and Starla.

We settle into the black leather couches in the comfortable living room. Miska and her mother appear with coffee and a white cake topped with a variety of wild red berries. Miska explains that these berries, some of which are sweet, others of which are quite tart, are grown in the mountains of Slovakia.

After we all enjoy the cake, Miska changes into a thick off-white sweater, and we all pile back into our winter coats to take a walk to her school.

SCHOOL DAYS

Miska's school logo.

Miska attends a bilingual Slovak-Spanish school, one of several specialized language schools in Slovakia. Sponsored by the government after the opening of Slovakia to the West in 1990, these schools were founded to improve the language skills of Slovak young people. Slovakia joined the European Union in May 2004 and Miska and her classmates are well-prepared Europeans.

From the fourth year on, all of Miska's core subjects, including Mathematics, Physics, and History, are taught in Spanish. Her classes run from 8:00 a.m. until 3:00 p.m. every day with 5-minute breaks between each class. The students only get 15-minutes for lunch! These schools are not for the lighthearted. Miska has an average of five hours of homework nearly every evening!

If I Could Be...

translated from Slovak

I would like to be elected to be the leader of my country. My country, Slovakia, is extremely beautiful; however, for several years now politicians have only been paying attention to politics and neglecting society. I do not think that this is good for us.

Drugs, sexual promiscuity, and crime are becoming dominant, nature is being devastated, and children are being controlled by technology. I would like my beautiful country to be clean and without waste. I would like to live in a country in which the mountain rivers and brooks are full of fish, in which I meet people hiking on mountain trails rather than people driving their cars. I want children to enjoy the scenery of our beautiful forests and mountains rather than the screens of their computers and TV sets. I want nature to be full of animals again and people in our country to be happy and satisfied.

I would like to improve the level of education and culture of people living in my country so that the people are knowledgeable and appreciate the cultural heritage of our ancestors. This will lead people to want to preserve national monuments and cultural traditions, which could then be passed down to the younger generation. I would like our nation to be healthier, not afraid of modern diseases, not living in stress, but leading healthy, simple, and, most of all, happy lives.

If I were the leader of my country, I would do my best so that people would be paid fairly for their work, so that they would receive a salary that allowed them to make a decent living. Instead of leaving to live abroad, they would be able to make use of their knowledge, wisdom, and skills here, in Slovakia.

Did You Know?

- The Slovak Republic became an independent country in 1993 when the Czechoslovak Federation dissolved. The capital of the Slovak Republic, or Slovakia, is Bratislava. The official language is Slovak, a Slavic language written in the Latin, rather than Cyrillic script.

- In Slovakia and other Eastern European countries, it is quite common for children to be given a nickname formed by adding a "ka" to the end of the first syllables of a girl's name, or "ko" to the end of a boy's name. My Slovak nickname would be Starlika! What would your nickname be?

Slovak Flag

Slovak Currency

- Miska mentions the Sisi books. Sisi is the nickname given to Elisabeth, the Empress of Austria (and Hungary) from 1854 until her death in 1898. Sisi, known for her courage and beauty, is still admired by girls in all of the countries that were once part of her empire, including Miska's Slovakia.

The rooftops of Bratislava.

Slovakia

Some words in Slovak

Thank you = Dakujem
Please = Prosím
Hello = Ahoy

Goodbye = Cau
Good morning = Dobré ráno
Good night = Dobrú noc
How are you? = Ako sa máš

Dasha Kiev, Ukraine

Dasha

Nationality: Ukrainian

Religion: I was baptized in the Eastern Orthodox Church when I was born (and I still have the gold christening dagger), but I am not religious now.

Languages: At home we speak both Ukrainian and Russian. I am learning English at school.

Brothers and Sisters: None. My mom, grandmother, and I live together in a two-room apartment in a nine-story building. My dad does not live with us.

Pets: A cat called Marusya. She is very independent and sometimes she bites me when I scold her. She wakes me up every morning by jumping up on my bed.

Hobbies: I collect cuddly toys.

Talents: My mom has said that I have a talent to be a reliable friend, but I am not sure this is a talent.

Favorite Sport: I like to watch synchronized swimming very much. I run and swim every day.

Favorite Books: Agatha Christie detective stories; The Fairy Tales of the Brothers Grimm; and Tree of Desire by the Ukrainian author, Victor Kusmenko

Favorite Food: My granny's Ukrainian borscht [beet soup]

Least Favorite Food: Fish. My mom and granny tell me it is good for me, but I wonder, can something be good for you if it is something that you do not like?

Whom do you most admire? I most admire my mom. She is beautiful, strong, and clever. I hope to be similar to her when I grow up.

Favorite Possession: I like my bed very much. I sleep very well in it and have dreams in color.

Do you help with chores at home? I try to help with everything. I dust, vacuum, wash the dishes, and go to the market to buy food.

Do you have your own telephone or computer? No, having a computer would be a very expensive pleasure for my family. But I belong to the computer club at school. My family has one telephone.

Do you use the Internet? No

Where would you most want to travel? I would like to visit Paris and New York City very much.

What comes to mind when you think of the United States? The Statue of Liberty

… and France? Perfumes and romantic love

… and China? Chinese food and the Great Wall of China

… and Kenya? Deserts and wild animals

What do you talk about with friends? School, since we spend a lot of time there

What do you want to know about other girls your age? How they spend their free time; deal with failures at school; and reconcile with their friends when they have quarreled

Dasha collects cuddly toys.

About Me

translated from Ukrainian

"I have stopped dreaming of having a father."

My name is Dasha. I was born in Zhytomir. My mother had gone there on a business trip and I was born early.

At that time, we lived in Kiev together with my dad. He is an artist-restorer and is very handsome. In my childhood, we would go to the seaside together where he would teach me how to swim. However, at that time, I was too young to learn. Then my mom and dad quarreled and we moved in with my grandmother.

Since then I have not seen my dad, although he lives on the same subway line in Kiev. He has never congratulated me, not even on my birthday, and he has never come to my school. At first I missed him very much. I even found a photograph of him and put it under my pillow so that he might remember me. But it was all in vain. Then my mother found the photo and asked me if I wanted to call him. But, then, I don't know why, I felt insulted and no longer wanted to call.

In general, the divorce of parents is terribly sad. I have some friends whose parents are also divorced. I sometimes think that we are not as happy as the other children, but we are drawn together by our shared fate.

Now, however, I remember less and less about this. My mom, grandmother, and I live in an amicable female collective. Of course, at first I very much wished my mom would remarry so that I would have a father with whom I could walk in the courtyard holding hands, like I have seen others do, and everyone would know that I had a father to look after me and protect me. But now, as I have grown up, I have understood that such a clever, kind, and talented man who would be worthy of my mom simply does not exist in this world. And so, I have stopped dreaming about having a father.

My grandmother and I take care of the house and our cat, Marusya. My mom earns the money and takes us on small holidays, or surprises us with gifts like new bedroom slippers, or suddenly a whole kilogram of bananas or ham.

"...the divorce of parents is terribly sad. I have some friends whose parents are also divorced. I sometimes think that we are not as happy as the other children, but we are drawn together by our shared fate."

Each year my mother tries to make my health improve because I had a lot of problems as a child: I often had a bad stomach because of nerves. My mom is a doctor. She is very much respected by other people and they always come to her for help, even by telephone. She often spends long periods of time on the phone with patients, and even when they do not heed her advice, she does not lose her patience and bang down the phone, she convinces them to listen to the doctor.

Dasha, her grandmother, and her mother: the "amicable female collective."

My grandmother is very old, but very cheerful. When there was the war against the Fascists [World War II], she was a young nurse and worked in the operating room assisting surgeons with operations. She had a very important blood type, and consequently, they often drew blood from her and flew it out to wounded soldiers who needed blood replacements. She saved many people. My grandmother received many honors and medals, but she only wears them on Victory Day.

My grandmother loves to dance and on New Year's my mom and I take turns dancing with her. She also likes to help people and to educate me. After my grandfather's death, my grandmother learned many "man's" activities: repairing the door of the wardrobe, the electric iron, or the peephole in the door.

There are sometimes difficult moments for us, for example, if we go on holiday and must carry heavy bags. We are not strong enough for this. However, we are accustomed to these difficulties and ask our friends to help. My family is very sociable and we have many friends.

Since my last birthday, I now have a vote in our family. They have already begun to consult with me—how is it better to make the omelet, with cheese or with tomatoes? And if I do not want shorter hair, nobody forces me

One of the many Kiev Pie shops near Dasha's home.

to go to the hairdresser.

I feel a sense of responsibility for the house while my mother is at work. Sometimes, though, I get scolded for the fact that I go for a walk and wander too far from the courtyard. Then I become silent and quietly worry.

If there were a worldwide committee of broken families, I believe that I would find understanding there. This is because only incomplete families (for example, a family without a father, or a family without a mother) would know what difficulties must be overcome, and how it is necessary to love and care for one another. You see, if someone in such a family becomes ill and dies, then there is no more family.

Therefore, it is necessary to protect each other as one protects one's own eyes. My mother is, for me, and I am, for her, the best good-luck charm. When we are together, nothing is terrible. And my grandmother is the base of our family. The most important thing now is her happiness.

Meeting Dasha by Starla

Before I visit Dasha, I first meet up with my translator, Anya. To get to Dasha's, we wind through Kiev and across the wide Dnipro River. The city looks to me like a large forest with bits of city sprinkled here and there. Outside of the city center, which includes large buildings and wide avenues, the city melts into woodland. Just above the treetops, the golden onion-shaped domes of Kiev's many Orthodox churches shimmer in the white sunlight, endowing the city with their exotic beauty and attesting to the city's rich history as the cradle of Slavic Orthodox culture.

As we drive to Dasha's apartment complex, where she and her family have recently moved, Dasha and her grandmother can be seen keeping watch from the windows of the sixth-floor apartment. When at last they see us, they throw open the windows to the frosty air, and enthusiastically wave to us to come up.

The apartment door bursts open and we are immediately ushered into the waiting arms of Dasha's mother and grandmother. They greet us with big hugs. Dasha does not rush forward. She stays in the background for a couple of minutes, taking in all of the activity. At last, she quietly approaches to say hello. Dasha is wearing a pair of red-and-blue plaid trousers and a dark blue sweatshirt. She is tall and slender with thick, dark brown hair cut in a shoulder-length bob. Her brown, doe-like eyes are partly hidden behind thick bangs.

Once inside the door, after we remove our shoes, as is customary in Ukraine, Dasha's mother directs us into the

Starla and Dasha.

kitchen for lunch. The small table is set with a new, white tablecloth and the family's best dishes. To my delight, I discover that we are having borscht, a flavorful soup that originated in Ukraine and is eaten throughout Central and Eastern Europe. It can be eaten hot or cold, and is usually served with a dollop of sour cream in the middle and a piece of black bread on the side. Dasha tells me, "No one prepares Ukrainian borscht as good as my granny," so I sit in anticipation as I watch Dasha's mother spoon out the chunky, scarlet-red liquid into each bowl. It is delicious! Dasha intends to master this dish, too, but for now, her granny only trusts her to cut the vegetables. Dasha explains, "There should be beets, potatoes, cabbage, onion, carrots, herbs, tomato sauce, and a small piece of meat with a bone. We often make borscht without the meat, but with sunflower seed oil, which I like just as well."

After lunch, we head outdoors for a short walk to Dasha's school. It is still sunny, but oh so cold! It is early spring and the grounds of Dasha's apartment complex are a patchwork of leftover snow and patches of green where bits of grass are struggling to grow.

Dasha's school is just a few minutes away from her new

UKRAINIAN EGGS

Ukrainians are highly skilled in arts and crafts. Among their beautiful creations is the Ukrainian Easter egg, called pysanky. The painted eggs go back thousands of years in history, when sun worshippers believed that eggs held magical powers. The eggs were decorated in different colors and designs rich in symbolism, and were believed to bring good luck to the recipient of the egg. When Christianity came to Ukraine in the 10th century, the painted eggs were turned into religious symbols, and the egg designs were given Christian meanings.

To make pysanky, wax and dye are used in a method very similar to that used in batik (a type of fabric-dyeing). After the design is drawn on the egg, layers of wax are added and removed while dipping the egg in different dyes to create an intricate colored design. There are great websites that offer step-by-step instructions for making your own pysanky! For example, check out www.learnpysanky.com.

apartment. In typical Soviet style, apartment buildings in Kiev are grouped together so many people live near one another. In between the many buildings, there are trees, courtyards, and playgrounds for the children. Sometimes there are cafés, bars, or little shops for the residents in the ground floors of the buildings. An advantage of these apartment villages is that all of the children in the neighborhood attend the same school. This means that all of Dasha's school friends live nearby.

On Sunday, my last day in Kiev, I have an important errand to run. I must get my hands on a Kiev Pie (Kyivsky Torte) to take home with me. Dasha explains that the Kyivsky Torte she served at her birthday party is a special type of cake made only in Kiev.

Before I leave Dasha, she takes out the diary she received as a gift for her birth-day. The diary is filled with colored pages with questions for Dasha's friends to fill in. Dasha and Anya help me make out the questions, which are written in Cyrillic. What is your favorite color: Blue, I write in English. What is your favorite flower: Roses. What is your favorite drink: Champagne, I write, as Dasha giggles and her face turns red. She was clearly expecting me to write Coca-Cola, as I am an American. She forgets I am an American living in Paris!

"Kiev pies are made only in my city."

SCHOOL DAYS

Dasha has classes six days a week, including Saturdays. Classes start at 8:30 in the morning and end at 2:15 in the afternoon. The children get several 15-minute breaks between classes during which they can have a snack, but they usually do not eat lunch until they have gone home.

There are 28 students in Dasha's class, 14 boys and 14 girls. Their lessons include Physics, Biology, Mathematics, English, Ukrainian, Russian, Ukrainian Literature, Foreign Literature, Geography, Home Economics, Music, Art, and Gym. Dasha's favorite subjects are English, Home Economics, Art, and Gym. The students do not wear uniforms to school, although each student has a green or brown blazer to wear for special school functions.

My Best Day

translated from Ukrainian

My happiest day was my 12th birthday. That day, I was allowed to organize a birthday party with my friends. We have a small apartment and do not often have visitors. This time, however, my mom said that it would be appropriate for her daughter to have a birthday party. How I waited for the day!

So much time has passed, but I still remember each minute of that day. Since my mom told me I could have the party I thought about and planned the menu and whom I would invite. I told my mom about each of my guests—eight classmates—so that she would know everybody and know what to talk about with whom, so that it would be interesting for everybody.

From the early morning I wanted to set the table. But I had to wait because we only have one table and we still had to use it to prepare some of the food. My grandmother and I made salad, sandwiches, and baked a piraguas [a Ukrainian dish that is like a pie with cheese, onions, and mayonnaise].

I planned to wear the most beautiful dress I had ever seen. My mom chose it and bought it for me as a gift and probably paid a great deal of money. But I must admit, I looked so beautiful in it! I was excited that my friends would see me in my beautiful outfit and maybe they would even envy me a bit.

It was snowing outside although it was spring according to the calendar. We had roses and blossoms in our room in beautiful vases. On the table, I laid a snow-white cloth and placed the plates and the various tasty and delicious dishes on it.

Then I waited.

I was so afraid that my guests would forget to come to the party, or that someone might suddenly become ill and be unable to come, or that their parents would not allow them to go out at the last minute. But they all arrived and were not even late! All of them: Galya, Sasha, Maxim, Igor, both Yaroslaws, and my older cousin Anya, with a friend Mitya.

I have never in my life received so many gifts! I do not know what friends give as birthday gifts to 12-year-old girls in other countries, but we usually give sweets, flowers, books, and toys. I received some boxes of remarkable chocolate, a silly furry jackrabbit, a large children's encyclopedia, a beautiful diary, a calendar, some cool stockings, and a bouquet of real white tulips.

Maxim even told me I was like a princess. And it even seemed to me that I was a princess at a fantastic dancing party. Maybe even Cinderella!

We sat at the table and drank lemonade from tall wine glasses and everyone toasted me. We had fun and I enjoyed myself so much. You see, in class I am just a regular schoolgirl—not even the best one—but at my party, everyone considered me to be the most beautiful and remarkable girl!

Then we danced and all the boys wanted to invite me to dance. I did not want to offend my friend Galya, but I couldn't refuse any of the invitations. Then we drank tea with Kiev pie. These pies are not made anywhere else, only in my city. And, we told silly stories and then went outside and played in the snow. Two snowballs hit me right in the face, but it wasn't painful because it was so funny. My hands were frozen because I had taken off my gloves after they had gotten wet. And I realized that snow isn't really cold, but hot—at least it feels so when my hands are freezing.

When it was dark, my mom and I took all of my guests home so that their parents wouldn't worry. So, my happiest day came to an end. But then the happiest night began because I had a wonderful dream. Actually, in the morning I tried to remember it, but I could not.

Peace! Dasha in her room.

If I Could Be...

translated from Ukrainian

If I were elected the president of my country...actually, I don't see how this could ever happen—that everyone would suddenly vote for me—because nobody knows me! But, I like my country, Ukraine, very much, and I think that the presidents we have had up until now have not understood what should be done for the country. They certainly pay a lot of attention to politics and diplomacy. They go to other countries and appear at youth concerts, but most people still feel that you cannot live very well in Ukraine. And, therefore, they go to live in other countries where it is happier and life is more carefree.

Some of my friends have left Ukraine with their parents. I thought that if we left also we could become rich and not be dependent on anyone, like the heroes in the American television series.

But, when my mother lived in Jordan for business one year, I understood why she wrote to us all of the time

The architecture of Kiev highlights a rich religious history.

that she missed us and Kiev. Because for us, our home is the best, once we had made some small adjustments.

And now I have figured out what kind of adjustments should be made and how to make them. What is important is that everyone be happy. But, first you must find out what happiness means for each person.

I am sure that many people would say that happiness is wealth. I agree that this is certainly good. When you have a lot of money you can buy your own car, rather than taking taxis when you need to go to the station or the airport. It's possible to purchase a pass to a beautiful health resort rather than staying in ones small and dirty room for a short stay at the sea. It is possible to have dinner in beautiful restaurants instead of eating fast-cooking vermicelli. I have never eaten in a restaurant, only in a café with my mom. Anyway, wealth is a wonderful thing, but not the most important thing.

It is really only possible to be happy when you have friends that you like, or a hobby, or a favorite job. Therefore, if I were president, I would invent many ways for people to find a hobby. For example, if a person likes

The towering steeples of the Kiev-Perchersk Lavra (Cave Monastery), built in the mid-11th century, can be seen in the hills above Kiev.

to grow flowers and is good at it, why not permit him to cultivate flowerbeds all around the cities, even capitals. Imagine how beautiful the city would be if in every city there were a gardener who loved his job. Then we would have roses everywhere, and people would smile and not tear them down, as it would be a pity to kill such beauty. And the person would be happy that his work pleased so many people. And we would be happy that we had such beautiful streets.

I have only used the gardener as an example. But, in general, if I were elected president, I would ask each inhabitant of Ukraine to write me a letter in which everyone would write what his favorite job is, or what he needs to make him happy.

I certainly understand that the president is a very busy person and to read the letters of all of the people who live in my country is impossible. (My mom has said that there are about 50 million of us.) So, I would create a committee to read the letters on happiness. When I understood the desires and capabilities of my people, I would try to help everybody. And then everyone would be happy, including me.

Did You Know?

put on their finest clothes and gather at the Victory monument in Kiev, a tall statue of Lady Victory. They bring flowers to pay homage to the soldiers who fought and died in the war.

- Formerly one of the republics of the Soviet Union, Ukraine became an independent state in 1991. Its capital city is Kiev and the official language is Ukrainian, a Slavic language written in Cyrillic script. Most Ukrainians, like Dasha and her family, also speak Russian.

- Since Ukraine's independence, the entire economic and political regime in the country has been transforming from a communist system to one that is market-based and democratic.

- In the past, Kiev, the capital city of Ukraine, was the center of Slavic culture, which is still the dominant cultural influence today in Eastern Europe. Slavic cultures share, besides a common history, a common alphabet (the Cyrillic alphabet), and a common religion (the Eastern Orthodox religion).

Ukrainian Flag

- Dasha was baptized into the Eastern Orthodox religion. This is a form of Christianity that is found throughout Greece, Central and Eastern Europe, and Russia. Eastern Orthodox Churches are recognizable by their onion-shaped domes.

- Victory Day, the day that marked the end of WWII in Europe, was May 9, 1945. This is an important holiday in Ukraine (and Russia) and is celebrated every year. Ukrainian families, including Dasha, her mother, and grandmother,

Ukrainian Currency

Some words in Ukrainian
Hello = Vitayu
Goodbye = Do pobachennya
Please = Proshu

Thank you = Dyakuyu
Good morning = Dobryy' ranok
Good night = Dobranich
How are you? = Yak mayetes

With a population of three million, Kiev is the bustling capital of Ukraine.

Ukraine

Belarus
Poland
Russia
Kiev
Romania
Sea of Azon
Black Sea
Dasha's home city

Kate Samara, Russia

Ekaterina Vladimirovna ("Kate")

Nationality: Russian

Religion: Eastern Orthodox

Languages: Russian and some English, French, and Latin. I am learning them at school.

Brothers and Sisters: None

Pets: Yes, a small white dog named Beema, a gray kitten called Mathilda, and some fish

Hobbies: Graffiti art

Talents: Drawing, art

Favorite Sport: Snowboarding and wakeboarding

Favorite Books: Jonathan Livingston Seagull by Richard Bach, The Neverending Story by Michael Ende, and The Picture of Dorian Gray by Oscar Wilde. All three repre-sent to me peace and beauty.

photo by Ludmila Reznick

Kate wakeboarding.

Favorite Food: Fruits chopped into small pieces with ice cream and double cream

Least Favorite Food: Soup and anything that looks like it

Whom do you most admire? Nobody really, but I can probably say my cousin, Anton.

Favorite Possession: My snowboard and my wakeboard

Do you help with chores in your home? Yes, I tidy up my room and I occasionally wash the dishes.

Do you have your own telephone or computer? I have my own cell phone and a computer.

Do you use the Internet? Yes, mostly for e-mail, or if I need to find information.

Where would you most want to travel? To Australia, because I know very little about it, and I have already been to many places.

What comes to mind when you think of the United States? Supermarkets; sky-scrapers; and hamburgers

...and France? Small narrow streets and the Eiffel Tower

...and China? Chinese bells because I have them in my room

...and Kenya? To take out a map and look where it is

What do you talk about with friends? What is most on my mind at the moment: clothes; boys; money; school

What would you most want to know about other girls your age? What they have on their minds

Kate's favorite books (in English!).

About Me
translated from Russian

Sometimes it seems to me that I am alone...absolutely alone. Nobody in this world can understand me. But really it is not so. Morning comes and with the morning come my friends as well. They remember me and we have a laugh together. What can be better than friends, especially when you are in a good mood? But if you are in a bad mood, you need friends even more. When I am in a bad mood, my friends always make it better. They simply say a few nice words that improve my mood. Then, I no longer feel like a white crow in this world, but feel part of it, like I belong in this society. This is most important for me at the moment. While a flower is growing, its stalk is not yet strong and it needs support. This is how I am now, and my friends are my support.

However, sometimes I get the impression that everyone lives inside their own shell and only for themselves. Or, maybe it is only I who lives inside my own shell. Sometimes it seems that everyone wants something from me and that nobody would do anything for nothing. And sometimes it feels that I cannot let anybody into my heart; it's open but nobody wants to get in. At these moments, I can't do anything with myself.

I am made of two parts: optimist and pessimist. When I wake up, I never know through what color glasses I will see the world today. People who know me have gotten used to this, and to those that do not know me, I always tell them in advance so as not to scare them away.

But my best friend always know right away what kind of mood I am in.

Only one thing really gets on my nerves: monotony. Every day being the same, getting up in the morning, going to school, then back home, then doing my homework, and going to sleep. Every day the same! I would go mad....On the other hand, you never know what might happen to you from one day to the next; I might meet new friends or maybe old friends will get in touch with me.

And school—I can't say that I like it, but it is fun. My friends are there and I spend most of my life there. Then, I have Sundays. I get tired more on this day than any other in the whole week, as I am trying to fit into one day all varieties of activities that I could not do during the rest of the week. And when it does not work, I am cross with the whole world. But when it does work, and without special efforts, then you understand what people live on the Earth for and the whole of life is beautiful!

I am a romantic, but, for some reason, nobody believes this. I love roses, I love the forest, I love my friends, I love my parents, and my dog. I love winter and summer, Nikolai Gogol (a Russian writer), and music. My cousin always wonders how I can like both Limp Bizkit (an American pop band) and Vivaldi. I can't listen just to rock or rap, for example. I don't understand people who think that if they like hip-hop and somebody else doesn't, then that person is hopeless and there is no point even to talk to him. Everyone has the right to their own opinion and it does not matter what style of

"...my friends say a few nice words, then I no longer feel like a white crow in this world..."

photos by Ludmila Reznick

"One thing really gets on my nerves: monotony."

Kate with her English teacher, Mrs. Kogan.

SCHOOL DAYS

Kate is in the seventh grade of a middle school/high school in the center of Samara. Last year, Kate and her classmates had to select a specialization: Humanities, Mathematics, or Science. Kate chose Humanities. Now her studies focus on literature and foreign languages. Her language classes are English, French, and Latin. In Literature, she studies Russian Classical Literature, Modern, and Foreign Literature, and Literary Theory.

Everyone takes Russian Grammar, Math, Biology, Physics, History, Geography, and Gym where they take horseback riding lessons in the school stables!

Kate takes horseback riding lessons in gym class.

Kate's family from left to right: her grandfather, cousin, father, aunt, grandmother, Kate, and her mother.

music he listens to. Most important is a person's personality.

I especially love my bedroom. It is a whole separate topic. My friends say that it is a museum because all the walls are covered in photographs, pictures, letters,

"I am a romantic, but, for some reason, nobody believes this."

and everything I get. But my bedroom is not a museum; it is my soul and all of me! It is my life from the start to present. It is my castle, in which only very close people can enter. My room does not exist without me, nor do I without it. We are two halves of one whole. I love my bedroom very much. I never feel lonely in my room, because from one wall my cousin looks at me, from another wall, my friends, and here I am on the Volga, and here I am at the seaside...and everything that has ever happened to me, everywhere I have been, everyone I have met, everything is here, in my room.

And I love evenings, especially winter evenings. Silver snow on the streets, and everywhere there are yellow lights like fireflies. In the glass sky, it looks as though somebody has stuck tiny, tiny stars like small pieces of grain. But really they are very big. Maybe somebody looks at us from above exactly the same way we look at things and thinks that we are tiny, although we are not.

Meeting Kate

by Starla

photo by Ludmila Reznick

Kate and Starla.

After a hair-raising flight from Moscow on a small, old, and over-crowded Russian airplane, here I am in Samara. Kate's town, named for the Samarsky River that flows into the Volga River, was called Kuibyshev in the 1930s. Like St. Petersburg, whose name was changed to Petrograd, then to Leningrad during the Soviet era, and back to St. Petersburg, Samara reverted to its original name in 1991. This name change happened after the fall of the Communist regime in Russia. When Samara was Kuibyshev, my visit here would have been impossible, as it was one of several "closed" cities in the Soviet Union, off-limits to foreign travelers. But times have changed!

The morning after I arrive, Kate's father picks me up at my hotel and drives me to their home. En route, the colossal Volga River, surrounded by dense woods of white birch and blossoming apple trees, competes for my attention. The land around Samara is vast. Everything is big: the forests, the fields, the Volga, the sky. I feel like a character in Dr. Zhivago [see sidebar]. It is therefore a surprise to meet Kate, a thoroughly modern Russian girl, conversant in English and downright trendy.

Ekaterina ("Kate" for short) lives in an eighth-floor apartment with her mother, Ludmila (Luda), and her father, Vladimir, near the banks of the Volga. They share their medium-sized apartment with their terrier named Beema, an aquarium full of tropical fish, and their fluffy gray kitten, Mathilda. On the day we meet, Kate herself resembles a cat as she sits across from me holding Mathilda. Kate is wearing a long linen dress, a beaded necklace, and slippers. She has a wide, glowing face, cat-like yellow eyes, and thick, black eyelashes. Her hair is cut in a trendy, layered style that frames her face attractively. I soon realize that this is just one of Kate's looks.

Kate's mother, Luda, is a photographer and the walls of the apartment are covered with her photographs—there is Kate with cropped blond hair, Kate with long black braids, Kate with long brown hair, and Kate with a short brown bob. Kate hates monotony, as she told you!

On the walls of Kate's cheerful and eclectic apartment, there are also photographs of the Volga River taken during all four seasons. In this part of the world, the seasons are quite dramatic. Summers are sweltering; autumns are a symphony of golds, reds, and browns; winters are snow-covered and frosty; the long-awaited spring seasons are explosions of new life. The blue waters of the Volga River accentuate the beauty of the environment all around. Kate explains that the people of Samara call the river, *Volga Matushka,* which means "Dear Mother Volga" in Russian.

The next day, we visit Kate's grandparents who live in a small village on the outskirts of Samara. I feel that we have been transported many decades back in time. The home is a small wooden structure that was built nearly 60 years ago and there is no indoor plumbing (this means no indoor toilets!) and no central heating. The home is cozy, nevertheless, and Kate's grandparents welcome us enthusiastically. Kate explains to me that I am the first foreigner her grandmother has ever met. Think of that!

Having lived her whole life in Soviet Russia, the majority of the time in a "closed city," Kate's grandmother had few opportunities to meet foreigners. I am certain, however, that the most memorable part of her day is watching the ease with which her granddaughter, Kate, is able to communicate with me in her very capable English. I try to imagine how these three different generations of Russians feel about all of the changes their society has undergone in just over a decade. How times have changed!

My Best Day

translated from Russian

"There is nothing more beautiful than mountains in snow, the crunching sound of snow under the snowboard... the feeling of flight, and wind blowing in your face."

It is difficult to say straight away which day was the best for me. There were so many of them! Some people say that the best days are birthdays. I don't agree with this, because on the day I was born nobody asked me if I wanted to be born into this world. Also, what was so happy about that day? They were taking me from one room to another, I was crying and, actually, I don't remember anything about that time. So how can I say it was happy for me or not? And holidays we have every year...Nothing is really exciting about them either! First, you are worried if everything is ready, then you are worried if guests will come, and then when they come you don't know how to entertain them.

But I think I have a best day in mind; I will start from the beginning. (After all, it's quite difficult to start from the end.)

Like most people I have a hobby, but it is not just a hobby, I absolutely adore it. And if it is possible to say so, this hobby is my life! It is snowboarding. There is nothing more beautiful than mountains in snow, the crunching sound of snow under the snowboard, icy frost, the feeling of flight, and wind blowing in your face. And aside from just snowboarding, there is also

photo by Ludmila Reznick

"I think about that time as if it were a fairy tale."

the pleasure of spend-ing time outdoors with my friends.

The first time I arrived at a ski resort, I was given a snowboard to try. I spent all day going head over heels, trying to do something with it. I felt straight away that snowboarding was the sport for me. Everything I love I share with my brother Anton because he is not just my relative but my best friend as well. Though he is my cousin, he has always been more like a brother to me from the day I was born, so I refer to him as my brother. I called him to join me the next weekend. That Christmas we both got snowboards.

All winter I spent with Anton in the mountains. I think about that time as if it were a fairy tale.

When the snow melted my family decid-ed to go to Andorra to the alpine resort. I did not even think twice of whom to bring—obviously I would ask Anton.

The "best day" that I am talking about was the last day of our ski vacation. I felt tired when I woke up and I was not in a good mood. The day before we had tried to snowboard all day but the weather was so bad. There was such a strong snow-storm that we could not see anything at all. I even caught a cold. But this is not all yet. It's okay that there was a snow-storm and it's okay that I was tired, everyone gets tired sometimes! But it was such a pity that it was the last day of our holiday! I had been waiting for this trip for half a year. I so much wanted to get away from the daily routine! And when I arrived here what did I see? Terrible weather, worse than we have at home, and nothing else! I was very disappointed.

On this day, I was afraid to open my eyes. What if there was only a white wall of snow outside the window? I was lying in my bed wrapped up in the quilt and wondering why everything was so unfair.

I would not have gotten out of bed if it had not been for Anton. I did not hear

photo by Ludmila Reznick

The white Russian winter.

his steps coming into my room. It was so dark and warm under my quilt and I felt tears come to my eyes. Suddenly, I heard a terrible wail right next to my ear. I jumped out of bed. Oh, I got so angry! I grabbed my pillow and started chasing him all over the room.

But then I suddenly stopped. The whole room was full of sunlight and out-side the white giants, the Pyrenees were shining as if made of crystal. We snow-boarded all day until it got dark. Anton nearly had to carry me to the hotel, as I was so tired I could not move my feet. I fell asleep as soon as my head touched the pillow and in my dreams I saw the mountains and snow and felt the wind blowing on my face!

My Cousin Anton

I am not afraid to say again that Anton is a real treasure. His best quality is iron nerves. And it helps me to be with him as I am very hot-tempered. I get bad-tempered for any small reason. For example, when the tea is too hot or when the porridge is not hot enough. (I understand perfectly that this does not do me any favors and I am trying to change myself, but it does not work very well.) I am amazed by his patience! I can run around and moan about the unfairness of life and try to prove that I am right when somebody sits at my favorite table (where I like to have my breakfast when we are on holiday) and he simply takes my hand and leads me to another table. And then for about ten minutes, he will listen patiently to my moans about life. Then when I have finished he will simply ask: "Would you like tea or coffee?" A legendary man.

"Everything I love I share with Anton because he is not just my relative but my best friend as well."

If I Could Be...

translated from Russian

"I would like to do something unusual, something outstanding... conquer the peak of a mountain, jump with a parachute, win a snowboard competition, or at least get rid of some of my bad points."

Who would I like to be? Perhaps, it would be easier to say who I would not like to be. I would not like to be a president, simply because I am not interested in politics. And I am happy with my life the way it is, so far. Frankly speaking, I do not desire power and I do not want to be responsible for millions of peoples' lives. I feel that I am not a Cleopatra and not a Caesar. I won't be able to come, to see, and to conquer. I don't have noble motives like to reduce taxes, equip orphanages with better services and utilities, increase wages, and reduce prices.

Please don't think that I only care about myself. I simply understand that it is not as easy as it seems. If it could be another way, everything would have been done by now. The thought of politics is not for me.

To explore the cosmos...interesting suggestion! First, I love traveling. Everything new and unusual always amazes me, and what can be newer and more unusual than the cosmos and the stars. But I understand that this trip would not be for one day or one year, but, perhaps, for dozens of years. And, I hate monotony. I am a changeable person. That is why a cosmos odyssey is not for me. For me, such a life would be like a prison, real confinement.

To become a film or pop star—I most definitely don't need that! To work every day for 12 hours, not to eat anything so to keep a good figure, no private life. What for? For crazy fans who would never leave you in peace? And the media who would turn your life inside out? No, thank you! I don't need such pleasure! But to be an actor in a small theater, this is better! To live a few lives at the same time: one time you are a princess, another time you are a fairy, or witch, or suffering from an unhappy love, or you are a bride! I would probably be happy with that. But then we know what little wages they get working in small theaters. How is it possible to have a proper family with such a job?

I have thought that I should become a lawyer. Lawyers will always be needed. And my performing skills might be needed as a lawyer. If I were to become a lawyer, I would be able to put my efforts into changing this world in a better way, even if only a little bit.

I would also like to do something unusual, something outstanding, for example, to conquer the peak of an enormous mountain, to jump with a parachute, to win a snowboard competition, or at least to get rid of some of my bad points.

I really want only one thing—to love and to be loved, to feel that I am not alone on this planet, that I am not an alien whom everyone is afraid of and does not understand. I want to feel sun every morning, not in the sky, but in my soul!

photo by Ludmila Reznick

In the summer, the Volga is used for boating, waterskiing, and in Kate's case, wakeboarding, jet skiing, and swimming. Kate even swims here in the winter. Brrrr!

courtesy of M.G.M.

Doctor Zhivago

Doctor Zhivago is a famous novel written in1958 by the Russian author Boris Pasternak. If you are in the mood for a wonderful epic story and beautiful romance, you must read it or rent the movie! It is the story of the life of Doctor Yuri Zhivago, a medical doctor and poet, and his great romance with the beautiful Larissa Fyodorovna. The beautifully written book earned Pasternak the Nobel Prize for Literature in 1958, but he declined it at the urging of Soviet authorities. The movie, Doctor Zhivago, starring Omar Sharif and Julie Christie, was filmed in 1965 during the height of the Cold War. Since Hollywood did not have access to the Russian countryside at that time, the film was shot in Spain.

Did You Know?

- Russia became the independent Russian Federation in 1991 following the dissolution of the Soviet Union (USSR). Russia is the largest country in the world in terms of area, stretching across 11 time zones.

- Moscow is the capital city of Russia. Russian, a Slavic language written in Cyrillic script, is the official language.

- The Cold War was the name given to the conflict between Communist countries (led by the Soviet Union) and democratic countries (led by the United States).

- March 8 is International Women's Day, an annual holiday in Russia celebrating women. Men and boys give small gifts, flowers and compliments, to girls and women. Even grade-school boys presenting small gifts and flowers to their girl class-mates.

- The Cold War era was characterized by mutual distrust, suspicion, espionage, and escalating tension over nuclear weapons. Much of the Soviet Union was "closed" to foreigners, and likewise in the US. For a time, even Disneyland and Walt Disney World were "closed" to Soviet citizens.

- Like Katia from Bulgaria, Kate's second, or middle name, Vladimiranova, is a "patronymic" meaning "daughter of Vladimir." Boys also have patronymics formed by adding -ovich or -ievich or -ich to the end of their father's name.

Russian Flag

Russian Currency

Some words in Russian
Hello = Zdravstvuyte
Nice to meet you = Ochen priyatno
Thank you = Spasibo

Goodbye = Do svidaniya
Good morning = Dobroe utro
Good night = Spokoynoy nochi
Friend = Droog

The Red Square in Moscow, Russia's capital city.

Russia

St. Petersburg, formerly Leningrad

Arctic Ocean

Norway

Sweden

Finland

St. Petersburgh

Moscow

Samara

Starla flew from Moscow to Samara

Kate's hometown

Kazakhstan

China

Mongolia

Asia & Oceania

The Great Wall . Tae Kwon Do . Shinto

Tatiana
Kazakhstan

Lavanya
India

Wanning
China

Natsupho
Japan

Angela
China

Dieu
Vietnam

Kiely
New Zealand

Alex
Australia

Turkmenistan
Uzbekistan
Mongolia
N. Korea
S. Korea
Afghanistan
Pakistan
Burma
Laos
Philippines
Thailand
Malaysia
Cambodia
Borneo
Indonesia
New Guinea
Indian
Ocean

Temple of the Emerald Buddha, Southeast Asia.

Cherry blossoms in Kyoto, Japan.

Aerial view of the coral reef around Australia.

Sydney Opera House in Australia.

Below: City night scene in Hong Kong, China.

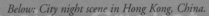

Bicycle cart in China.

Angela Nanjing, China

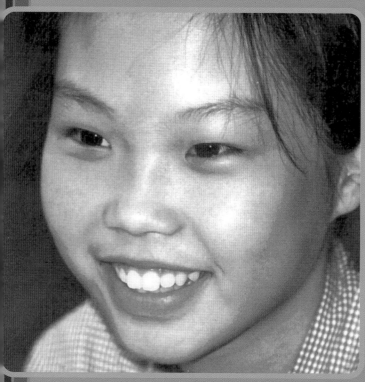

Anqi ("Angela")

Nationality: Chinese
Religion: None
Languages: Chinese, and I am studying English.
Brothers and Sisters: None
Pets: Yes, a pair of birds
Hobbies: Singing and playing the electric piano
Talents: Singing
Favorite Sport: Riding bicycles and playing badminton
Favorite Books: Several Chinese books called *I am the Flag-Raiser Today* by Qin Wenjun, and *I Want to Be a Good Child* and *Days of Being Naughty* by Huang Beijia. This last book is about the daily lives of two boys who keep getting into trouble.
Favorite Food: Prawns (these are big shrimp)
Least Favorite Food: Eggplant
Whom do you most admire? Intelligent people who have their own opinions
Favorite Possession: My electric piano

Angela's favorite possession is her electric piano.

Do you help with chores at home? Yes, washing dishes, washing vegetables, and mopping the floors
Do you have your own telephone or computer? No
Do you use the Internet? No
Where would you most want to travel? The Disney Theme Park
What comes to mind when you think of the United States? Strong and prosperous
...and France? Famous perfume
...and China? Capital well known throughout the world
...and Kenya? Unfortunate refugees
What do you talk about with friends? Study; daily life; popular movies; and music stars
What do you want to know about other girls your age? I want to know about their life and study.

Angela with her parents and her younger cousin Enya.

About Me

translated from Chinese

Enya and Angela enjoy their milkshakes.

My name is Anqi. I am a student at Huilong Bridge Elementary School in Nanjing. Shortly before the International Children's Day this year, I entered into an election contest for senior leader of the Young Pioneers with three other students. This was the most unusual and exciting day in my life.

The election contest was to begin in the afternoon. In the morning, I practiced my campaign speech. Although I told myself, "Don't be nervous," again and again, I felt quite nervous. Knowing I was to take part in the election contest, my friends warmly encouraged me. One said, "I believe you will win." And another said, "After success, don't forget to treat us!" The crowd burst into laughter and I was not as nervous as before.

The afternoon came very soon. Ms. Xu, the Young Pioneer Counselor, asked the candidates to go to the broadcast room. I felt nervous again, and I ran to the broadcast room in a hurry. As soon as I got there, the bell rang. Classes began to distribute ballot tickets and I could sense the rustle of paper. My heart beat faster and faster as if there were a rabbit bouncing in my chest, and the hand holding the speech text was sweating. The order in which the campaign speeches would be delivered was decided by class number. Since I was in Class 4, Grade 5, I was to be the last of the four candidates. I thought that I had enough time to prepare, and I read the speech text again and again.

The other three candidates gave their campaign speeches one by one, and each of them gave a good performance. Then, it was my turn. When Ms. Xu passed the microphone to me, I was so nervous that I nearly dropped it. With quivering hands, I cleared my throat and began to read the text, "My name is Anqi…." My heart didn't calm until I finished my speech. I could clearly hear applause bursting out from the classrooms.

Next, it was time for the voting. The students were thinking and deciding carefully and I was agitated. I tried to imagine the result: elected, not elected, elected, not elected….

Ms. Xu got the voting results of every class very soon, and she calculated the total result quickly. By that time, I had gone back to my classroom to await the results. "Now, I declare," my heart beat faster again and I felt as if the air was frozen, "the senior leader of Young Pioneers this year is—Anqi!" To the sound of warm applause, I smiled broadly.

This was the most unusual and exciting day in my life because it was a good chance for me to build my self-confidence and strengthen my courage.

> "Although I told myself, 'Don't be nervous,' again and again, I felt quite nervous. My heart beat faster and faster as if there were a rabbit bouncing in my chest…"

Young Pioneers

The Young Pioneers is the youth group for children aged 7–14. Young Pioneers are honed to become leaders within the Communist Party. They learn the history of the party, the importance of respecting authority, and the merits of doing good deeds. Yearly, the leaders of the Young Pioneers gather for a national congress on International Children's Day.

Meeting Angela
by Starla

Angela (that is Anqi's "English" name that she likes her new American friends to use) is dressed in a magenta Disney tracksuit with a scarlet-and-white checkered blouse underneath. She is in her last year of primary school, so her hair is cut in a short pixie hairdo. She has pulled it back from her forehead with a small, pink barrette. We are meeting in my hote, and Angela is with her Aunt Suni, Uncle Frank, and Enya, her nine-year-old cousin. Angela and Enya are holding hands as they approach.

Angela's hometown of Nanjing, located in the southeastern region of China, is not far from Shanghai. The easiest way to get there is to take the train, Shanghai to Nanjing, through the calming Chinese countryside. I am happy to get a break from Shanghai, a bustling metropolis that can be overwhelming with all of its people, cars, skyscrapers, billboards, twisting elevated highways, lights, horns, noises, and more people everywhere! During the train ride to Nanjing, Chinese music is

The Shanghai-Nanjing train.

broadcast over loudspeakers, and young Chinese women come through the aisles with thermoses of hot water for the Chinese soup, noodles, and tea, which the passengers have brought onboard.

Like most children in China, Angela and Enya don't have siblings, but they live in the same house together, along with their parents and grandparents, and are being raised like sisters. We sit down in the hotel's restaurant that overlooks an elaborate garden, and we order cool drinks. Angela and Enya are having milkshakes in large parfait glasses with twisting straws. As we sip our drinks and talk (Angela's aunt and uncle speak English), Angela and Enya exchange furtive glances and giggles—just like sisters.

During the conversation, we quickly establish that Angela was born in the Year of the Horse. One of the characteristics of children born under this sign is that they are outgoing and popular among their peers. Angela is, in fact, very popular at school, so much so that last year she was elected to be senior leader of the Young Pioneers. This is similar to being elected class president. Angela explains that, as Young Pioneer leader, she must set an example for the

Clockwise from top: Starla, Angela, and Enya.

other students and carry out many responsibilities. Every Monday morning, she presides over the Flag Raising Ceremony at school. Every two weeks, she is in charge of determining the contents of the school bulletin board, and throughout the year, she is in charge of organizing school activities like Arts Week and various competitions between classes. She also represents the school at important events, such as the International Children's Day Ceremony, which is celebrated in China on June 1.

In preparation for the election, Angela distributed for the students and teachers, a personal resumé, in which she introduced herself and described her character and ambitions. For these elections, students do not run campaigns, put up posters, or employ catchy slogans, like you might see in a student council election in the United States. The students in Angela's school vote for candidates based on their resumés and their speech which is given over a loudspeaker on Election Day.

Chinese lanterns in red, of course. In China, red is the color for good luck.

My Best Day

translated from Chinese

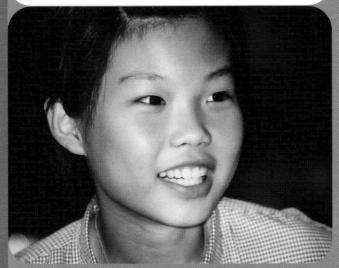

Angela

Jiangxin Islet in Nanjing, China, is a wonderful place. It is an islet in the middle of the Changjiang River. Perhaps it got its name (which means "islet in the middle of the river") from this. I had heard before that Jiangxin Islet abounded in grapes and that there was a Grape Festival in July and August every year. I had been eager to visit there for a long time, and finally I achieved my wish this summer. Dad took me there just before the opening of the Grape Festival.

Dad and I got to the ferry very early that day (since Jiangxin Islet is in the middle of the river we had to take a ferryboat to get there). There were many big ships berthed near the bank. Dad and I got onto the ferryboat. "Hoot-hoot"—the steam whistle sang and the ferryboat set sail. Standing on the deck, I was so excited—the Changjiang River was rolling and roaring with great waves, there were lots of people on the deck, and "Grandpa of Wind" brought us a soft wind. The scene was beautiful and I was very happy. "Hoot-hoot"—the steam whistle sang again. We had arrived at Jiangxin Islet!

When we went ashore, we met Uncle Xiao, Dad's colleague. Uncle Xiao lives on Jiangxin Islet and he came here especially to meet us.

Riding in a red tour bus, we arrived at Uncle Xiao's home. Uncle Xiao Lu took out two bunches of grapes from the fridge for us. Wow, grapes! They are my favorite fruit! I put the grapes into my mouth one after another, and I had no time even to speak. After a while, I had made a hill of grape skins in front of me and I recalled a (Chinese) tongue twister about grapes: "Don't spit out grape skins while eating grapes, but spit out grape skins while not eating grapes." Thinking of this funny tongue twister, I cannot help laughing.

The grapes here deserve the reputation they enjoy. They are very sweet and tasty. The grapes are the size of a Ping-Pong ball and the color is glossy and purple. Just looking at them makes your mouth water. Uncle Xiao told me that these grapes are a new variety called *Jufeng* (meaning "huge and abundant"). When you peel off the thin skin, the flesh of the grape is like a fat and pretty baby. When you put it into your mouth, you can feel it is juicy, sweet, and quite tasty.

After eating grapes, we went to the vineyard behind Uncle Xiao Lu's house. The grapevines were like green dragons twisting and twining round the trellis. This trellis was not made of wood but of iron wire, and unlike the grape trellises used in Tulufan (a famous grape-growing area in Xinjiang, China), they were not in the shape of pillars. There was a sea of green leaves! Why, there were also hundreds of uniform white bags fastened on the trellises. Looking far into the distance, it was like lots of white spray in the green sea and it was very beautiful.

I was surprised because I couldn't see any grapes, so I asked Uncle Xiao, "We have come here to pick grapes,

Can You Say Angela's Tongue Twister in Chinese?

Here it is in English: Don't spit out grape skins while eating grapes, but spit out grape skins while not eating grapes.

Now try in Chinese: Chi pu tao bu tu pu tao pi, bu chi bu tao dao tu pu tao pi.

"...these grapes are called Jufeng meaning 'huge and abundant'."

Uncle Xiao, but where are the grapes?" Uncle Xiao told me that the grapes were inside the white paper bags. I see! *Jufeng* grapes were grown this way. And the bags were not ordinary bags. They were especially made for *Jufeng* grapes. There was a wax coating on the surface of the bag to protect the grapes from dampness and insects. Uncle Xiao also told me that this method has many other strong points: the size of the grapes is bigger; it is considered "green" food because there is no pollution from insect repellents; after the grapes are ripe, no matter whether they are green or purple, they are sweet; and the flesh is thick while the pits are small. Uncle Xiao's explanation made me come to an understanding all of a sudden.

At this time, Uncle Xiao gave us two pairs of scissors, one for Dad and one for me. I was surprised again, "We can pick grapes just using our hands, why do we need to use scissors?" Uncle Xiao and Dad laughed. Dad said, "The grapevine is thick and strong, so using scissors will be easi-er and quicker." Then, I stepped into the vineyard with scissors in my hand. Uncle Xiao taught me how to pick the grapes. There was a small hole in the white bag to let air in and so people can observe the growing condition of the grapes. After looking through the hole, I cut the ripe grapes with the scissors and left the unripe ones. When cutting the grapes down, I did not tear the bag, or the grapes would have fallen down from the vine. The bag was fastened at the top, so I unfastened it and took the grapes out. Under Uncle Xiao's direction, I picked grapes one bunch after another.

Looking at the countless grapes on the grapevines, I recalled the ordinary peasants who grew grapes. They watered the grapes and fertilized them, and a whole year's hard work won a month's harvest for them. Their work was not easy!

The day spent on Jiangxin Islet was the best and most unique day for me, because on this day I gained a lot of knowledge and experienced the happiness of harvests.

Angela and Enya walk home for lunch every day.

SCHOOL DAYS

Angela and Enya attend the same public primary school in Nanjing, and walk there together every morning. School starts at 7:30 in the morning and ends at 4:00 in the afternoon. Angela has 50 classmates, both boys and girls, who all wear school uniforms.

Angela's school subjects include Chinese Language, Mathematics, English, Arts, Gym, Music, Science, Nature, and Civics. In Civics, students learn how to behave in society, at school and at home. Angela's favorite subject is English. The children change classrooms for each subject. The children do not have personal lockers or desks, so they must carry all of their schoolbooks with them for the entire day. They have a half hour for lunch and may eat at school, or go home to eat. Angela and Enya walk home for lunch every day.

There are various clubs, or "interest groups," at the school such as the Chinese Group, Math Group, or English Group, where the children can deepen their knowledge of specific school subjects. There is also a computer interest group that Angela belonged to when she was younger. Sports clubs are only for the boy students at Angela's school.

School is very competitive for Chinese children, particularly at Angela's age. Students must prepare for a middle-school examination, which will determine where they can attend middle school, and greatly influence where they will eventually attend high school.

If I Could Be...

translated from Chinese

Everyone has her own goal and dream. If you ask me "What is your dream?" I will tell you proudly that I want to be an astronaut who explores outer space.

As a child, I liked to read books about the universe very much. Mum and Dad bought a lot of books about the universe for me, such as *Outer Space*, *Human Beings and the Universe*, and so on. I never get tired of reading these books. As a result, my knowledge about outer space is increasing constantly. Now I can answer questions such as "Does human life exist on the Mars?" or "Who was the first person exploring outer space?"

I hope I will be an astronaut enjoying great fame both at home and abroad in the next 20 years. At that time, I will travel to outer space in a special spaceship that I will design. I will call it *Success*, implying that exploring outer space will be a success. It will be specially made according to people's different needs. Its outside design will be streamlined, beautiful, and practical. The spaceship will be operated automatically. Wherever you want to go, just call the name of the place by microphone and then the spaceship will take you there. When you reach the place, the spaceship will land automatically and put down the ladder. If you want to take some photos, you can just sit there and click the screen, and the spaceship will take many valuable pictures for you at your command. I believe that spaceships in the future will be what I have described.

How do you like my dream? It is quite wonderful, isn't it? In fact, we can turn this dream into reality if only we study hard starting now and all the countries work together to grasp the technique of making this spaceship. If we do this, I believe we can change "not have" to "have" and "impossible" to "possible" because both mankind and human society are progressing!

As for being elected the leader of our country, it is everyone's dream, including mine. However, my aspiration to be a country leader is not as strong as my dream to be an astronaut. I don't want or expect to be a music star or a movie star. And I don't think I can win a gold medal at the Olympics since the results of my P.E. course are not very good (although not too bad). So I will only cheer for the athletes at every Olympics.

CHINA'S SPACE PROGRAM

"Taikonaut" is the Chinese counterpart for the American astronaut and Russian cosmonaut. In October 2003, China became the third nation in the world to achieve manned space travel. Cosmonaut Yuri Gagarin, of the former Soviet Union, was the first man to orbit the Earth in 1961. John Glenn became the first American astronaut to do the same in 1962. After 21 hours in orbit, Chinese "taikonaut" Yang Liwei, aboard spacecraft *Shenzhou 5*, became the third man to orbit the Earth—making Angela's dream of space travel that much closer to reality.

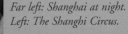

*Far left: Shanghai at night.
Left: The Shanghi Circus.*

Year of the Rat
1936, 1948, 1960, 1972, 1984, 1996
Noted for your charm and beauty, you are a perfectionist with big ambitions and you work hard to achieve your goals. Generally thrifty with money, you are easily angered, but also love to talk with your friends. You are compatible with people born in the Years of the Dragon, Monkey, and Ox.

Year of the Ox
1937, 1949, 1961, 1973, 1985, 1997
Patient and eccentric, you speak very little but can be quite eloquent when you do. You are easygoing, and mentally and physically alert. You have strong opinions, are easily angered, have a fierce temper, and can be remarkably stubborn. You are compatible with people born in the Years of the Snake, Rooster, and Rat.

Year of the Tiger
1938, 1950, 1962, 1974, 1986, 1998
You are sensitive, given to deep thinking, greatly sympathetic, and respected by others. You are powerful and courageous, but can also be short-tempered, indecisive, suspicious, and have conflicts with those in positions of authority. You are compatible with people born in the Years of the Horse, Dragon, and Dog.

Year of the Rabbit
1939, 1951, 1963, 1975, 1987, 1999
Articulate, talented, ambitious, you are also virtuous, have excellent taste, are financially lucky, and kind. You love to talk with friends, you are clever, conservative, and wise. You can be evasive and do not say what you are really thinking. It seems you are always planning your next move. You are compatible with people born in the Years of the Sheep, Pig, and Dog.

Year of the Dragon
1940, 1952, 1964, 1976, 1988, 2000
You are healthy, energetic, honest, sensitive, brave, inspirational, and trustworthy. You tend to be soft hearted, which sometimes gives others an advantage over you. You are also excitable, short-tempered, and stubborn. You are compatible with people born in Years of the Rat, Snake, Monkey, and Rooster.

Year of the Snake
1941, 1953, 1965, 1977, 1989, 2001
You are deep, wise, reticent, lucky, sympathetic, and helpful to those less fortunate. You are calm on the surface but passionate inside. You have doubts about other people's judgments and prefer to rely on yourself. You are compatible with people born in the Years of the Ox and Rooster.

The Chinese Zodiac
The Chinese calendar is a lunar calendar, meaning that it follows the movement of the moon, and it dates from 2600 BC! The entire lunar cycle takes 60 years, or 5 cycles of 12 years. That is why 12 years must pass before another generation of Sheep or Dragon are born. Since the start of the New Year is based on the moon cycles, it can fall anywhere between late January to February!

Rat

Pig

Dog

Ox

Rooster

Tiger

Monkey

Rabbit

Sheep

Dragon

Snake

Horse

Year of the Horse
1942, 1954, 1966, 1978, 1990, 2002
You are popular, cheerful, skillful with money, perceptive, talkative, wise, talented, and good with your hands. You like to entertain large crowds, and are very independent. You rarely listen to advice. You can be impatient and hot-blooded. You are compatible with people born in the Years of the Tiger, Dog, and Sheep.

Year of the Sheep
1943, 1955, 1967, 1979, 1991, 2003
Elegant and highly accomplished in the arts, you are also shy, usually deeply religious, and passionate about your beliefs. You are wise, gentle, and compassionate. You can also be pessimistic, are sometimes puzzled by life, and tongue-tied. You are compatible with people born in the Years of the Rabbit, Pig, and Horse.

Year of the Monkey
1944, 1956, 1968, 1980, 1992, 2004
You are the changeable genius of the Chinese zodiac—clever, skillful, flexible, inventive, and original. You are a good problem solver, possess common sense, have a deep desire for knowledge, and an excellent memory. You are strong-willed, but your anger cools quickly. You can also be overly agreeable, impatient about your projects, and become bored too quickly. You are compatible with people born in the Years of the Dragon and Rat.

Year of the Rooster
1945, 1957, 1969, 1981, 1993, 2005
You are a deep thinker, capable, and talented. You like to be busy and are devoted beyond your capabilities and deeply disappointed if you fail. You are often a bit eccentric, and can be timid, selfish, and outspoken. You are compatible with people born in the Years of the Ox, Snake, and Dragon.

Year of the Dog
1946, 1958, 1970, 1982, 1994, 2006
You are very loyal and honest, a good leader, know how to keep a secret, care little for wealth, but always seem to have money. You find fault with many things and are known for your sharp tongue. You are compatible with people born in Years of the Horse, Tiger, and Rabbit.

Year of the Pig
1947, 1959, 1971, 1983, 1995, 2007
Whatever you do, you do with all your strength. You are quiet, honest, and extremely loyal. You keep friends for life, possess a great thirst for knowledge, and are very well educated. You also tend to be quick-tempered and impulsive, but you hate arguments and quarreling. You are compatible with people born in the Years of the Rabbit and Sheep.

Did You Know?

- Nanjing, formerly called Nanking, is the capital of Jiangxu Province in the southeastern part of China—officially known as the People's Republic of China (PRC).

- China was ruled by a series of Dynasties for over 3,000 years. In 1911, the Qing Dynasty was overthrown by the Chinese Nationalist party headed by Dr. Sun Yat-sen.

Chinese Flag

- Since the break-up of the Soviet Union, China, Cuba, and North Korea remain the world's last Communist nations. Unlike Cuba and North Korea, China has opened up several free economic zones and is very active within the world community.

Chinese Currency

- Throughout China, particularly in the larger cities like Beijing and Shanghai, people wake up at 6:00 in the morning and join hundreds of others for morning exercises. In Shanghai, the people converge on the river quay (the Bund) to start their day with Tai Chi, fan dancing, sword dancing, kite flying, and even ballroom dancing.

- In China, the last name, or family name, goes before one's given name in writing, as well as in formal introductions.

Some words in Putonghua Mandarin

Hello = Ni hao	Please = qíng
Yes = Shì	Thank you = Xie xie
No = Bú shì	Goodbye = Zài jiàn
	Friend = Péng you
	How are you? = Ni hao ma?

Fan Dancing on the Shanghai Bund.

China

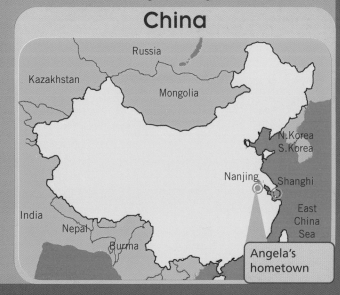

Russia

Kazakhstan

Mongolia

N. Korea
S. Korea

India

Nanjing   Shanghi

Nepal

Burma

East China Sea

Angela's hometown

Wanning Beijing, China

Wanning

Nationality: Chinese

Religion: None

Languages: Chinese, and I have just begun learning English at school.

Brothers and Sisters: None

Pets: None, although I used to have some birds.

Hobbies: Playing badminton; drawing pictures; reading; making up short stories; playing Peace Chess; and skipping rope

Talents: Skipping rope and playing badminton

Favorite Sport: Badminton

Favorite Books: *Little Angels in the Forest*; *Les Miserables* by Victor Hugo;

and *Chi-Bi Marubo*

Favorite Food: Chocolate

Least Favorite Food: Cake

Whom do you most admire? Painters and artists

Favorite Possession: My collection of books in the *Little Angels in the Forest* series

Do you help with chores at home? Sometimes I clean the table or the shoe cabinet.

Do you have your own telephone or computer? No

Do you use the Internet? No

Where would you most want to travel? Tokyo, Japan

What comes to mind when you think of the United States? The Statue of Liberty

…and France? The Eiffel Tower

…and China? The Great Wall

…and Kenya? African, dark skin

What do you talk about with friends? Studies

What do you want to know about other girls your age? About their hobbies

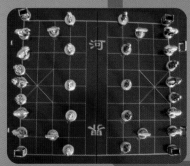

Wanning's favorite game, Peace Chess.

Peace Chess

Wanning's favorite game, Peace Chess, is the most popular board game in the world based upon the number of people who play it. In the game, the Black Palace and the Red Palace strategize to cross a river (which is symbolized by a line across the middle of the board). According to legend, the game depicts a stalemate in a real battle that occurred over 2000 years ago. In that stalemate, the armies were deadlocked on either side of a river in Southern China. Peace Chess is a re-enactment of this stalemate…it is up to the players to see who prevails in the battle in a more peaceful fashion!

If I Could Be...

translated from Chinese

If I had to choose among many jobs, I would choose sports as my career without the least hesitation. And I would hope to win a gold medal at the Olympics through my great efforts.

Why am I eager to be an Olympic gold medal winner? Whenever I see on TV Chinese athletes standing atop the awards stand and the five-starred red flag rising slowly to the powerful national anthem, I feel as excited as the athletes. This is the proudest and most exciting moment for us Chinese and this is the moment I am most yearning for. I often dream of that precious moment: I am standing on the awards stand with a gold medal hanging around my neck. My face shines red before the bright red national flag. Flowers, hand-clapping, and cheers of joy overwhelm me. I feel so happy and excited!

However, being an Olympic gold medal winner is not exactly easy. It requires hardships and great efforts, tears, and sweat. I know that this is a beautiful and faraway goal, but it is also my ultimate dream. My results in my physical education course are not very good. I cannot run the fastest or jump the farthest, but I have tried my best and I will always try my best. I am very thin and weak, so I hope I can strengthen

Beijing street with China's national flag waving above.

my body through physical exercises.

Championship and gold medals are not far away from me because they represent Olympic spirit in my heart. When I meet setbacks in my life or study, I recall many Olympic champions, such as Deng Yaping, Kong Linghui, Fu Mingxia, and so on. They practiced in chilly winters and burning summers. Their sweat dripped like rain showers; they fell down and bled. They overcame a lot of difficulties. How persevering and strong they are! Their spirit influence and encourage me. I will follow these models and face challenges in my future life and study bravely.

Being an Olympic gold medal winner is not only my dream but also the motive in my life. Every Olympic champion is my example. I will study hard and do exercises hard, and be a useful person for the development of China in the future. At the same time, I wish that I could win a gold medal at the Olympics. Imagine how happy and proud I would be standing on the awards stand!

China and Population

Have you noticed that both Wanning and Angela do not have siblings? This isn't a coincidence. It is the result of China's "one family, one child" policy. To control population growth, the Chinese government has encouraged families to have only one child. Thus, Wanning is an only child, as are the majority of the students in Wanning's class at school, and nearly all of the children she encounters on a daily basis. None of them have brothers and sisters! There was concern that the one-child policy would result in generations of spoiled children. In fact, these children are excelling beyond their peers in other countries in everything from foreign languages and mathematics, to music and the arts.

Wanning with her aunt and uncle.

Chinese Painting

Wanning's afterschool activity, Chinese painting, is very specialized. It is traditionally done in black ink on white silk. The subject of the work is usually either Chinese calligraphy or Chinese symbols. The Chinese symbols may be animals, insects, or plants, all of which have specific meanings. The speed with which the artist completes the painting, as well as the number of brush strokes used (the fewer the better), are as important as the quality of the finished painting in judging the talent of the artist.

A rooster symbolizes good luck; bamboo means long life.

Meeting Wanning
by Starla

Wanning means "Concentrated Perfection" in Chinese, and that is what she looks like as she sits gracefully at the very edge of a large fluffy sofa. Her shiny black hair is cut in a short pixie-style, typical of all Chinese primary-school students. She is dressed in a Mickey and Minnie Mouse T-shirt, a white jacket, black tracksuit pants, and white leather sneakers.

Wanning lives in Beijing, the capital city of the People's Republic of China, in an apartment with her mother and father. Rather than meet at Wanning's home, however, we are at the hotel where I am staying. Wanning is waiting for me along with her mother, father, her older cousin, Colleen, and Colleen's boyfriend. As I approach, Wanning's elegant family stands up to shake my hand. Wanning quietly steps out from behind her mother and tentatively holds out her little hand for a handshake. Wanning's father and cousin speak English so they are translating for us. Wanning speaks a form of Mandarin Chinese called Putonghua, which is the official language of China. We sit down in the hotel lounge and order tea.

Through the large window of the hotel lounge, we can see the wide, crowded, tree-lined avenues, where bicycles have the same rights as cars.

Wanning means "Concentrated Perfection" in Chinese.

It is the Golden Week holiday, which begins every year on Worker's Day (May 1) and there is an unending sea of people enjoying the sights of Beijing. In fact, 2 million tourists are here for the festivities. Couple that with the fact that we are already in the world's most-populous country, and that adds up to a lot of people! More than 1.2 billion people call China their home. That is nearly one-quarter of the entire world's population. On top of that, much of the population is concentrated in the Eastern part of the country, where Wanning lives. With so many people living so closely to one another, it is important for people to get along.

What I Most Want The World To Know
translated from Chinese

I most want people around the world to know what I am thinking. Because if people around the world understood each other better, there would be less misunderstanding, less suspicion, and fewer quarrels, and then the world would become more peaceful and happy.

My Best Day

translated from Chinese

My happiest day was when my mom bought me three little parrots. I loved them very much. I named the boy wearing a green coat, Guangguang, the girl in the yellow coat, Nini, and the other girl in dark blue, Tiantian. Tiantian had a bad habit. She liked to be at Guangguang's side all the time. Wherever Guangguang went, she would follow. Sometimes Guangguang turned his head to her as if to say angrily, "Why do you always follow me?"

But Guangguang liked chasing Nini. I thought that Guangguang shouldn't blame Tiantian for following him, because he himself always followed Nini. But, I didn't know their thoughts.

Still, Guangguang was the naughtiest one. He liked

"My mom bought me three little parrots."

bouncing up and down and twittering from morning to evening; he did not eat at feeding time; he pecked noisily at the cage; he ate his rice very noisily in the early morning, waking me up. When I ran to the balcony to "punish" him, he acted as if he had done nothing wrong. He was so lovely! Sometimes, I let them bathe in the sun.

Nini liked singing very much. When the sun rose, she would hold her head high and sing. Nini had no bad habits. However, no matter how many bad habits Tiantian and Guangguang had, I liked them better.

But one day, the three of them flew away. I always wonder: What are their lives like now? Are they hungry? Do they get wet in the rain? Thinking of them, I feel very sad. When I hear birds singing, I always look out of the window hoping to see my three naughty, lovely parrots. I miss them very much.

Did You Know?

these historic sites are crowded market streets with not only traditional Chinese medicine shops and tea houses, but also McDonald's and Starbucks chain stores.

One of the many giant portraits of Mao Zedong in Tiananmen Square.

- Beijing, the city where Wanning lives, was the capital city of China under the Yuan, Ming, and Qing dynasties. (Nanjing, Angela's city, was the capital before that). These three dynasties contributed to the building of the Forbidden City, where the Emperor and his entourage lived. Regular Chinese people were not permitted to enter the vast grounds.

The Forbidden City.

- Since the 1950s, school children like Wanning have been making goods, from arts and crafts to fireworks, as part of the socialist school curriculum.

- Beijing is a mix of the ancient and ultra-modern. The Forbidden City is surrounded by tall red walls and just in front is massive Tiananmen Square, with its giant portraits of Mao Zedong. Surrounding

The Great Wall of China.

China

Kasakhstan

Mongolia

Kyrgyzstan

Where Wanning lives

N. Korea

Beijing

S. Korea

Yellow Sea

Nepal

Bhutan

India

Burma

Hong Kong

Dieu Hanoi, Vietnam

Thu Dieu ("Dieu")

Nationality: Vietnamese

Religion: None

Languages: Vietnamese and English

Brothers and Sisters: An elder sister

Pets: Yes, a cat

Hobbies: Swimming; reading comic books; looking for the history of Hittites and Egypt on the Internet

Talents: Speaking English; making jokes

Favorite sport: Swimming

Favorite Books: *5000 stories about the Ancient World*; *Sakura* (a comic book); *The Oxford Guide to English Grammar*

Favorite Food: Chicken; beef; and pork

Least Favorite Food: Vegetables

Whom do you most admire? The princess in the fairy tale

Favorite Possession: A small collection of comic books

Sakura, Dieu's favorite comic book.

Do you help with chores at home? Yes: cooking, washing dishes, cleaning the floor, washing clothes...etc.

Do you use the Internet? Yes, my favorite website is www.shoujoinitalia.net.

Do you have your own telephone or computer? Yes, I have my own laptop computer.

Where would you most want to travel? The United States

What comes to mind when you think of the United States? The Statue of Liberty

...and France? Eiffel Tower

...and China? Kung Fu movies

...and Kenya? Hot, sunny

What do you talk about with friends? About the boys in our class

What do you want to know about other girls your age? Do they have boyfriends at the age 13 or do they think it's too early?

About Me
translated from Vietnamese

Everybody wants the people around to know them as a wonderful, admirable person. I am like that too. In class, I am known as a tough, fearsome girl. Even the boys are afraid of me. It's a good feeling to have. The girls admire me and consider me to be the leader of the girls in class. Even the boys do not dare to hit me. In this age, people probably no longer value feminine traits like they used to. Of the people who know me, some think that I am a girl without any feminine qualities, one who is no good. Others think that I have a unique personality and should be respected. It is hard to control what other people think about you.

My parents often tell me that if I am not feminine, it will be hard to find a husband. But I have been this way since I was little. My mother told the story that when I was still in her stomach, one time I kicked so hard that she was bumped into my sister, who was sitting next to her. At first, my parents thought that I would be a boy and had a boy name ready for me. When I came out, my father had to rush to find me an appropriate name. When I heard my mother's story, I wondered if my father was sad when he found out I was a girl.

Why have there always been such differences between boys and girls? Maybe the boys are stronger, but so what? On the intellectual side, girls are not any less capable than boys are. These days, even a woman can become president. Perhaps because I was born under such funny circumstances, I have always thought that I have to do something so that people won't think so little of girls.

In class, I am an ordinary student, with no subject that I clearly excel in over my friends. I am not a very smart girl in studying. The head of my class, a boy, is a very good student. He is so good that he gets to participate in the competition for the best students in the city.

"I will enjoy all the time I have now."

Because of that, he becomes an idol in the minds of other students. For the girls, the important thing is to make a good impression with the boys. We hope they have good impressions of us...the better the impression, the more wonderful we feel.

My class is so fun. The students always get together to chat or poke fun at each other. Everyday, we gather at the large, familiar tree of our class to talk about things that happened to us. Some talk about fun things in their families. The girls gather to gossip, while the boys get together to play soccer. Those who haven't done their homework sit down near the tree to copy their friends' homework. I think my class must have the most fun in school. Usually, when the school announces days off, everyone would be very happy. However, I think staying at home is more boring than going to school. There are boring things in school, but at least I always have friends to talk and play with the whole day.

I think I would be very bored once I pass the high school age. Then, I won't be as happy as I am now. Therefore, I will enjoy all the time I have now.

My life is generally good. It may even be a life that other girls my age wish for. I often have demanded more from my parents. Now, I realize that I was wrong to do this. I have enough, maybe even too much. With this life, I don't have much to wish for. I can only hope I have the ability to fulfill my parents' wishes and to repay what they have done for me. People often say that life is not fair. I must be so lucky to have a life this good. For 13-year-old girls, a life like this is already wonderful.

"Why have there always been such differences between boys and girls? Maybe the boys are stronger, but so what? On the intellectual side, girls are not any less capable than boys are."

Meeting Dieu
by Starla

Dieu can be very intimidating. For starters, her name in French means "God." She is tall, very pretty, and not afraid to speak her mind. She likes to pretend she is lazy (I don't believe she really is) and she enjoys intimidating the boys in her school. While this has brought her the admiration of the girls in her class, she sometimes worries that she is not feminine enough. This is not a typical worry for girls who come from a country renowned for their graceful, quiet, and beautiful women.

Dieu's desk.

Dieu is from Hanoi, Vietnam where she lives with her mother and father in a small house, which has a living room and kitchen on the first floor, and her parent's room, her bedroom, and her studying room on the second floor. She has an older sister, who is currently studying abroad in England.

Dieu's father always takes the time to explain her homework if she doesn't understand.

Both of the girls in Dieu's family speak excellent English. As Dieu explains, this is thanks to her parents. Although she is sometimes afraid of her father because he can be very strict, he is also very intelligent and always takes the time to explain Dieu's schoolwork to her if she doesn't understand.

Her mother is very good at English and works in a foreign embassy in Vietnam. Dieu is very proud of her parents and gains great inspiration from them.

On weekends, you will find Dieu in jeans and a T-shirt. (There are not too many skirts in her wardrobe.) She usually spends her Saturdays going to the market shopping with her mother in the morning, and watching TV and relaxing with her father in the afternoon. If she is with friends, they may go to the movies, the local entertainment center to play games, Sword Lake (the most famous lake in Vietnam), or to get ice cream. When friends come over to Dieu's house they sit around on the floor watching videos, eating snacks, talking about school and their teachers, and maybe sometimes talking about boys.

As you can see from her essay, Dieu knows that she is very fortunate to live the life she does. There is a lot of poverty in Vietnam and the surrounding countries of Laos and Cambodia. This whole area of the world became a pawn of the Cold War and its aftermath. In the case of Vietnam, the country lost a lot of financial support from the Soviet Union when it dissolved in 1991. Nevertheless, through hard work and study, Dieu's parents have improved their lives for the benefit of Dieu and her elder sister, and it is clear that Dieu recognizes and appreciates their sacrifice. One of her ambitions is to have her parents live with her when they are older.

For now though, Dieu is enjoying being a young teenage girl—a simple comic book or a CD of her favorite boy-band would be among the greatest gifts you could give her.

And she can still get away with acting lazy, noisy, and funny, and scaring the boys in her class at school, all the while daydreaming about being the princess in the fairy tale and imagining the handsome prince on the white horse riding up to her.

SCHOOL DAYS

Not surprisingly, English is Dieu's favorite class in school, and she is among the best students in her English class, although her teacher thinks that she can be a "difficult" student. (OK, she tends to be a little loud…and remember how she pretends to be lazy?)

Dieu's classes include English, Mathematics, Literature, Physics, Biology, Chemistry, History, and Geography. School is six days a week, Monday through Saturday, from 7:15 a.m. until 12:00 in the afternoon. The eveninghomework load is not too bad, althoughit depends on thelesson and the time of year.

Dieu with her friends.

Nevertheless, summer is Dieu's favorite season precisely because there is no homework. Dieu wears a uniform to school, which consists of a white shirt and blue trousers.

My Best Day
translated from Vietnamese

My best day was yesterday, the first day I was able to cook a full meal for my parents. I was so embarrassed. Most other kids, particularly the girls, probably already knew how to cook since they were nine or ten. But not me. I only know how to cook now, three months before my last birthday. Actually, I knew how to cook a few simple dishes. However, it was only yesterday that I was able to cook a full meal for my parents.

My older sister went abroad to study in England two years ago. Since then, my parents have showered their attention on me, causing me to be lazy. When anyone mentioned cooking, I felt lazy. However, I have to admit I felt complete and wonderful when I was able to cook a full meal for the first time.

After I finished cooking, my heart beat faster than usual because my parents were about to enjoy the first meal I cooked. I was excited and nervous, yet unsure how my parents would enjoy the meal. It's hard to describe the feeling. I felt happy and liked the thought that my parents will have a good meal that I prepared for them. It was a feeling I never had before.

It was the first time I went to the market by myself. Usually, I went to the market with my mother to help her with carrying the bags. My mother did all the purchasing and bargaining with the vendors. By myself, I wasn't sure what I wanted to buy. After walking around the market twice, I bought two bags of tofu. Then after another round, I bought some more meat and shrimp, and then went home. But food shopping was only the first step.

The hardest part was to stand in the kitchen to cook. I was used to being in the kitchen, but it was only to help my mom with her chores. Now, I stood here alone with a pile of pots and pans, and unprepared raw meat and vegetables. I wasn't sure how I was going to cook

"I will become a capable woman, but I won't just stay at home to be a housewife. I will find employment in society just like a man. I am sure other girls have the same thought."

THE LUNAR NEW YEAR

The largest festival in Vietnam is the Vietnamese Lunar New Year called *Tet Nguyen Dan* (which means "Feast of the Three Firsts"). This is celebrated on the 23rd day of the 12th month of the lunar calendar used in Vietnam (usually corresponding to late January—early February). Tet is the first season of the new year.

The lunar calendar (which is also used in Angela's and Wanning's China) follows the movement of the moon, and this is where it gets its name from. It dates from 2600 BC, and the entire lunar cycle takes 60 years, or 5 cycles of 12 years.

During the holiday of Tet, Vietnamese families honor other family members and ancestors, cleanse themselves of the previous year's troubles, and prepare for the New Year and the start of spring. There are many special foods and rituals that are prepared and followed as part of the Tet festivities.

Language lesson:
Happy New Year
(to be said during Tet):
Chuc Mung Nam Moi

them. The smell of boiling oil and the crackling sound of firewood were familiar. But somehow, this time they felt much better than usual. The air in the kitchen became hotter, similar to the burning feeling I had inside, unsure whether I had cooked well.

Cooking was hard work. I tasted the food many times to make sure they were just right. I was so happy after putting them on the plates and seeing that they looked good. At other times, when my mother brought delicious dishes from the kitchen, I wasn't as happy as I am now. An ordinary dish, even slightly burned, prepared by my own hands made me feel wonderful.

I brought the dishes from the kitchen to the dining room. After setting up all the dishes on the dining table, I felt so good looking at the sight. I waited impatiently for my parents to come home from work, hoping that they would enjoy the first meal made by their daughter.

Yes, I admit that I am a lazy person. I am laziest when it comes to doing household chores. I am also lazy with doing my homework. But after cooking this meal, I began to like cooking. I like to watch my parents eating the meal I cooked. It makes me feel that I have done something to help my parents and make them happy.

I am sometimes lazy and sometimes hard working. If no one reminds me, I won't ever remember to do the household chores myself. But once I start doing it, I would do a very good, thorough job. This personality of mine is strange, but what can I do? It's my personality.

Remembering back, I still think yesterday was so wonderful. My parents said that the meal I cooked was delicious. I also thought it was delicious. Is this the happiness of a housewife? But saying that is probably too early since I am not yet a housewife. Nevertheless, if you want to have this feeling, why don't you go into the kitchen to cook? I've failed at cooking many times and only attained success this time.

As a girl, not knowing how to cook will be a problem, making it hard to find a husband. Being capable at doing housework is a good trait for women, one that I need to fully use. I will become a capable woman, but I won't just stay at home to be a housewife. I will find employment in society just like a man. I am sure other girls have the same thought. Women are not any less capable than men are.

Oh, yesterday was so wonderful that I found it hard to go to sleep. I just laid there smiling, remembering the meal. Today, I cooked the meal again. Usually, my mother still has to cook after coming home from a tiring day of work. Today, she could sit down to eat dinner as soon as she came home. Seeing my mother smiling happily and forgetting her tiredness, I felt so good. I thought I was becoming a truly capable young woman. My father came home late. As soon as I heard the horn of his motorcycle, I had a hot bowl of rice ready for him on the table. His face had a smile as bright as mother's smile. The creases on his face seemed to be more and deeper every year. My mother also has grown skinnier. Perhaps, this year it will be different.

If I Could Be...
translated from Vietnamese

Who doesn't have a dream? I have dreams too and many of them. For a girl, the dream is usually to have a "prince on a white horse" appearing in her life. I have the same dream too, to have a handsome, tall, nice man who wants to be my boyfriend. But it is a dream that is hard to become reality. Where do you find such a man these days? Even if there is such a man, what is the chance that he would like me? That's why those dreams are hard to become reality.

But if we talk about more realistic dreams, then my first dream is to pass the exam to go to college. Since I was little, my parents have spent all their time to take good care of and educate me. My parents work very hard and save every penny. They ignore their own wants and needs, all because of me. I am very grateful for everything they have done for me. I have became a grown, well-adjusted person, all due to my parents, their sweat, and sacrifices.

My parents just wish that I will go to college, then be able to find a good job, and have a good family. Thus, the dream is not just mine, it's my parents' too. I want

The gardens at the Emperor's Tomb.

"The dream of finding a 'prince on a white horse' is just a dream of the adolescent... It is probably similar to dreams of other young girls my age. I know from sitting dreamily in class and hearing the girls get together to gossip about the handsome boys."

to be able to go to college, so that I won't let my parents down. I feel that I am much luckier than other children in my country. I have a father, a mother, and a warm, loving family that provides everything I need. I have three full meals a day and enough warm clothes to wear during the cold winter days.

There are many children my own age, or even younger, who never knew their parents' faces. Daily, they wander in the dusty, dirty streets to beg for a living. Wearing dirty clothes, their skin turned dark and leathery from exposure to the relentless tropical weather. They don't even get to go to school and don't know how to read, let alone to talk about finding a job later to make a living. Where are their lives headed?

Every time she sees these children in the street, my mom would tell me, "See there. These children are younger than you and they have to shine shoes or beg for a living. You have to realize how much luckier you are. You have to work harder. You only have to play and study, how hard can it be? Don't disappoint me and your father."

Perhaps it is because I only have to play and study that I become complacent and don't have the drive to work hard. Now, I have set a dream for myself, the same dream that my parents have. First, I have to try hard to make it to college, to deserve everything my parents have done for me. They only hope I can go to college and receive a good

education so that later I will have a way to make a good living and to have a good life.

Right!

What other romantic, faraway dreams do I have? The most wonderful dream can only be to have a happy life. For me, to have a happy life means to go to college, according to my parents' wishes, to find a good job, to have a family with an honest, good man, and to bring my parents to live with me. Perhaps, this "happy life" dream, for me, is the main dream. It sounds simple, but this dream is a luxury. If everyone can have a life like that, then why would anyone dream to have it? Because a life like that is hard to have, people dream to have it and I dream to have it too.

I can guess my parents' dream. It has always been the same. My parents wish for me to be successful in life and that they can live with me even when I have a family of my own. My parents want to be next to me, to be able to observe as I grow up, to see the daily changes in my life in the future, and to help me in life, even with the little things. To carry out the dream of my parents is my biggest dream right now.

Additionally, I have other smaller dreams. I have mentioned above that I want to become a capable housewife, but still be able to find a job in society—a good office job with a decent salary.

Vietnamese Food

There are many varieties of Vietnamese food that are now popular all over the world. Some of world's choicest restaurants in New York, Paris, and London are Vietnamese. Boiled rice (*Cam*) is the basic food that may be served with dishes of tofu, pork, seafood, fish, and vegetables sautéed in hot vegetable oil. Other famous dishes include sticky rice cakes (*Banh Chung*), eaten especially during Vietnamese New Year Celebrations (*Tet Nyugen Dan*), hot and spicy soup with noodles called *Pho*, and crispy spring rolls (*nem*) that are eaten wrapped in a lettuce leave with a sprig of mint. Delicious! Today, it is possible to get authentic Vietnamese food in many places throughout the world where Vietnamese people have re-settled. (Many South

Vietnamese fled the country when it fell to the North in the 1970s.)

Like in other Asian cultures, knives and forks are not used during meals, only chopsticks and spoons. Therefore, all meats and vegetables are cut into small pieces before cooking.

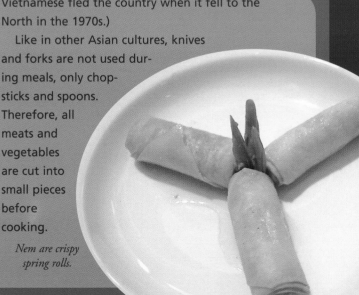

Nem are crispy spring rolls.

Did You Know?

- Vietnam is located in Southeast Asia. China is on its North, Laos and Cambodia are to the West, and the Gulf of Tonkin is to the East. In 1945, Vietnam was divided into two countries, North Vietnam and South Vietnam. It reunified in 1975. Today, Hanoi is the capital of Vietnam, and Vietnamese is the official language.

- You may have noticed Dieu's emphasis on the importance of her parents in her essays. In Vietnam, a person's first loyalty is to their family. There is a saying in Vietnam that while Westerners have health insurance, unemployment benefits, social security, foster homes, nursing homes, and psychiatrists, the Vietnamese have family.

- As with Angela's and Wanning's China, in Vietnam the family name is always spoken and written before a person's given name.

- Vietnamese culture was influenced by the Chinese because it was ruled by Chinese Dynasties for over a thousand years. During this time, Confucianism, Taoism, and Buddhism were introduced, all of which are still prevalent in Vietnamese society today.

- In the early 1960's, American troops were sent to Vietnam to fight the Communist forces of North Vietnam, which they called the Viet Cong. Many in Vietnam today refer to the "Vietnam War" (which is what Americans call it) as the "American War."

Vietnamese Flag

Vietnamese Currency

- The war in Vietnam cost America many human lives and much money, so they withdrew their troops in 1973. Shortly after that, South Vietnam fell to the forces of the North, with the fall of Saigon, which was renamed Ho Chi Minh City.

- The Vietnamese language, like Chinese, is monosyllabic, meaning that all words have only one syllable. Also like Chinese, the Vietnamese language has tones (six of them), which change the meanings of words.

- Today, Vietnam remains a Communist country. Along with Merida's Cuba and Wanning's and Angela's China, it is one of the last countries in the world with a Communist political, social, and economic system.

Some words in Vietnamese

Hello = Xin chào	No = Không
Goodbye = Tam biêt	Thank you = Cám o'n
Yes = Có, Vâng, Da	Nice to meet you. = Râ't hân hi
	Friend = Bahn

The Emperor's tomb near Hue.

Vietnam

China

Hanoi

Gulf of Tonkin

Laos

Dieu's home city

Thailand

Hue

South China Sea

Cambodia

Gulf of Thailand

Natsupho
Hitachi-Ota City, Japan

Natsupho

Nationality: Japanese

Religion: Shinto

Languages: Japanese, and I am learning English at school.

Brothers and Sisters: I have an older sister, Shoshun, who is away at university.

Pets: None

Hobbies: Reading

Talents: Cooking

Favorite Sport: Volleyball

Favorite Books: *The Copycat Killer* and *The Dragon is Sleeping* by Miyuki Miyabe and *The Magician in Hell* by Yojin Yokkaido.

Favorite Food: Coffee jellies. This is like a coffee-flavored jelly, which is soft to eat.

Least Favorite Food: Carrots; green peas; and celery

Whom do you most admire? Sungawala Michizane. He is a historical Japanese figure, who symbolizes study and learning.

Favorite Possession: My books

Do you help with chores at home? I help with the cooking, especially for festivals and holidays.

Do you have your own telephone or computer? No, but my family has a computer.

Do you use the Internet? Yes

Where would you most want to travel? Kyoto, Japan

What comes to mind when you think of the United States? The FBI; Abraham Lincoln

...and France? The Eiffel Tower

...and China? The Great Wall

...and Kenya? Elephant tusks

What do you talk about with friends? Favorite CDs and books

What do you want to know about other girls your age? Nothing in particular

Sungawale Michizane.

"I was raised surrounded by books."

Origami: Paper Sculptures

Origami is the art of paper folding—a popular pastime for Japanese kids. Folding is easiest if the paper is thin, strong, and able to hold a crease. The paper is often ornate, dressed with patterns of flowers or geometric forms. It is amazing to see the transformation of these single sheets of paper into 3-D figures of animals, people, and objects.

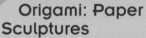

If I Could Be…

translated from Japanese

Natsupho in her school uniform.

In the future, I would like to be either a writer or an artist.

First, I would like to explain why I want to be a writer. I have loved to read stories ever since I was small. I read everything from fantasy to suspense, from mystery novels to romance novels. My older sister and my father both love to read, so I was raised surrounded by books. Because of that, I read more than most people do. Fortunately, in elementary school, we had a "reading time" intended to help our imaginations grow, and I was able to read every book I could find. I have continued to do that to the present day. In particular, *Bakuhohan*, a Miyuki Miyabe novel that I read in my second year of junior high school made a big impact on me. It made me think, "Wow! So there are really people who can write this well!" My mother also said that Miyabe's writing abilities are wonderful.

I had never really liked

Miyuki Miyabe's first English book. Now you can read a mystery by Natsupho's favorite author!

mystery novels very much before, but since this writer appeals to me so much, I have also read *The Dragon is Sleeping*, *R.P.G.*, *Dream Busters*, and *The Murderous Twilight of Shitamachi, Tokyo*. Of all writers, Miyuki Miyabe and Kurobito Kaito write the stories that I find easiest to read.

Because of my admiration for these two writers, I often think, "Wouldn't it be great if someday I could express my own feelings and the feelings of others like they do?!" Because of that, I have the dream of one day becoming a writer.

Additionally, I would also like to become an artist, but that wish is very similar to my thoughts of becoming a writer. I would like to express my feelings, through pictures or words. It may be selfish of me, but that is what I truly feel I want to do. I did not choose the other possibilities for the reasons I have already explained.

Natsupho's school friends say "Peace!"

"I would like to be a writer or an artist… to express my feelings through pictures or words. It may be selfish of me, but that is what I truly feel…"

Meeting Natsupho by Starla

It is early spring in Japan and the flooded rice fields of the Japanese countryside look like small square mirrors or sheets of glass reflecting the morning sunlight. These gleaming fields are dotted with colorfully dressed rice planters sowing their rice seeds by hand, which has been the tradition for centuries. The rice will grow all summer and make its final push in August—"high summer"—before being harvested in the autumn. Natsupho was born in August and her unusual name means "high summer."

Natsupho and her father are standing outside their house as I arrive with my Japanese friend, Mrs. Furukoshi, who is translating for us. The weather is mild and Natsupho is dressed in a peasant-style, flowered blouse, a white zippered sweatshirt and jeans. Her layered black hair is pulled into a short ponytail and she wears small wire-rimmed glasses. Japanese teenagers are renowned for their shyness, so I am grateful when 13-year-old Natsupho confidently welcomes me, adding a bow and a gentle handshake. She then guides us into the house, where we remove our shoes before entering. In Japan, one never enters a home, or many public establishments for that matter, without removing one's shoes and putting on a pair of slippers.

Natsupho means "high summer."

We enter the living room through the sliding paper doors. This calming room contains only a small wooden table surrounded by satin pillows on the floor, a large ebony-colored wardrobe, and a short shelf with a vase of beautifully arranged flowers. The floor is covered with tatami mats, a traditional Japanese floor covering made from woven straw. Mrs. Furukoshi and I are invited to kneel on the pillows at the small table as Natsupho and her mother bring out tiny porcelain cups and pour us a light-colored tea from a small teapot.

To accompany the tea, Natsupho's mother serves us little round pink cakes that are carefully arranged on small wooden plates. They are called sakura cakes and are made from cherry blossom plants. Presently in season, these cherry blossoms have exploded into a sea of pink and white fluff all over Japan, falling to the ground just as quickly as it had appeared.

Natsupho lives in Hitachi-Ota City, northwest of Japan's capital, Tokyo. Hitachi-Ota City is surrounded by Japanese countryside and is near the Pacific Coast. Like the rest of Japan, Hitachi-Ota City has modernized rapidly, but still manages to maintain a uniquely Japanese feeling and atmosphere. Natsupho is proud of her community, but nervous about the impact of progress on the environment in her town.

In Japan, there are many festivals and traditions to mark the passing months. Many of these festivals have their roots in Buddhist or Shinto religious traditions.

Natsupho's uncle is a Shinto priest.

Natsupho's uncle, who is the resident Shinto priest at the Shrine, has his hands full overseeing ceremonies and the day-to-day spiritual activities in Hitachi-Ota City. Natsupho and her father take me to visit her uncle at the Shrine. When we meet him, he is dressed in a purple silk robe with a sash and a turquoise skirt-like hakama—the traditional clothing of the Shinto priest.

People come to the Shrine to leave prayers and receive blessings. They write their prayers on small pieces of paper, which are then tied onto tree branches or onto a small trellis. There are literally hundreds of pieces of paper, and they look like a flock of tiny white birds perched there. Natsupho explains that when the trellis and tree branches are full, the priest takes down the little prayer papers and offers them to the spirits inside the Shrine.

School Accessories

Hello Kitty and Pokemon are the most popular products for children in Japan, and a variety of school supplies—notebooks, pens, and organizers—are decorated with these fun and adorable animated characters. It is amazing to see the lengths to which Japanese students will go to express their individuality and creativity, with every pencil and eraser making its own little statement. This may be because in Japan, all children, including Natsupho, wear a uniform to

school. Natsupho's uniform, typical for middle-school girls, is a dark blue skirt and a dark, blue-and-white sailor shirt. She wears this with white ankle socks and black shoes or sneakers. School regulations on how to wear the uniform are quite strict, often going as far as directing what kind of socks and shoes can be worn, and what kind of backpack the students may carry. Luckily, the children still have the opportunity to show off their individualism by carrying distinctive pencils, pencil boxes, notebooks, and charms.

A bag of Hello Kitty candy that Starla got in Japan.

Did You Know?

- Japan is one of the most densely populated countries on Earth. There are 1,500 people per square mile of habitable land! Tokyo is Japan's capital city, and Japanese is the official language.

- Japan was isolated from the rest of the world for centuries. It was ruled by a series of emperors, who were believed to have descended directly from the Sun God. For a time, Japan was also ruled by warrior (*samurai*) chiefs each called *Shogun*. Japan opened itself to the world in the mid-1800s.

Japanese Flag

- Shinto is the original religion of the Japanese people and has strongly influenced Japanese culture. In Shintoism, people worship sacred spirits called *kami*, which are believed to inhabit most natural elements and even inanimate objects.

Japanese Currency

- The cherry blossom (*sakura*) is the Japanese national flower. The fragile cherry blossom bursts into life and then falls to the ground in its prime. The art of cherry-blossom viewing, or *hanami*, is an important national pastime for all Japanese.

A typical Japanese rice field.

Japan

Russia

Sea of Japan

N. Korea

S. Korea

Pacific Ocean

Tokyo   Hitachi-Ota-City

Natsupho's home city

Some words in Japanese

Yes = Hai
No = Iie
Thank you = Arigato

Goodbye = Sayounara
Hello = Kon-nichiwa
How are you? = O-genki desu ka
Friend = Tomodachi

Tanya Karaganda, Kazakhstan

Tatiana ("Tanya")

Nationality: Kazakh, of Korean descent
Religion: Protestant
Languages: Russian, and I am learning English at school.
Brothers and Sisters: None
Pets: None
Hobbies: Playing computer games
Favorite Sport: Tennis
Favorite Books: *Evgeny Onegin* by Aleksandr Pushkin; *Evenings on a Farm near Dekanka* by Nikolai Gogol; and *"Mcuri"* by Mikhail Lermontov
Favorite Food: All Korean cuisine

Least Favorite Food: Lamb
Whom do you most admire? Bruce Willis
Favorite Possession: Cuddly teddy bear
Do you help with chores at home? I help my grandmother by mopping the floor and taking out the garbage.
Do you have your own telephone or computer? Yes
Where would you most want to travel? Disneyland in Paris
What comes to mind when you think of the United States? The Statue of Liberty
...and China? The Great Wall
...and Kenya? Black people and Africa
What do you talk about with friends? Homework
What do you want to know about other girls your age? Where they live; where they study; what they do every day; and what their hobbies are

"I am a very athletic girl and I like tennis a lot."

If I Could Be...
translated from Russian

When I was 11 years old, my granny and I were watching the sports news about professional tennis. I liked this sport right away. Frankly speaking, I am a very athletic girl and I like tennis a lot. The next day we were watching Wimbledon. It was very late at night but my granny let me watch it to the end and I really enjoyed it.

Then I started asking my mum and granny if I could join a children's tennis training group. We knew that one of our relatives, Oleg Borisovich, is a sports coach at the sports complex based at the Polytechnical University. So it seemed that I should not have any problems joining a tennis club. But they said "no" to my mother and I don't know why. I was very disappointed, but later I had to accept it, as I did not have any choice.

I was suffering because of this for a few years. Then my auntie came to visit us and I told her about my great desire to play tennis. She promised to help me. I told her that it is the dream of my life. I remember my first tennis training at the tennis club. I had training sessions five times a week. It was a great pleasure for me. It was the most enjoyable thing in my life.

My dear auntie bought me a tennis racket. At first I was in a group for beginners, then they moved me to the next higher level. I have taken part in the tennis competition in Astana twice already. The competition is for "The Cup of the Capital City." Last year I was sixteenth in this competition and this year I was fourth. I intend to carry on with my training. If it is necessary, I will take private lessons to be the best. I think it will be a great day when I play at Wimbledon. I will have to play against the most serious competitors, but I am going to win anyway. I will be on television and the whole world will hear about me. I will be the top player at Wimbledon.

"I always had a dream to go to the Arab Emirates."

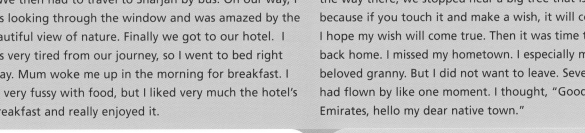

My Best Day

translated from Russian

I always had a dream to go to the Arab Emirates and one day our family decided to go there. I found out about this trip on the same day we were leaving and I was very happy. On the way to the airport, I was trying to imagine what it would be like to get on the plane and fly. Our plane was a Boeing 737. I fell asleep right away after we boarded. I woke up when the stewardess came to us with a tray full of nice food. I had my meal and went to sleep again. I woke up only when our plane was landing.

We then had to travel to Sharjah by bus. On our way, I was looking through the window and was amazed by the beautiful view of nature. Finally we got to our hotel. I was very tired from our journey, so I went to bed right away. Mum woke me up in the morning for breakfast. I am very fussy with food, but I liked very much the hotel's breakfast and really enjoyed it.

Every day after breakfast we would go to the beach, then have lunch and a *siesta* (a little sleep). In the evenings, when it had cooled down we would go to town for a walk and look around the shops.

We also visited Abu Dhabi and the Indian Ocean. On the way there, we stopped near a big tree that is famous because if you touch it and make a wish, it will come true. I hope my wish will come true. Then it was time to go back home. I missed my hometown. I especially missed my beloved granny. But I did not want to leave. Seven days had flown by like one moment. I thought, "Goodbye Arab Emirates, hello my dear native town."

Did You Know?

- Kazakhstan is in Central Asia, with Russia on the North and China on the East. Kazakhstan was part of the Soviet Union like Kate's Russia, Michaela's Slovakia, Dasha's Ukraine, and Katia's Bulgaria.

- Kazakhstan has two official languages: Kazak and Russian.

- The Kazakhs, of Turkish descent, make up more than half of the country's population. People of Slavic descent, such as Russians, make up about one-third of the population. Other ethnic groups include Ukrainians, Uzbeks, Germans, Chechens, and Koreans, like Tatiana and her family.

Kazak Flag

Kazakhstan

Russia

Karaganda

China

Uzbekistan

Caspian Sea

Tanya's home city

Lavanya New Delhi, India

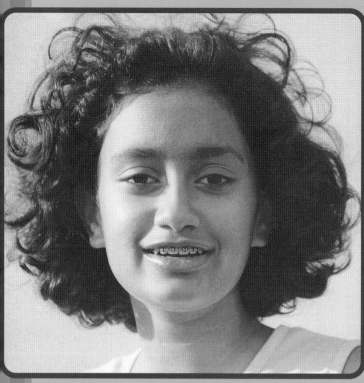

Lavanya

Bijli ("lightning"), and two Great Danes called Titus and Cleopatra. I also have a cow called Devaki and a calf called Jatraprasad.

Hobbies: Singing and dancing
Talents: Writing
Favorite Sport: Badminton
Favorite Books: The Last Jungle On Earth by Randhir Khare; The Alchemist by Paulo Coelho; and Boy Meets Girl by Meg Cabot
Favorite Food: Idlis—fermented steamed rice made into cakes
Least Favorite Food? Moong dal, a type of lentils.
Whom do you most admire? My father
Favorite Possession: My red chiffon skirt
Do you help with chores at home? I want to but nobody lets me.
Do you use the Internet? Yes, and my favorite website is Orisinal.com.
Do you have your own telephone or computer? I have my own computer.
Where would you most want to travel? Spain
What comes to mind when you think of the United States? Terrorists

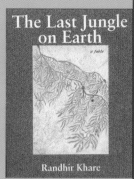

The Last Jungle on Earth
a fable

Randhir Khare

This fable is written by Lavanya's father and is dedicated to Lavanya and her brother.

Nationality: Indian
Religion: I follow what I like best in Hinduism and Christianity.
Languages: English and Hindi
Brothers and Sisters: One brother
Pets: I have dogs. There's a boxer called Aandhi (meaning "storm"), a cocker spaniel called Maximus, a mixed-breed dog called Ruby, a Labrador called Kajol ("black kohl" for the eyes), a Himalayan sheep dog called Toofaan (meaning "typhoon"), a half boxer/half Dalmatian called

Credit: Shamona Stokes

...and France? Poodles
...and China? The color red
...and Kenya? Elephants
What do you talk about with your friends? Shopping
What do you want to know about other girls your age? How do you live life without worrying about the future?

"I have a cow called Devaki and a calf called Jatraprasad."

About Me

Have you ever taken a peek at a map of the world? If you have, you would have come across a triangular chunk of land sticking out of the south of the Asian continent into the Indian Ocean. On the west side, you'd have seen the Arabian Sea, on the east, the Bay of Bengal, and way to the north, the freezing ice caps of the Himalayas! Well, that's my country—India.

A lot of people think that India is a country of elephants, magicians, snake charmers, sadhus, and slums. Too bad, because they're wrong. Of course, we have all of this and more. Much more. It's the "much more" that I'm going to tell you a little about.

The country is made up of many states, each with its own language, customs, eating habits, and ways of dressing. It's just like a continent by itself—each state a country! I sometimes get freaked out when I think about all this "difference." How does it all stay together and call itself a country? Is it because we are surrounded by the sea and the mountains and have really nowhere else to go? Or is it that we all feel comfy enough to hang around here and get on with our lives? I don't know. All I know is that we get along with each other most of the time. Sometimes we

Lavanya in front of her grandmother's portrait.

squabble over this and that, but it's normal with neighbors, don't you think?

Now I'm going to confuse you a little more. Not only do we have a whole lot of states, but we also have a number of religions like Hinduism, Zoroastrianism, Sikhism, Islam, Christianity, Judaism, Jainism, and more. Then we have tribal people who follow their own religions that are thousands and thousands of years old.

Hold it! I'm not finished yet. Here's another dose. This country is made up of villages, towns, and cities, each with their own type of living.

Phew! Sorry about this! I don't mean to scare you!

Credit: Shamona Stokes

Sequined slippers from a market in New Delhi.

"So here I am, a 13-year-old girl plonk in the middle of it all, living in New Delhi, the capital, one of the big cities where people turn up with dreams, hoping that they can make them happen.

Well, I have my own bag of dreams..."

So here I am, a 13-year-old girl plonk in the middle of it all, living in New Delhi, the capital, one of the big cities where people turn up with dreams, hoping that they can make them happen.

Well, I have my own bag of dreams, which I will share with you sometime.

Living in India has helped me to accept all types of differences—different religions, customs, beliefs, foods, and ways of living. This fills my whole life with lots of variety and makes it far from boring. I always find it interesting to learn about and discover new people. It helps me realize that however different anyone is from me, he or she is a human being with feelings, hopes, joys, dreams, and sadness. I don't like to imagine that because someone is of a different religion it gives me the right to be rude and hurt that person. Living in India has taught me acceptance and the realization that I am human and must live in harmony with other humans.

This makes me realize that by becoming a writer, I will be able to build a bridge between different religions and cultures in India. As an Indian writer, I will be able to explain to people all over the world that India is unique and different because it is a place where different types of people can live peacefully side by side.

Let me tell you one thing for sure—I don't spend all my time being serious! A lot of my time is spent doing things that most city girls my age don't do—like roller-blading in squelchy mud, playing a game called "try to snap my leg off" with my dog Kajol, taking a keen interest in burping competitions, or making horrid salad dressing and burnt cookies at 360 degrees Farenheit while our maid runs around the house, screaming "fire fire."

When I'm not doing all this, I sit and read stacks and stacks of books. And when I am not reading stacks and stacks of books, I chat with my friend and neighbor over ...side. Sometimes I visit my best friend, Ambika, who lives ten houses away from mine. We chat and listen to music.

During my summer holidays, I travel to the city of Pune along with my younger brother, Raghu, to spend time with our dad who lives there. Pune is the opposite of Delhi. While Delhi is a big zooming city, Pune is quiet and has lots of interesting places to visit. It's a historical city that has a number of forts nearby, and is a good holiday spot, quite unlike the other cities in the State of Maharashtra.

Every holiday in Pune, we take a trip to a place called Malavali that is in the mountainous Western Ghats. We travel there by a local train with my dad and then trek from the station to a group of ancient 2000-year-old Buddhist rock caves near a village called Bhaje. I always find it very interesting and beautiful. The unique part of all this is that we have to climb many hundreds of steps up a hill to reach the caves. Once we are there, we explore the amazing stone carvings and stupas [ancient Buddhist mounds]. From the top, we can see the plains lying at the foot of the hill like green velvet carpet.

Credit: Shamona Stokes

"We trek off deeper into the woods and collect exquisite rock crystals."

When we descend, we trek off deeper into the nearby woods and collect exquisite rock crystals. We add them to our collection of stones that come from all parts of the country. There are stones from the sub-Himalayan Tose River, some from the jungles of Dangs in the State of Gujarat, some from the tribal jungles of Jhabua in western India, some from the deserts of Kutch, and others from places like the Blue Mountains of the Nilgiris in the south of India. We also have seed fossils and a Stone Age spearhead! The history of India is in these stones.

So there you are, I'm a different girl in a different country.

An ancient Buddhist temple in India.

Meeting Lavanya

by Starla

Who is Lavanya? A loud, spunky, pushy Indian girl who loves chocolate and South-Asian food. That is how Lavanya thinks her friends would describe her. How would her teachers describe her? According to Lavanya, they would say she is, "A very bright, quiet, and sensitive girl." Regardless of whom you ask, Lavanya is always reading and discovering new, crazy, interesting things about her amazing country. That is, unless it is a weekend, in which case, she is probably lounging around in her pajamas, on her bed, tucked in the pink silk bed sheets, with her fuzzy blue blanket and embroidered pillowcases, eating cheese pancakes, and watching cartoons!

When it isn't the weekend, or a holiday when Lavanya is enjoying time in Pune or Dehradoon (in the Himalayan foothills where her family has a little farm next to a river), she is probably in school. After her school day, and after finishing all of her homework, Lavanya enjoys hanging out in her room some more…"the only place where I can be myself. " She likes to play loud music, yak on the phone with her friends, and read books. Lavanya's mother is constantly reminding her that her room looks like a tornado just went through it, but as Lavanya says, "At least it doesn't look like a museum or an advertisement for interiors!"

In New Delhi, there are plenty of things for 13-year-old girls to do in the afternoons, like go to the shopping malls, the cinema, or to one of the hundreds of coffee shops around the city, but it is quite rare for groups of girls to go out on their own. Usually, teenage girls go out in town only with their parents. And when they meet their friends, it is at one another's homes. This is partly because many parents wouldn't consider it safe to send their girls out alone, but mostly because, in Indian culture, it is not the custom for girls to go around by themselves. Or, maybe it is because of the crazy antics (burping competitions?) that they might get into if they are on their own.

Lavanya also has a serious side, which comes out when she talks about the predicament of girls and women in India. India is a country of contradictions. It is one of the few democracies to have elected a woman to the highest office of Prime Minister. At the same time, girls—especially in the villages—are sadly undervalued in parts of Indian society. This prejudice does not affect Lavanya directly for many reasons—primarily because of her family's privileged background and education, but also because she is an urban Indian girl living in the capital city. Things might have been different had she been born in a small village. Regardless, Lavanya does not believe the mistreatment of women in her country is just a problem for other people to worry about. Nor is it a topic Lavanya is willing to ignore, as you will see.

SCHOOL DAYS

Lavanya attends a coed school, where, as in most schools throughout India, the children wear uniforms. In Lavanya's school, the girls sport a knee-length denim skirt and a blue-and-white striped shirt. In school, Lavanya studies English language, English literature, Hindi, Sanskrit, Mathematics, Geography, History, Biology, Physics, and Chemistry. She loves English and Biology (although not the life-cycle of frogs) and is less fond of Sanskrit and Mathematics. This is a small problem, because she has Math homework every night of the week. Oh, well.

Lavanya in her school uniform, with her dog, Kajol. "A typical day means getting up too early and wrestling with the dog for the blanket."

My Best Day

Birthdays are always great fun. Some are even wild. But the birthday to beat all birthdays was my 12th. It all started when I got up way too early...long before everyone else. So I trotted off and made myself a breakfast of chocolate sandwiches and a glass of orange juice, brought it back to my room, and treated myself to breakfast in bed while Kajol my dog sat salivating next to me.

While Kajol stared at me eating my chocolate sandwiches, I watched "Popeye the Sailor" smacking Bluto on television. By the time Popeye got to give Olive Oyl a kiss, my mum walked in loaded with presents and the opening ceremony began.

I think it lasted about half an hour and then the day unfolded with lots of unexpected excitement and magic.

My first visitor, my friend, Aditya, strolled in like he was in his own house. Kajol, who had had her eyes on his chubby legs, finally got the opportunity. She broke free of her chain and went for his legs, chasing him on and off the bed until I got the chance to grab her tail and stop her.

Other friends started turning up and very soon the party was swinging. First, we watched the movie One Hundred and One Dalmations. Popcorn was consumed in great quantities as we watched those spotted four-legged wonders complete their journey home. By that time, everyone was ready for more action, so we had a burping competition.

Now that was fun! You know what a burping competition is, don't you? Well, each participant stands in front of the judges and burps. The judges choose the

"...the day unfolded with lots of excitement and magic."

winner depending on loudness, length of burp, and if the burp is unique in any way. Obviously, Aditya won the burping competition because he could burp out a whole song!

Once the burping competition was over, it was time for lunch, and the hungry horde attacked the fabulous spread. Mum had made sure there was something special for everyone. But in Aditya's case, it didn't make much of a difference because all food is heaven for him.

I'd expected everyone to chill out before we started the dancing, but that wasn't part of their plan. On came the music and everyone began to move to the beat of "Saturday Night Fever." And so, as the fever rose higher and higher, the room began to look more and more like it was about to burst into flames.

Then the fever slowly gave way to a coolness as dancer after dancer slipped into a state of calm. When everyone had reached this state, we began chatting and telling jokes.

When we ran out of jokes, we began watching the movie Harry Potter and the Chamber Of Secrets. Actually it wasn't easy deciding on this movie because all the girls wanted to watch Sweet November and all the boys wanted Die Another Day. So we settled for Harry Potter, which wasn't that violent.

Slowly, my friends began to leave, one after another until only 14 of them remained for the slumber party. The slumber party officially began when the pizzas were ordered and the living room floor was cleared to put out sleeping bags. The bags were placed in a large circle with the makeup in the center, along with some scarves and flowers to use as props.

When the pizzas arrived, everyone ate a slice and then went into the center of the room and got their makeup put on by Devesha. Now, a little bit about Devesha: She's a bubbly, enthusiastic, and creative makeup artist. She knows how and when to use the right shade of eye shadow.

When everyone was ready and had their props in place, the fashion show began. The judges were Raghu (Lavanya's brother) and his best friend, Arjun.

One at a time, each of us walked the ramp and the winner was chosen on the basis of her creativity and originality. After nearly 20 rounds, the judges dozed off to sleep and we never got to know who the winners were.

At around 3:00 in the morning, my mother decided to shoo us into our sleeping bags and switch off the lights. She had hardly left the room when one head after another appeared out of the bags and the party limped back into action. At 4:00, we couldn't keep our heads on our shoulders so we finally crashed. The party had officially ended.

Lavanya in a bright green lacha (shirt-and-skirt set).

I think that this was a special day because I had the company of all my friends and we got a chance to be ourselves without adults constantly interfering and organizing us. This is also the reason why this day was so different from all the others. It's not usual for me to have so many friends around at one time. The week goes by with a routine of school, homework, tests, and other horrifying realities of life.

A typical day means getting up too early, wrestling with my dog for the blanket, dawdling to the bathroom and falling asleep there, and then getting a yelling for doing so. After that, it's struggling to finish breakfast in time for the bus. At the bus stop, listening to my best friend lecture me about the evils of arriving late. Then pushing through the never-ending day plastered with molecular equations, algebra, and the biology teacher going on about the lifecycles of frogs. Then it's surviving lunch and the journey home, far too pooped to do very much else.

Now can you see the difference?

Sanskrit

There are 18 official languages recognized in India's Constitution. English is the language used for government and administrative business. One of 18 languages in India is Hindi, which Lavanya speaks. Hindi is spoken by 30 percent of the population. Sanskrit, which Lavanya studies in school, is another official language of India. One of the most ancient languages in the world, Sanskrit derives from the same source as Latin and Greek and, because of this, these languages share some common words. Sanskrit is written in Hindi (in Devanagari script). To learn more about Sanskrit you can go to www.ukindia.com and go to the Sanskrit link!

बाला *Girl*

पठ *Read*

लिख *Write*

हस *Laugh*

अम्बा *Mother*

जनक *Father*

खेल *Play*

वद *Speak*

धाव *Run*

चल *Walk*

अश्व *Horse*

सिंह *Lion*

गज *Elephant*

If I Could Be...

LAVANYA KHARE, PRIME MINISTER OF INDIA TALKS TO THE NATION ON TELEVISION:

People of India, I thank you for electing me your leader, the second woman in India to be given this honor. This is a big responsibility that you've handed me and I hope I will live up to your expectations.

I know that the Miss Universe pageant is on tonight and you'd love to switch channels, but what I am going to talk to you about is much more important. I'll try to keep it as short as possible so please stay tuned in and listen.

I am going to talk to you about women. Not like the ones you are waiting see in the pageant tonight, but the thousands and thousands who live in our country but remain unknown. Many of them are never respected, are given no chance to speak for themselves, and have been condemned to neglect.

Also, all of you know that female babies are often killed right after being born. And what is their crime? Being a woman! You know exactly what I am talking about.

The life of a woman is a constant struggle in every possible way. In small villages all over India, it is always the boy who is fed first and only when he has eaten enough will the girl get any food. Because of this, the girl child is weaker and more vulnerable to illnesses. Many of these illnesses are fatal. If the girl

"People of India, I thank you for electing me your leader."

An Indian wedding.

does survive this stage of life, she will remain downtrodden. Whatever a girl does, she cannot win the same respect given to a boy. Thanks to this, the boy child is sent off to school and given a chance for further studies, while the girl is kept at home and made to do housework. This is just like jhadoo (broom) practice to prepare her before marriage.

Even though it is illegal, many of you still demand dowry from the young woman's parents. This is like the bride's parents giving money to their future son-in-law to take charge of their daughter. How can anyone treat a woman like this?

Why can't you accept that a woman is a human being? She deserves the same rights as everybody else. In the eyes of our Constitution, a woman has the same rights as a man and should be treated that way.

If given a chance, women have the ability to effect change. Look into the past and you will find that there have been many women who have overcome terrible difficulties to make life better for others.

How can we now help our women all over the country to discover themselves and make this country a better place to live in?

As your Prime Minister I ask for your support to make my vision for a stronger Indian woman come true. I believe I can make this happen and I trust that you will stand by me.

Here's what I don't want:

- I don't want a female child's life to be taken away before she can discover the joy of living.
- I don't want the girl child to be treated unequally in the family.
- I don't want early marriage and the giving of dowry to be practiced.

• I don't want men to treat their wives like household servants.

And here's what I want:

• I want every girl child to have a caring home, proper nutrition, a good education, and the opportunity to enroll for colleges or try for jobs.

• I want women to make the most of their abilities.

• I want men to stop underestimating the power of women.

• I want women to stand up for their rights and demand equal opportunities.

Now you'll surely want to know how we're going to make this possible. This can't happen overnight. I can't force you to believe in me. You have to trust me. It all begins with trust. Along with trust, we must have the right attitude.

Credit: Shamona Stokes

"I want men to stop underestimating the power of women."

So let's begin now, this minute.

If you have a girl child in your home, ask yourself these questions:

• Do I treat her the same way as all the others in the family?

• Have I given her the same opportunities as my other children?

• Am I helping her realize her potential?

• Have I spent time with her to find out what her hopes and fears and dreams are?

The answers to these questions will tell you where you stand—on the side of progress or backwardness. In the days to come, you will get to know what I plan to do. Until then, look into your own heart and listen to what it has to say. Good night. Enjoy the Miss Universe pageant if you must. Beauty also has its own type of power.

Did You Know?

• The population of India is over one billion and it will probably surpass China as the world's most populous country by 2020.

• Lavanya writes about the differences in the treatment of boys and girls in India. This is easily seen in India's literacy, or reading, rates. For boys, the literacy rate is 70 percent; for girls, it is only 48 percent.

Indian Flag

Indian Currency

• In 1967, Indira Nehru Gandhi became India's first female Prime Minister. She was assassinated in 1984 by Sikh extremists.

• Did you notice that Lavanya has a cow named Devaki and a calf named Jatraprasad? In the Hindu religion, cows are considered sacred.

• Renowned for its spirituality, three of the world's oldest and largest religions came into being in India—Hinduism, Buddhism, and Jainism.

Some words in Hindi
Hello = Namaste
Goodbye = Alavidha (Namaste)
Yes = Ha

No = Nahi
Please = kRipyaa
Thank you = dhanyavaad
Friend = Saheli

India

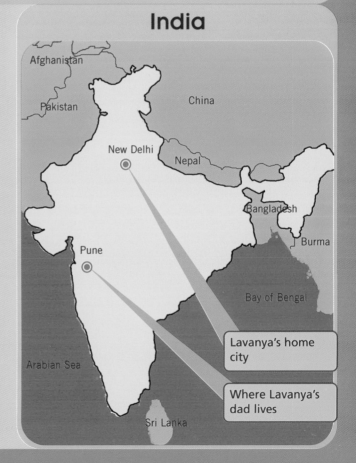

Afghanistan

Pakistan

China

New Delhi

Nepal

Bangladesh

Burma

Pune

Bay of Bengal

Lavanya's home city

Where Lavanya's dad lives

Arabian Sea

Sri Lanka

Kiely Whangaparaoa, New Zealand

Kiely

Nationality: New Zealander

Religion: Roman Catholic

Languages: English, and I am learning Latin and Maori.

Brothers and Sisters: I have two younger siblings, Grace and Isaac.

Pets: We have two budgies, Romeo and Juliet; two fish, Splash and Sabrina; a dog, Skye; and a cat called Mitzi.

Hobbies: Netball (I play for a club); reading; seeing my friends; bush trekking; swimming at the beach; riding horses (when I can); riding my bike; roller blading; cooking; sewing; writing; artistic ventures; drama; and generally having fun.

Talents: I enjoy a lot of sporty things, but this does not mean that I am good at them. I am a rather academic person and am good at English, vocabulary, writing short stories, mathematics, science, and social studies.

Otherwise, I am a good cook, OK at drama, good at drawing and art, and good at long bush treks.

Favorite Sport: Netball and horse riding

Favorite Books: Harry Potter and the Goblet of Fire by J.K. Rowling; I Am Not Esther by Fleur Beale; and The Tiggie Tompson Show by Tessa Duder

Favorite Food: Watermelon sorbet with lime ice cream. This is a fruity, icy dish that I first had when I was in Wellington. Yummy!!!

Least Favorite Food: Any kind of meat (I'm a vegetarian, which means I don't eat meat) smothered in gravy and mushrooms. Yuck!!!

Whom do you most admire? Tessa Duder and my uncle, Campbell Walker

Favorite Possession: Other than my pets—my photo album. It holds heaps of memories.

Do you help with chores at home? Yes, I hang out the wash, set the breakfast table, bake the week's biscuits, cook dinner sometimes, clean my room, do the dusting, and I do paper runs three times a week.

Do you have your own telephone or computer? I share a cell phone with my sister, but otherwise no.

Do you use the Internet? I rarely use the Internet except for schoolwork.

Where would you most want to travel? Argentina, probably, as they have such a lovely culture that is so different from New Zealand's.

What comes to mind when you think of the United States? The White House

...and France? French restaurants

...and China? Cantonese music

...and Kenya? The African Pridelands

What do you talk about with friends? Whatever is happening; at the moment, our school drama production.

What do you want to know about other girls your age? What their schooling is like, since it probably differs from country to country

My Best Day

"My family is really important to me."

The most memorable and enjoyable day I've had so far was probably the Millennium day. This was not just because of the new Millennium itself, but also because of where I was and with whom I spent that day.

The night before Millennium day had been a huge success despite the dreadful weather! After a barbecued dinner and a fireworks display over one of Coromandel's many beaches, we all trooped up to the family batch for the final countdown. The deck erupted with cheers after three off-timed tries at the countdown. We had finally gotten it right! Two thousand years gone by and another lot just beginning!

When we woke up in the early hours of dawn expecting a fantastic sunrise, we were sadly disappointed. Low, blotchy, gray clouds were hanging in the sky obscuring the sun and the few rays that managed to poke through were dull and fading. However, the scene was still spectacular to me. My large and extensive family, hugging and staring, as we watched the last of 2000 years melt away. After sleeping for another good four hours, we woke up to a day of fun stretching before us.

Here I was, in our batch and bush combination in Coromandel, which is one of the most special places I know, with the people I love the most. Already the day was off to a fantastic start. If you don't know, a batch is a holiday home usually found near one of New Zealand's abundant beaches. It may be a sparse bungalow with little furniture or a fully-equipped house. But every batch has one thing in common—lots of sleeping space for friends and relatives!

Anyway, after a huge breakfast and a big Happy Birthday to my uncle, Greg, we set off for the sand castle competition. We were put into teams at the beach across from us and set out to make the biggest and best sand castles ever.

My cousin, Georgia, and I made a large and unique sculpture of New Zealand, covered in shells and pohutakawa flowers. We won the prize for the most original sculpture.

We then went back to the batches to have a bit of a rest before the tree-planting ceremony. We had six trees representing the six family lines,

> **"I was in one of the most special places I know, with the people I love the most. Already the day was off to a fantastic start."**

One of New Zealand's many exotic plants.

which we were planting to signify the end of 2000 years and the beginning of a new Millennium. I thought this was a really great idea, having these trees growing as we did. Now generations of Hannafords would be able appreciate why the trees were there and they would become a mark in our family history. My aunts and uncles had a great time planting the trees and mak-ing as much of a mess as they could.

By now, the uncles had gotten lunch ready. There were huge lumps of lamb that had been roasting on spits all day; it made me want to puke from the smell every time I neared the back deck (I'm a vegetarian).

There were piles of salads, barbecued food, and mouth-watering Coromandel potatoes. (Coromandel potatoes are a tradition in the summertime. They're cooked over an open fire and the smell alone is enough to make you think you're in heaven.). Mmmm.

We must have taken nearly two hours to digest all that scrumptious food, but the fun couldn't stop there. The adults had designed a scavenger hunt that tested not only our skills in detective work, but also our knowledge of Coromandel and our family history. We had heaps of fun and a tough time working out the clues, but in the end, my cousin, Fred, and I won the quest by milliseconds as Fred's brother, Michael, came speeding up behind us on the path.

Much later that afternoon, just before Mass started, my one-year-old cousin, Mae, was baptized. I thought that it was really special that she was baptized on New Year's Day, particularly as most of her family was present and able to celebrate it with her. We enjoyed the Jubilee church ceremony, and afterwards had our traditional ice cream in town.

That evening we had group photos. It was fantastic—86 of us sitting there in our "Hannaford 2000" T-shirts of all assorted colors, grouped on the soft turf of the barbeque grounds.

That was a wonderful end to a memorable day. My family is really important to me and being with them in Coromandel helped to make that day so special for me. Things like hearing stories about Nan Hannaford (my great-grandmother), the planting of the trees, and looking at the huge family photo boards of us in Coromandel made such a fun-filled day just about perfect.

These little things showed not only how much my family cherishes being together, but also how important Coromandel and our history is to us.

A Kauri tree in New Zealand.

Meeting Kiely

by Starla

Did Kiely mention that she's a vegetarian?

Kiely lives with her mother, brother, and sister in a house in Whangaparaoa (pronounced fong-a-roar), which is a suburb of Auckland, the largest city in New Zealand. Whangaraparoa is a cove with a harbor, white-sand beaches, and mesmerizing sunsets. Today, however, Kiely and her family are visiting her grandparents in the busy city of Auckland. Kiely is wearing a black T-shirt, a denim skirt, and black sandals. Her skin is lightly tanned with a healthy glow, and her light green eyes are clear and bright. She has shoulder-length hair that curls at the ends. Her whole appearance suggests a healthy, outdoor lifestyle, typical of Kiwis (that's the informal nickname for New Zealanders).

In early autumn, Auckland, which lies far north on New Zealand's North Island in the Southern Hemisphere, is still warm and tropical. Nevertheless, on most afternoons it gets cloudy for an hour or two. As the clouds gather overhead, they transform into one thin long white cloud, reflecting the narrowness of the landmass below. In fact, the Maori name for New Zealand, Aotearoa, means "Land of the long, white cloud." White-sand beaches run for miles in downtown Auckland, which is laid-back with an eclectic charm. Kiwis are out in abundance, dressed casually in T-shirts and jeans, sampling oysters at booths along the beach. Little children run about barefoot and carefree.

Kiely's mum, Stella, calls us in for lunch and we all sit down around the large family dining room table. Stella serves us all a heaping spoonful of ratatouille made with eggplant, zucchini, tomato, and onion, and served with a fresh green salad and warm, chewy bread. There is no meat, fish, or chicken. This is because, as Kiely mentioned, she is a vegetarian. She has been a vegetarian since she was just eight years old, when she decided to stop eating red meat. About one year ago, she stopped eating chicken. (She is not a vegan though, which means she still drinks milk and eats eggs.) I ask her why she decided to become a vegetarian. She says it is hard to explain why. "Basically I didn't like eating the flesh of other creatures." Hmm, when she puts it like that, I contemplate becoming a vegetarian, too! In order to ensure that she doesn't miss out on any nutrients, Kiely takes iron supplements, a multivitamin, and gets proteins from dairy products like milk, cheese, and eggs.

Kiely has her photo album with her. She shows me photos of her huge family on Millenium day at their batch in Coromandel, which is a peninsula across the bay from Auckland. Kiely's mother has 8 siblings and Kiely already has 18 first cousins, not to mention all of the second and third cousins, aunts and uncles, and great-aunts and great-uncles.

In her spare time, of which there isn't a lot, Kiely likes to write creative stories. She recently won a short story writing competition for all of Auckland. Her story was printed in a book with the other New Zealand finalists and she was invited to attend a conference for all of the finalists, where she met the New Zealand prime minister!

Ratatouille

2 large onions
2 green peppers
2 cloves garlic
2 small eggplants
4 zucchini
1 small head of celery
1 tsp cumin seeds
500g ripe tomatoes
1/3-cup oil
1 tsp dried basil
1 tsp salt
black pepper

Heat oil in a shallow pan, add sliced onion, crushed garlic, and cumin seeds; cook slowly until soft. Add the eggplant, cut into cubes, sliced zucchini, peppers cut into strips, and sliced celery. Mix well, cook quickly for 5 minutes. Add peeled, chopped tomatoes and seasonings, cover and simmer for an hour, stirring occasionally. Then remove cover and allow mixture to cool down until most of the liquid has evaporated and mixture is thick. Serve cold. Serves 4–6.

A picture of Auckland Tower. Auckland is laid-back, with an eclectic charm.

Trouble on the Track
a creative story by Kiely

"I thought that doing a story would be a better way to show not quite my every day life, but a bit of what New Zealand and my surroudings are like. So here it is...'Trouble on the Track!'"

"Is everything ready mum?" I asked excitedly.

"You know it is, Kiely," my mum answered from the kitchen of our not-so-large house in Whangaparaoa, Auckland. "And don't worry, they'll be here soon."

It was the morning of my 13th birthday and some of my friends were coming over for the day. We would be going off for a day of activities and I was hoping my friends would turn up soon so we could get started. I couldn't wait!!!

"Beep, beep!" called the horn outside—the first of my friends had arrived.

"Hi Kate!" I shouted, leaping out the door to greet her.

"And it looks like Georgia is just behind you," I exclaimed as Georgia's car also pulled up in our driveway. "You all ready for a great day?"

Georgia ran to meet us and soon both Ria and Aliesha had joined our throng.

"Right girls," said mum, herding us into the house as we babbled on non-stop, "Here's the plan: we'll have presents and some snacks and then I'm afraid we'll have to get going, we don't have long 'til we have to be at the horse-riding venue. After that we'll have lunch and a swim at the beach."

After opening a pile of presents, most of them containing clothes and craft sets, we climbed into the car and set off for Parkiri, a beach north of Whangaparaoa.

"I wonder if we'll get to ride on the beach."

"I hope I don't get a tall horse, I'd look a fool trying to get on!"

"There are so many of us! We're either going to take out all the horses or they're going to run out."

"I'm going to explode if we don't get there soon!"

My friends all voiced their opinions exuberantly as we neared our destination.

I, however, was too sick to speak. The flat and straight-farmed country roads had turned into horrendous twisting paths, curving their way through the vertical hillside.

It had better not take much longer!!!

Thankfully, the sharply falling-away drops smoothed out into scenic terrain, dotted with farms, houses, and sheep, and edged by a wide strip of sand with waves crashing onto it: The beach!!!

"Yahoo!!!" We screamed as we ran into the fenced corral.

"Nearing the beach, the horses became frisky..."

A few other people were there as well, and soon we were well acquainted. Peering over the corral fence, Kate called to me.

"Would you look at this," Kate whispered excitedly. "There have to be about 30 horses out here!" She sounded impressed.

At that moment, a woman entered the corral. She was wearing jodhpurs, a broad hat, and a big smile, and looked very horse-y.

"I'm going to be your trail guide for today, and I suggest you all go and get yourselves hard hats so that we can get started," she said, gesturing towards the tack room. Soon we were all ready with our horses saddled up, and trotting toward the bush.

It was a typical New Zealand countryside scene. There were large pine trees mixed between the dry, brackish gorse. Ahead of us lurked a deep stream, which the horses had to cross, allowing the water to slap against their shoulders.

Nearing the beach, the horses became frisky, nipping and pawing at the golden sand. My horse, Sparrow, a tall Appaloosa with a mind of his own, took it upon himself to let all the others know who was boss—him. My hands were so full trying to control him, that I barely had time to appreciate the white, rolling waves pounding onto the beach, startling the horses.

With my friends and their horses around me, we cantered down the barren beach, the sea spray and horses' manes in our faces.

"This is so much fun!" called Aliesha over the roar of the waves.

"I know," I replied as we turned onto a broad sandbank and then up a tall sand dune.

My friends, family, and I waited at the top of the hill for the other riders and our guides. As the last rider neared the top, his horse stopped, trembling. Its feet pawed the ground and suddenly the sand slid away from under it. Both horse and rider were thrown backwards down the dune. My knees went weak as both horse and rider landed with a thud at the bottom of the dune.

The horse got up immediately, shaking its head, and ran off, terrified. So there was no damage done to the horse, but what about his rider? It seemed to take hours for our guide to run to the rider and check him over. At last the rider's eyes fluttered open.

The guide called to us, "I think his leg's broken. I'm going to wait here with him, you guys will have to go on by yourselves and get a car to transport him back."

We stood there shocked for a moment, digesting this information, and then my mum came out of the stupor.

"Which is the shortest route?" she asked shakily.

The guide gave us the instructions, which seemed to involve a lot of lefts, and rights,

and we set off gloomily.

After half an hour of hurried riding through the scenic New Zealand bush, we came to a derelict farmhouse.

"This isn't right…" began my mum slowly.

"No, of course it isn't!" I cried angrily. "This is that house you pointed out to us on the way, and eight kilometers later we arrived in Parkiri. How will we ever find our way? There isn't even a driveway or track to follow!"

My younger brother, Isaac, burst into tears at this.

"It's okay," I said comfortingly to him. "We're just going to have to go backwards, that's all."

And so we did. That is until…

"We've lost the trail again!" I wailed desperately. "How will we ever…"

At that moment I was cut short by a thundering of hooves. A wild-eyed horse came galloping towards us. It was the one that had fallen over before and ran off. It streaked past us, heading for the…"I've got it!" I shouted whooping with joy. "We've just got to…"

Ten minutes later we arrived at the corral. It turned out we hadn't been that far away in the first place.

We soon heard an ambulance driving off with the injured rider. Our guide made us a strong brew of tea back in the tack room.

"I hope I never go through that again," she said, sighing and leaning forward. "But what I really want to know is, how did you find your way back? This place is a maze!"

"Well," my mum said, "when that frightened horse came streaking past us, Kiely had the bright idea to follow him, remembering that horses always know where the food's kept, after all!"

The women's netball team in New Zealand is named after the Silver Fern.

Netball

Netball is Kiely's favorite sport. Originally called "Basketball," netball was invented in 1891. The objective is to score points by throwing a ball through a basket at the opposite end of the court. However, in netball, there is no dribbling up or down the court with the ball. The only way to advance the ball is by passing. New Zealand has a professional women's netball team called the Silver Ferns. Kiely likes the sport, but isn't so crazy about her uniform: "We have to wear white polo shirts, navy pleated skirts that fly up around your hips when you run, navy bibs with our number, sneakers, and, would you believe it, these special undies which everyone tends to see whenever you move."

If I Could Be...

I would love to be an Olympic Medalist in the future. I enjoy most sports, both watching and participating in them, but if I were to win an award in the Olympics, I would prefer it to be in equestrian sports. I would choose this not only because I like horseback riding and have a competitive spirit, but also because I would like to do it for my country.

I love living in New Zealand, it is a really beautiful country filled with extremely nice people and I would be proud to represent it in any way. I think New Zealand does really well for such a small country and being able to support it would be an enormous opportunity.

Apart from that, equestrian sports, and a lot of other sports, such as netball, are extremely pleasurable for me and being able to excel in any of these sports would be really exciting as well as a great experience. I also enjoy a bit of healthy competition and being with and competing against the Olympians of all other nationalities and cultures would be a great chance to learn from them.

The other options sound fantastic as well, especially the one about being able to explore outer space. But they are not really as "me" as the option of winning gold at the Olympics.

With exploring outer space, the downsides probably are that I'd be really scared we were going to fall out of the sky or fly into a black hole or some such thing. And, I don't think I would like the discomforts of being in

"I love living in New Zealand...I would be proud to represent it in any way."

space, such as floating around all the time and having to be strapped down (though flying would be fun for a little while) and having to eat dehydrated food. Also I'm not really interested in anything beyond the planet Earth unless it's going to fall on us. But then again, I might be able to gain a lot information that could be used back on Earth, so it would definitely have some enjoyment to it.

Becoming the prime minister is the second best option, but I don't think I'd enjoy it because of all the responsibility of having to look after my country and decisions to keep it going. It would definitely be a hard job. I would also not be able to have my normal everyday life anymore or be able to spend a lot of time with my family and friends.

Me? A movie or pop star? Somehow I don't think so. Although I enjoy a bit of drama and improvisation, that sort of lifestyle would totally not suit me. Having to give up my time whenever my theater company wants me and only for a rerun of a scene or photo shoot would be really inconvenient! Also, pop stars and movie stars come and go so quickly that it would not be a stable career to pursue.

I think the choices I have made, and the reasons I have given for making my choices are all quite sensible for me; though, as I said, I would enjoy all of them. But, it is likely that none of these options will be achievements that I actually make. But, it is always nice to dream about them.

SCHOOL DAYS

Beginning this year, Kiely is attending a Catholic all-girls school in Auckland. Classes begin at 8:45 in the morning, but the school is quite far from Kiely's home in Whangaparaoa and so she catches a bus at 7:20. There are 36 students in her class. Throughout the week, her lessons include Mathematics, English, Social Studies, Religious Studies, Music, Technology, Science, Art, and Gym. She is also taking Latin and Maori as her foreign languages. (Her choices were Japanese, French, Latin, and Maori.) I ask Kiely which is more difficult, Latin or Maori. She says Maori is more difficult, by far, because it is so different from English. All the same, Kiely loves her new school, especially the all-girl environment, which she describes as really friendly and easier to work in than a coed school.

Did You Know?

- New Zealand was an uninhabited, isolated landmass in the South Pacific for around 80 million years. During that time, many plants, flowers, ferns, trees, insects, birds, and other wildlife flourished. Many of New Zealand's plant and animal life exist nowhere else on earth, and some even date from prehistoric times!

New Zealand Flag

New Zealand Currency

- Whangaparaoa, the name of Kiely's town, is a Maori word that means "Bay of Whales." Maori is the language of the Maori people from Polynesia who first settled in New Zealand. Both Maori and English are official languages in New Zealand. The names of most places in New Zealand are in Maori.

- A Kiwi is a native New Zealand bird, a fruit grown in New Zealand, and the nickname for people from New Zealand. The Kiwi bird can't fly and has very bad eyesight, so they have nostrils at the ends of their beaks so they can sniff out insects.

- Bush trekking, also called "tramping," is a national sport in New Zealand, and it is just what it sounds like, a tramp (okay, a walk) through nature trails in New Zealand's bush. You can go for one day or for several days. The entire country is organized so that people can fully enjoy trekking, complete with excellent toilet facilities just off the trails.

Auckland Bay at dusk. Auckland means "long white cloud" in Maori.

New Zealand

Whangaparaoa

Auckland, where Kiely's Grandparents live

Tazmanian Ocean

Kiely's hometown

South Pacific Ocean

Some words in Maori
Hello = Kia ora
Goodbye = E noho rä
Welcome = Nau mai

Family = Whänau
Very Good = Ka pai
Love = Aroha
Friend = Hoa

Alex Hoppers Crossing, Australia

Alexandra ("Alex")

Nationality: Australian

Religion: Anglican

Languages: English, and I know a bit of French, Chinese, Italian, and a little bit of German because of school.

Brothers and Sisters: I have one half-sister who is older.

Pets: I have a dog that is part Australian cattle dog, part Mastiff. Her name is Roxy and she is four years old.

Hobbies: I collect stamps and I am in the Australian Scouting movement.

Talents: I can sing, act, draw, and swim well.

Favorite Sport: Swimming; volleyball; and rugby

Favorite Books: Any books of the *Harry Potter* Series and *Artemis Fowl* by Eoin Colfer. This is a story about a child-prodigy criminal mastermind who falls in with a group of evil fairies.

Favorite Food: Mango, a jellybean-shaped fruit that is orange in color and tastes amazing

Least Favorite Food: Probably spinach; it's green, leafy, and tastes disgusting. Popeye eats it from a tin.

Whom do you most admire? My parents

Favorite Possession: My dog; my dark blue denim jeans; and my bedroom

Do you help with chores at home? Sometimes folding and hanging clothes and vacuuming

Do you have your own telephone or computer? I have my own computer.

Do you use the Internet? I use the Internet when I can get around to it, but I love using it. *Dolly* magazine's website is my favorite.

Where would you most want to travel? All over the universe

What comes to mind when you think of the United States? McDonald's and Disneyland

...and France? Pépé le Pew

...and China? The Great Wall

...and Kenya? Remarkable African animals like the rhinos and hippos

What do you talk about with friends? What we do at home

What do you want to know about other girls your age? Are they anything like me?

Alex with her dog, Roxy.

Alex's room and her favorite pair of jeans.

The uniquely Australian spread that Alex loves and her mother swears by.

About Me

The Aussies call Koalas "tree-droppers" because they are always falling out of trees.

My full name is Alexandra Courtney (but don't go spreading that around). My friends call me Alex and my best friends call me Al. Isn't it funny how your name gets smaller the closer you are with someone. My closest friends, Mariah, Rebecca, and Katie are known as Mya, Bec and KT to each other and myself.

Anyway, getting back to the point, I live in a two-story house with my mother, Jan, my father, Phil, and my dog, Roxy, who is an Australian cattle dog cross. I have an older sister who is married with a bouncing, one-year-old boy named Matthew and a 15-year-old stepdaughter named Rebecca. They have a grumpy Himalayan cat called Bogart. As you've probably guessed, I'm not really a cat person.

I attend Heathdale Christian College (non-denominational) and am in year seven, the first year of high school in Victoria (which if you don't know is the southernmost state on the Australian mainland). I enjoy singing, dancing, football (Aussie rules), listening to music (tried to learn the clarinet, but thought I'd do everyone a favor and listen to others instead), playing around on my computer, friends, people, enjoying myself, and having fun, a lot of the time with Scouts.

My favorite subjects at school are Home Economics and Drama. My least favorite subjects at school are Geography, L.O.T.E (Language Other Than English), and Math. I would just like to say that any person the same age or around the same age as myself who likes Math is mad or extremely determined to get somewhere in life. If so, I wish you the best of luck. If you are mad, I suggest a psychiatrist.

I'm basically an all-rounder, though, and so far am doing well in all my 11 subjects, surprising my parents and most of all myself.

Now just to get the facts straight:

1. I do not have a pet kangaroo although I've heard spunky Heath Ledger does.

2. Kangaroos and Koalas (there is no such thing as a Koala Bear) do not live in my backyard, on my street, or even in my suburb.

3. I do say "G'day Mate," but I'm only joking around with my friends; I say "Hello" to greet people normally.

4. Most Australians only call someone "mate" when they have forgotten their name.

5. People who have barbeques every night are a dying breed and are sometimes considered a bit freakish. Weekends are a different matter.

6. I live on a street, not on an Outback property with sheep. Don't get me wrong, many people in Australia do live in the Outback. I'm just one of the city slickers.

7. I don't eat witchetty grubs for breakfast, lunch, or tea. (I presume they taste like chicken, if you're wondering, since everything tastes like chicken).

8. If you tried to ride a kangaroo in Australia you would most likely be sent to jail.

9. We do not "throw" or "chuck another shrimp on the barbie." Shrimp are served in five-star restaurants because they are tiny and expensive. Prawns, however, are

Scouting Skills

Alex has learned a lot about nature through the Australian Scouting movement. She has also met children from all over Australia and done amazing things, like white-water rafting, rock climbing, rapelling (climbing down a steep cliff with a secured rope), and lots of camping. She has learned how to pitch a tent and tie knots, as well as advanced first aid, safety planning, and mapping. Alex also participated in a survival camp where she had to live alone in the Australian bush for a weekend with just a few items such as tin foil, plastic bags, coat hangers, and a pocketknife.

excellent on or off the barbie.

And finally…

10. Australia is the best place to live or be in the world and don't let anybody tell you differently. (Ireland could be a good second, although I've never been there.)

And as part of any good tour, some of the native language:

"Ankle biters" are children.

"G'day" means hello.

"Mate" is another name for anybody you meet or see.

"Mozzie" is a mosquito, an annoying insect that sucks your blood (A little like your brother or sister if they were a vampire).

"A bludger" is a lazy person who basically does nothing (Or a Quidditch ball for those of you who have read *Harry Potter*).

I guess I wanted you all to know these things about me because it's what I would want to know about you. There's really not much else I can say about myself. I'm pretty smart, I think. I've got a nice personality and a great sense of humor, blah, blah, blah. I'm just repeating myself. I really hope this essay has given you a taste of what I'm really like. If it hasn't, you'll just have to come to Australia and find out for yourself.

SCHOOL DAYS

Alex attends a private school, which is why I assume she wears a school uniform. But then I learn that, like in China and Japan, nearly all students in Australia wear uniforms. Australians believe that students should not be distracted by fashions. Moreover, girls are not to wear makeup or distracting jewelry, and hair should be pulled off the face so as not to impede vision. Alex likes wearing a uniform because it keeps the kids from competing about their clothes. In the summer, the girls

wear a tartan dress with short sleeves. In the winter, girls wear a knee-length skirt and a dark blue sweater (see left).

There are 30 students in Alex's class, 15 girls and 15 boys. Her classes include French, English, Mathematics, History/Geography, CLS (Christian Life Studies), Creative Arts, I.T. (computers), Home Economics, Drama, and Gym. The children get several breaks throughout the day and a whole hour for lunch. School is out at 3:30. In the evening, Alex usually has about one to two hours of homework.

Alex's winter uniform.

Meeting Alex by Starla

Alexandra ("Alex" for short) is a tall, athletic 13-year old with thick, curly hair and big blue eyes. Her auburn-blonde hair has natural blonde highlights and a shiny hue acquired from many hours in the chlorinated swimming pool. Alex has on a red sweatshirt with USA written on it, her favorite pair of blue jeans, and sneakers.

Alex lives in a big redbrick house with her mother and father in a residential subdivision outside of Melbourne. This subdivision is surrounded by vast areas of cattle grazing lands and open fields dotted with clusters of Acacia trees.

Australia is an immense country-continent and wide, open spaces are abundant. Luckily, Australians are not deterred by long car drives. As Alex's father explains, it is not unusual to drive one hour just to have a pizza at your favorite pizzeria.

It is the beginning of autumn in the Southern Hemisphere, and the foliage in and around Melbourne, which is quite far south, is already turning red, yellow, and gold. Thick pullovers and warm overcoats hang in the fancy store windows in Melbourne's European-style city center. I have been invited to stay the weekend with Alex's family and the house is bustling with activity when I arrive. Alex's father and his friend are in the computer room, where three computers (one belongs to Alex) are linked together, allowing three adults to play computer games against each other. In the spacious living area, Alex's two-year-old nephew, Matthew, is scuttling around under everyone's feet. Several women are busying themselves in the kitchen, which opens onto the living area, and another group of friends is minding the barbecue. It is Saturday afternoon, and Saturday afternoons in Australia usually mean "barbecue."

Alex has offered me her bedroom for my short stay while she moves into the guest room (the one with the television). One can tell a lot about a person from her bedroom and Alex's has a lot of personality. It is also very organized. Various knickknacks and souvenirs, picture frames, candles, and books are creatively displayed on the dresser and bedside table. The bed, covered in a multicolored quilt, is adorned with a very well-thought-out arrangement of decorative pillows and cuddly toys. (I take a mental picture of this so that I'll be able to replicate it in the morning when I make my bed.) Her clothes hang in an orderly fashion in the walk-in closet. A poster of the Australian actor, Heath Ledger (mentioned in her "About Me" essay), is tacked up on the back of the door.

Sunday morning I awake to preparations for another barbecue. In Australia, Sundays, like Saturdays, also usually mean "barbecue." More friends are coming over and there is a lot of chopping and mixing going on. Alex and I are the last ones up and we each make ourselves toast for breakfast. As I spread butter on my toast, Alex takes out the Vegemite for hers. Like most Australians, Alex has grown up eating Vegemite and usually has it on toast for breakfast. It is a very healthy, uniquely Australian spread made of yeast extracts, dried vegetables, and salt. I tried some and it is probably fair to say that if you did not grow up eating Vegemite, it will not quickly become your favorite food. Alex's mother swears by Vegemite any time Alex gets a cold. At Alex's house, it's a big spoonful of Vegemite over chicken soup any day.

Did You Know?

- Australia is the only country on the planet that is also an entire continent. It is located in the Southern Hemisphere between the South Pacific Ocean and the Indian Ocean. New Zealand is its closest neighbor.

Australian Flag

- Like New Zealand, Australia's isolation resulted in the flourishing of unique wildlife. Some of Australia's unique animals are the koala, kangaroo, platypus, spiny anteater, and the ostrich-like emu.

Australian Currency

- As Alex mentions, koalas are not bears, but are marsupials, like kangaroos. Koala is an Aborigine word that means "no drink" because koalas quench their thirst on the Eucalpytus leaves they chew. These leaves don't provide very much nutrition, so koalas must preserve energy. They do this by sleeping nearly 20 hours a day and moving slowly. They tend to fall asleep on their tree branch and—boom! fall to the ground.

Some words from Australia

Great = Bonzer	A cold = Wog
Broken = Bung	Swimwear = Swimmers
Sheep = Jumbuck	Bobby pin = Hair slide
	Good = Nerpy

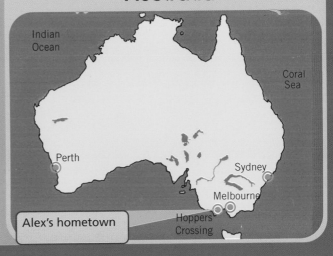

An Australian sunset.

Australia

Indian Ocean

Coral Sea

Perth

Sydney

Melbourne

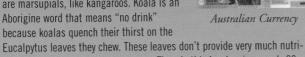

Alex's hometown

Hoppers Crossing

Africa & the Middle East

Hadil
Egypt

Naz
Turkey

Shani
Israel

Meera
Abu Dhabi

Morocco

Algeria

Libya

Saudia
Arabia

Mauritania

Mali

Niger

Chad

Sudan

Yemen

Oman

Priscilla
Kenya

Senegal

Guinea

Nigeria

Central African
Republic

Ethiopia

Sierra
Leone

Ghana

Ivory
Coast

Cameroon

Liberia

Gabon

Congo

Zaire

Philomena
Kenya

Atlantic Ocean

Angolia

Zambia

Namibia

Zimbabwe

Botswana

Katasi
Uganda

Ilke
South Africa

Rachel
South Africa

Louise
Uganda

Temple grounds in Israel.

Above: Mosque in Turkey.

Below: Kuwait Towers.

Kampala, Uganda.

Below: Ostrich in Africa.

Istanbul train station in Turkey.

Philomena Nairobi, Kenya

Philomena

Least Favorite Food: *Ugali* and kale. *Ugali* is a maize meal that is cooked with a little water. It is a staple food in Kenya. Kale is a green leafy vegetable.

Whom do you most admire? My mother

Favorite Possession: My family

Do you help with chores at home? Yes, I help by holding the baby, cooking, cleaning, and dusting.

Do you have your own telephone or computer? No

Do you use the Internet? No

Where would you most want to travel? Canada

What comes to mind when you think of the United States? Scared of racism

...and France? French language and art

...and China? Chopsticks

...and Kenya? Culture

What do you talk about with friends? Boys and their irrational behavior

What do you want to know about other girls your age? If their life is picture perfect; if they are not stressed or depressed about their families; if they enjoy life

Nationality: Kenyan

Religion: Christian

Languages: English; Kikuyu; and Kiswahili

Brothers and Sisters: I have two sisters, Sheila and Pauline, and an older brother, Stanley.

Pets: None

Hobbies: Swimming; hiking; and solving mysteries

Talents: Swimming; singing; and dancing

Favorite Sport: Swimming

Favorite Books: *The Famous Five* by Enid Blyton; *Jane Eyre* by Charolotte Brontë; and the *Nancy Drew* mysteries

Favorite Food: Chicken and french fries

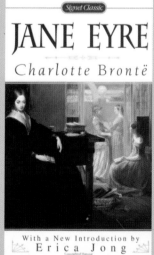
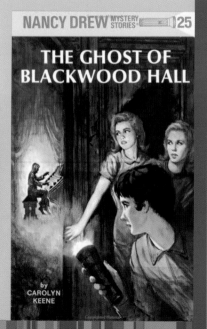

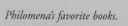
Philomena's favorite books.

My Best Day

Many happy or sad events take place in our daily lives. Some of these events affect us in one way or another. The events that have happened in my life in the past two years have in one way or another changed my point of view about life.

My happiest day was the day I went home from school full of questions in my mind because my mother had told us that she had a surprise for us when we arrived home.

When we arrived she was beaming with pride. She did not hesitate to tell us that she was pregnant. At first, the room was silent. She was getting a fourth baby ten years after the last one.

During that period, my mother had always wanted another child and finally her prayers were going to be answered. It took us quite some time to get over the fact that she was pregnant. She would tell us to feel her tummy and feel the baby kicking. It was an absolutely wonderful experience, one which I will never forget.

"Pauline has changed our pespective about life." Philomena, upper right, with her family; baby sister Pauline front and center.

> "I may be gloomy, sad, or discouraged, but the smile on Pauline's face is enough to drive any storm away."

The day the baby was due my grandfather came to check on us. My mother had not yet left for the hospital. We prayed with her and wished her all the best. We could see that she was in a lot of pain, but her faith in God kept her going.

She did not want us to see her in pain, so she sent us to the shops to buy unnecessary items. My younger sister and I danced with joy as we went to the shops. When we arrived home we found out that she had only just left for the hospital.

My sister and I stayed up wondering, hoping, and praying that both mother and child would be safe. On Monday morning when I arrived in school, the teachers and pupils flocked to me and started asking various questions. I could not wait until evening when I would get home and finally meet my new sister or brother.

But when we arrived home, my mother had not yet come from the hospital. She didn't arrive until late in the evening, and when she finally came home, I started crying. It was a relief to know that she was safe and that God's hand had been with her all the time. We named my new baby sister Pauline, meaning "little preacher," because she was God's

"My younger sister and I danced with joy as we went to the shops."

blessing to us.

Pauline has changed our perspective about life. She has left a mark in our lives and I'm grateful to God because the blessing he bestowed upon us is not comparable to all the wealth in this world. I may be gloomy, sad, or discouraged, but the smile on Pauline's face is enough to drive any storm away.

Meeting Philomena   by Starla

Philomena and Starla

Within the grounds of a large all-girls high school in Nairobi, Philomena —a sensitive Kenyan girl of Kikuyu descent—is probably missing her family.

Philomena is boarding away from her family for the first time. She has an older brother, Stanley, who attends an all-boys boarding school, a younger sister, Sheila, and a baby sister, Pauline. Philomena's favorite possession is her family.

At the school, the girls only get to see their families every three months, at the end of each term, and they are not generally permitted visitors. It is, therefore, a special exception for Philomena's parents and I to be allowed to interrupt Philomena's school day before the end of the term. She is very happy to see us.

When Philomena appears in the reception room, she is dressed in her school uniform: a forest-green, knee-length skirt, white blouse, light gray-green sweater with the school emblem, white bobby socks, black shoes, and leg warmers. It is winter after all, and although it isn't exactly

freezing, most of the girls are wearing leg warmers around their ankles because it gets chilly in the classrooms. (It is also quite fashionable.) Philomena's hair is pulled back into a small ponytail, and her big, brown eyes fill with emotion when she sees all of us waiting to greet her.

After a joyful reunion with her parents, Philomena turns to me and hugs

Philomena with her mother and father.

me like a long-lost friend. We sit down on a bench in the school foyer to talk. Words and emotions pour from Philomena, almost as if she is taking part in confession. She is clearly delighted to have someone new to talk to. Philomena explains that she had two best friends at school, Crystal and Maryann. They had great fun together and talked about everything all the time. Then Crystal moved to the United States with her family, and what's worse, Maryann will be changing schools next year! Philomena is a little worried. What will she do without her two best friends?

As we are talking, the principal of Philomena's school walks up to us and introduces herself. She is very proud of Philomena, and offers to take me on a tour of the school. The school has very impressive

The Equator and Nairobi

The Equator is an imaginary line of latitude that divides the Earth into the Northern and Southern Hemispheres. The latitude at the equator is 0. The equator crosses Kenya, Uganda, Colombia, and of course, Ecuador, among others. In these countries, the days are 12 hours long every day of the year.

Have you heard that water flows down drains in opposite directions in the Northern and Southern Hemispheres? This is called the Coriolis effect, and it makes hurricanes rotate in opposite directions in the two hemispheres. Is the Coriolis effect really noticeable in bathtubs, sinks, and toilets? The experts say "No", but I saw it with my own eyes when crossing the equator in Kenya!

Starla at the Equator Crossing.

back at the end of each term, the family enjoys evenings together talking, eating dinners, visiting the neighbors, and being entertained by Philomena's little sister, Pauline.

During the term, Philomena also eats all of her meals at the school, and spends weekends there as well. On Saturday and Sunday, she washes her clothes, does home-work, sleeps in, and does whatever else is necessary to prepare for the next week. The girls must stay on

facilities for the 500 boarders: an up-to-the-minute com-puter lab, science labs, tennis and netball courts, and a tan-talizing swimming pool. A new library is under construction. The school used to be exclusively for European (i.e., non-African) students, first boys, then just girls. The first Kenyan–African and Kenyan-Asian girls were admitted in 1962.

Despite the impressive school grounds, Philomena would rather be living at home. She keeps a photograph of her family next to her bed in the dormitory where she sleeps, and she waits impatiently for the terms to end so that she can go home. When she and her older brother are

The tantalizing pool at Philomena's school.

campus, even in the evenings. Sometimes movies are shown in the cafeteria for entertainment.

Overall, Philomena explains, the school is quite strict. She seldom complains, though, because she knows how impor-tant her education is. Leaving Philomena, and seeing her say goodbye to her parents is like pulling heartstrings. But, thankfully, I know that in just one more week she will be going home to them.

Philomena with her best friend, Maryann.

SCHOOL DAYS

To make the school terms pass more quickly, Philomena fills her days with studying, swimming, and talking about books and boys with Maryann. Philomena studies 12 subjects throughout the year: Mathematics, English, Kiswahili, Business Education, Computers, Home Economics, Chemistry, Biology, Physics, Geography, History, and Religious Studies. Her favorite class is History. After classes, the students can study in the library, read newspapers in the reading room, or use the computers in the computer room.

Checking e-mail in the computer room.

If I Could Be...

When I grow up I would want to become a pediatrician because I love to work with children. I was inspired to become a pediatrician when I was walking along the streets of Nairobi and met these young children. Their state of health was horrible. They seemed as if they had not eaten for weeks. Their bodies were covered in wounds and I felt so guilty inside that I could not do something to help them. Due to the economic hardships in the country, the poverty level has increased and the crime rate increases every week.

The total number of unemployed citizens is 14 million. Most of the population is the youth. Kenya is among the world's top leading countries with the highest number of street children. These children are a major target for various deadly diseases. Their parents live under less than a dollar each day and can barely afford to pay

Maasai children are happy in their mud huts, but Philomena wants to help Nairobi's street children who are not so lucky.

any medical bills. Therefore, I feel as if it is my obligation to help the children of Kenya.

Traveling to outer space can be exciting, yet become the most dangerous thing in your life. It requires a lot of self-confidence, which I do not have. You have to keep your mind focused on positive things, but we tend to think the opposite. I think of the engine not working, lack of enough oxygen, and getting lost in space, and parting with the ones I love.

Being elected the leader of a country is a huge responsibility. One must be ready to carry a huge burden. The choices and decisions that you make will affect someone's life in one way or another. It can affect someone's life both physically and emotionally. The public always points fingers at you. You might act as if you're not hurt, but hiding the problem only worsens it. In Kenya when a law is passed and the president signs or agrees with the contents, he holds the future of Kenyans in his hands.

To be president takes a lot of hard work and determination. You should have a positive mind and stick to what is best for the country. Most corruption cases are reported among the highest politicians, especially the president. This can spoil the name of the president and many people will think that you're the cause of all the problems facing the country. It is best that you be someone who does not become stressed when criticized for wanting the best for your country.

At this stage of adolescence, many young people have role models. A role model is someone you aspire to be in the future. Role models should set good examples for their fans. Many role models are found in the entertainment industry. Pop stars and movie stars influence young people a lot. The type of music pop stars produce carries a message that affects the fan directly or indirectly. An example of this is rock music. Not all rock music is bad, of course, but I think that some of it does involve cults and brainwashing.

Philomena reading in her classroom.

To be a movie star you have to sacrifice a lot. It may mean fame and glamor, but once you flash back and think of all the things you have missed out on, it hurts to the inner core. You never get the chance to make your own decisions. You have to do it their way. In the film industry it is like selling your body. You have no self-esteem and no self-dignity. Why sell your body when you can try something much better like teaching or being a lawyer? Some of these little things are what encourage sexually transmitted diseases. All in the name of making money. It is not worth it. Others become anorexic because of slimming themselves just to be in the right shape. People will mock you and despise you, and instead of giving your community a good name, you are giving it a bad one. I prefer to be just plain simple me.

To win a gold medal at the Olympics is not bad. It will bring pride and happiness to your country. I guess it's okay except for the training part where you need to keep on training and straining yourself. Otherwise it is also a very commendable achievement.

What I Most Want The World To Know

I would like the world to know that I'm a bit shy, but full of life inside. I'm a great fan of culture. I love adventure and mysteries. I do not get moody or gloomy. I just think about something nice that has happened and start smiling all day long. I love making new friends even though it's hard because in school I barely have any true friends. I want what's best for the world and I pray someday that I'll get the chance to explore it.

Women of the Maasai.

Maasai Mara

One of the finest wildlife sanctuaries in Africa, the Maasai Mara National Reserve, is located 270 kilometers (about five hours by car) from Nairobi, Philomena's home city. It is filled with hundreds of different birds and mammals, including wildebeests and antelopes. The Maasai people, with a total population of half a million, live a traditional, semi-nomadic existence in Kenya. Their homes are mud-covered straw huts and their primary source of income is livestock.

A leopard lounging in a tree; an elephant; and a giraffe.

Did You Know?

• Kenya is located in East Africa and is bordered by Uganda, Sudan, Ethiopia, Somalia, Tanzania, and Lake Victoria. It has a long coastline on the Indian Ocean. Nairobi is the capital city of Kenya, and both English and Kiswahili are official languages.

Zebras enjoying a drink.

• English is used for business and government, and Kiswahili is used for everyday life. Kiswahili (the "ki" means language) is close in origin to the Bantu languages spoken by many of Kenya's native tribes. It is spoken more than English is in the more rural areas of Kenya, outside the main cities. Most Kenyans also speak a specific local dialect, in addition to Kiswahili and English.

Kenyan Flag

Kenyan Currency

• Kenya was ruled by many foreigners, including the Portuguese and the British, before gaining independence in 1963. The independence movement began after World War II and culminated in the Mau Mau Rebellion.

• The Kikuyu tribe is the largest in Kenya. They are traditionally farmers and were instrumental in the Mau Mau rebellion that led to Kenyan independence. Joseph Kenyatta, Kenya's first African president, was a Kikuyu.

• The Mau Mau Rebellion was a four-year uprising against British control in Kenya from 1952 to 1956. It was led by a secret guerilla organization called the Mau Mau.

Some words in Kiswahili
Hello = Jambo
So long = Tutaonana
Please = Tafadhali

Thank you= Asante
Girl = Msichana
Friend = Rafiki
Nice to meet you = Nafurahi kukuona

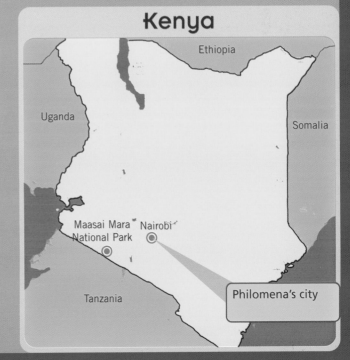

Kenya

Ethiopia

Uganda

Somalia

Maasai Mara National Park   Nairobi

Tanzania

Philomena's city

Priscilla Nairobi, Kenya

Priscilla

Nationality: Kenyan, but my parents are from the Indian state of Goa

Religion: Catholic

Languages: English; Kiswahili; French; and a little Konkani, which is my parent's language

Brothers and Sisters: I have a little brother, Mitchell.

Pets: Until recently I had a pet parrot named Larry. He was an African parrot with shades of gray feathers on his body.

Hobbies: Watching movies

Talents: My talents are acting and arguing with people; I practice arguing and building my vocabulary thanks to my brother, Mitchell. I use and test the vocabulary words I learn at school with Mitchell and he doesn't understand a thing!

Favorite Sport: Soccer. I mostly play attack defense.

Favorite Books: *Bridget Jones' Diary* by Helen Fielding; *Matilda* by Roald Dahl; and *Jane Eyre* by Charlotte Brontë

Favorite Food: Pizza with olives, pepperoni, sauces, and anything else you want to add. Don't get crazy and add ice cream. It doesn't taste nice. Believe me.

Least Favorite Food: Sushi, which is raw fish, and rice, because we eat it too often

Whom do you most admire? Ben Affleck

Favorite Possession: My wardrobe

Do you help with chores at home? Only when necessary. I help wash dishes and make the beds (even though it takes me very long—darn bedsheets!).

Do you have your own telephone or computer? Yes, I have my own phone and computer.

Do you use the Internet? Yes; my favorite site is the fashion website.

Where would you most want to travel? Hollywood; Hawaii; Ibiza; and Italy

What comes to mind when you think of the United States? Brilliant actors

...and France? French accents

...and China? The Chinese alphabet

...and Kenya? Total disaster!!!!

What do you talk about with friends? Wealth and fame

What do you want to know about other girls your age? How their everyday life compares to mine

Some of Priscilla's favorite outfits.

My Best Day

Priscilla at home.

Most people would describe the best day they've had in the past two years as "adventurous," "painful but worth it," or "fun." But the best day I've had in the past two years is described as "Patash." Obviously this word does not exist in the dictionary, nor does it exist in any human vernacular. "Patash" is a word I invented to explain anything that I myself cannot describe, even with big vocabulary words. "Patash" can be considered a description of something good or something bad, depending on how it is pronounced. In my case, this strange word expresses excellence, happiness, and memorable. Now that you know what "Patash" means, I can tell you how "Patash" the best day I've had in the past two years was.

It was a very dull Saturday morning. Everybody in my family including me was reluctant to do anything that required effort. We were just so lazy that putting on a pair of socks was tiresome, hard work. Usually after breakfast, a person's second priority is reading the newspaper. So, when I successfully reached the breakfast table without bumping into any walls and had my breakfast, I flipped the first few pages of Nairobi's *Daily Nation* newspaper. The only thing I read in the newspaper is the cinema guide or profiles on actors and movies. It took only a few seconds before my favorite page of the morning paper was displayed. As I slowly perused the guide, a title caught my attention. This title was *Pearl Harbor*.

I, at first, was not anxious to see this movie, but upon seeing its preview, I promised to be the first person to buy a cinema ticket for it.

Suddenly, my eyes burst wide open and a surge of energy surged throughout my whole body. I quickly ran upstairs into my room, picked up the telephone and called a friend of mine, and told her to meet me at the cinema at two o'clock in the afternoon. I gave her no option.

I could barely wait to get into the cinema to see *Pearl Harbor*. I was so excited that I reached the cinema a half an hour early, bought tickets, and waited "patiently" for my friend. As I waited, I bought loads of popcorn because I knew I would need it. Finally, my companion arrived. She didn't have quite an opportunity to greet me properly, as I literally dragged her into the cinema hall. I was getting very impatient as more and more movie previews appeared on the screen. If the movie didn't start soon, I was likely to throw all my popcorn on the person sitting in front of me, and hence, cause a lot of havoc like I normally do. At last, I saw the title *Pearl Harbor* on the screen and was no longer restless.

I watched the movie with great enthusiasm and interest. In fact, for the first time, I didn't utter a word to any of the people sitting on either side of my seat. After seeing the best movie of the year (according to me), I was

> "'Patash' is a word I invented to explain anything that I myself cannot describe, even with big vocabulary words."

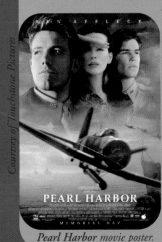

Courtesy of Touchstone Pictures

PEARL HARBOR

Pearl Harbor movie poster.

silent and not a word slipped out of my mouth.

Upon arriving home that day, I thought about what kind of lives the actors and actresses in the movie led before having an acting career and before starring in a movie of great potential such as *Pearl Harbor*. I took into consideration Ben Affleck—who was in a rehabilitation center after starring in the movie—and all of the other characters. As all these thoughts went through my mind, I realized that all those actors and actresses had to put in a lot of effort to become who they are today. They had to sacrifice to succeed.

You still don't know why this was the best day I've had in the past two years. Well, this was the best day I've had in the past two years because seeing *Pearl Harbor* made me realize that I wasn't going to be successful with the help of someone else. I had to succeed on my own.

This day was nothing compared to a typical day because on a typical day I would never be able to realize how important it is to become what you want to become and then make the best of it. If I hadn't seen *Pearl Harbor*, I wouldn't have realized how important it is to follow your dream. Realization made this day the best day I have had in the past two years, and probably the best day I will ever have in my life.

Meeting Priscilla by Starla

Starla with Priscilla and her family.

Priscilla has her eyes on Hollywood. Talkative (in several languages), self-confident (her e-mail address includes the words "mentally hot babe"), and funny—if she makes it to stardom one day I would not be surprised.

She keeps a close eye on her celebrity idols, knows all of the latest fashion trends, and is even improving on the language of Shakespeare by making up her own vocabulary when no existing words in the English language will quite do the trick. She does all of this from Nairobi, Kenya in East Africa.

Priscilla is wearing a denim jacket with pink, embroidered butterflies, flared jeans, and platform black sandals when we meet. Each finger on both of her hands sports a ring—ten small silver rings in all—and she wears silver hoop earrings in her ears. The silver jewelry matches her braces. Her waist-length, black hair is doubled up and tied in a loose ponytail, making it appear half its length. All in all, Priscilla's look is very hip and trendy. So, I am somewhat surprised when she introduces herself ("Hello, I am Priscilla, it is lovely to meet you"), with an accent and diction like the Queen of England. I quickly learn that Priscilla spent the last few years attending a British prep school in Nairobi, where she acquired the accent. (She can speak with an Indian accent when she wants to.)

Priscilla's parents are originally from the Indian state of Goa. Her mother has lived her whole life in Kenya, and her father came to Kenya 25 years ago. Priscilla still has family in India, and has been there twice to visit. When asked if she feels more Kenyan or Indian, though, Priscilla responds, without hesitation, that she feels more Kenyan. This is because she has lived her whole life in Kenya and hasn't experienced Indian life at all; that is, if you exclude the very Indian influences of her family, the extensive Indian community in Nairobi, and her current school.

Priscilla lives in a house in a residential subdivision about 15 minutes outside of Nairobi. According to Priscilla, this subdivision is BORING!!! For fun, she meets her friends at the large mall or movie theater.

A flamingo in Kenya.

SCHOOL DAYS

Last year, Priscilla left a mixed British prep school to attend a private all-girls religious school in Nairobi. It is run by Indians from the province of Gujarat who practice Jainism, a form of Hinduism. The Gujarati Indians take education very seriously, and to get in, Priscilla had to perform exceptionally well on her Common Entrance Exams. The majority of the girls at the school are Gujarati, although there are also some bright girls from other parts of India, and of Kenyan origin. The girls all wear school uniforms.

Priscilla studies Biology, Chemisty, Physics, Mathematics, English, Literature, Art, Computers, and a foreign language. Priscilla chose French instead of continuing with Kiswahili this year. Biology and Chemistry are her favorite subjects, but she also loves creative writing. Priscilla loves being at an all-girls school. Here's why: In the coed school, the girls were hesitant to participate in class for fear of saying something the boys might think stupid. There were also lots of little things to worry about, like who was wearing what and where to sit in class. If a girl sat next to a boy, rumors would start that she liked him. Most important, she couldn't be sarcastic or ironic because the boys couldn't figure out if she was being serious, funny, or just plain weird! At the new school, it's much more relaxed, all of the girls are sarcastic and ironic and everyone "gets it." Priscilla wraps up her description of the differences between schools by saying: "If I acted like I do at my new school, everyone would think that I had a brain transplant that didn't work!"

Did You Know?

- Kenya is named after its mountain, Mount Kenya, and means "the place where there are ostriches." On very clear days, the thin, jagged finger of its peak can be seen from miles away.

- Kenya's population is 99 percent African and between 30 and 70 different tribes call Kenya home. The non-African population is made up of European, Arab, and Indian people. Many of the Indians in Kenya come from Goa, like Priscilla's parents.

- Ties between Goa and Kenya go way back in history. Goa is located on India's Gold Coast along the Arabian Sea. It was a Portuguese colony for 450 years, and the headquarters of the Portuguese Viceroy for Africa. Late in the 19th century, many Goans sailed across the Arabian Sea and Indian Ocean to Kenya.

- Many of Nairobi's tourist sites feature orphaned animals that have been rescued from the wild. They are cared for by professionals until they are able to return to the wild.

The giraffe grabs food pellets right out of his visitor's hand with his warm, sticky, blue tongue.

Some words in Konkani

Yes = Vai	Girl = Cheddum
No = Nakam	Good morning = Deuborodissdium
Friendship = Ixttagot	Good night = Deuborirattdium
	Thank you = Deoboremcoruum

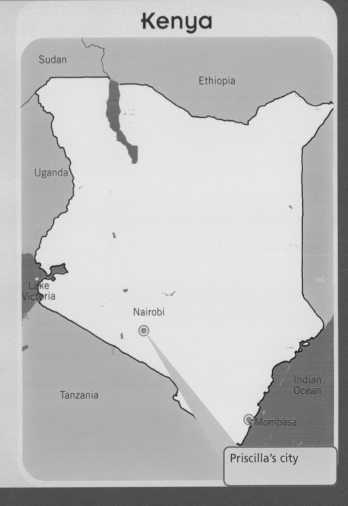

Kenya

Sudan

Ethiopia

Uganda

Lake Victoria

Nairobi

Tanzania

Indian Ocean

Mombasa

Priscilla's city

Katasi and Louise

Katasi

Nationality: Ugandan

Religion: Protestant

Languages: Luganda and English

Brothers and Sisters: A brother named Sendawulas

Pets: An angel fish

Hobbies: Listening to music

Talents: Singing and dancing

Favorite Sport: Basketball

Favorite Books: *Where the Red Fern Grows* by Wilson Rawls; the *Harry Potter* books by J.K. Rowling; and *Island of the Blue Dolphins* by Scott O'Dell

Favorite Food: Chicken Matooke and Rice

Least Favorite Food: Pumpkin

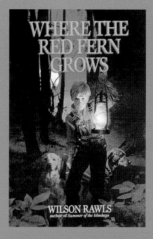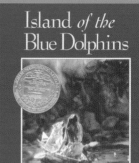

Two of Katasi's favorite books.

Whom do you most admire? My grandfather, Professor Senteza Kajubi

Favorite Possession: (No response)

Do you help with chores at home? Yes, I help to wash dishes and dirty clothes and clean the house.

Do you have your own telephone or computer? Yes

Do you use the Internet? Yes, my favorite website is Yahoo.com.

Where would you most want to travel? Puerto Rico

What comes to mind when you think of the United States? Many diverse people

...and France? Beautiful scenery

...and China? A great population

...and Kenya? Many wild animals

What do you talk about with friends? What happens at school

What do you want to know about other girls your age? If they have the same interests as me

*Katasi recently moved to the United States, and she spends her summers in Kampala with her father. She also sees a lot of her cousin Louise when she visits Uganda.

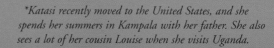

Cousins in Kampala*, Uganda

Nationality: Ugandan

Religion: Protestant

Languages: Lugandan and English

Brothers and Sisters: I have a sister named Zally, two brothers named Juko and Sam, and an older half-sister named Beverley.

Pets: Yes, two dogs, Bambi and Pony

Louise's favorite food is pizza.

Hobbies: Athletics; reading; and playing

Talents: Singing; dancing; and running

Favorite Sport: Running and basketball

Favorite Books: Secret Seven books by Enid Blyton, and *Mr. Canta and Healer of Souls*

Louise likes Enid Blyton books.

Favorite Food: Pizza

Least Favorite Food: Rice

Whom do you most admire? Jesus

Favorite Possession: My piano

Do you help with chores at home? Yes, washing, making the beds, sweeping, and mopping

Do you have your own telephone or computer? No

Do you use the Internet? No, I don't.

Where would you most want to travel? South Africa

Nakayenga Louise ("Louise")

What comes to mind when you think of the United States? It's fun.

Louise (left) and Katasi (right) with Louise's half-sister Beverley (middle).

...and France? Too much French (I don't know how to speak French.)

...and China? Karate

...and Kenya? It's more fun than Uganda.

What do you talk about with friends? Vacation

What do you want to know about other girls your age? Nothing in particular

Lake Victoria

Lake Victoria, also known as Victoria Nyanza, is bordered by Uganda, Kenya, and Tanzania. It is widely accepted as the source of the Nile River, the longest river in the world. It also provides a good example of different countries—Uganda, Kenya, and Tanzania—working together, since each of these three countries depend on the lake for all aspects of daily life. In particular, the fishing industry is an important part of their national economies. There have even been recent discoveries of new species of fish living in the lake!

About the size of the Republic of Ireland, Lake Victoria is also the world's second largest freshwater lake, after Lake Superior in North America. British explorer John Hanning Speke became the first European to sight Lake Victoria in 1858. He named the lake for Britain's Queen Victoria; it was also known to the Arabs as *Ukerewe*.

Meeting Katasi and Louise by Starla

Louise, Starla, and Katasi.

In Uganda, a girl's last name is used as her first name, followed by an African name, and finally the given name. The given name is the one used between friends and family. Therefore, Nakayenga Louise introduces herself in a very soft voice as "Louise." Louise is with her cousin, Katasi, who, at first, has an equally soft voice; that is, until she starts to feel more comfortable and she really starts talking. She talks about life in Uganda, her new life in the United States, what is different, what is the same. She asks lots of questions as well: How many girls are going to be in the book? Is she going to be in the book? Is her cousin Louise going to be in the book? When will she know?…Katasi is certainly not shy.

We meet in Kampala, the capital city of Uganda, for lunch at a fast-food court called Nando's, which is the girls' favorite restaurant. Louise's oldest sister, Beverley, has arranged for the meeting and taken both girls out of school for a couple of hours. (Katasi, out of school for the summer in Massachusetts, is attending the last weeks of school in Kampala, in order to spend time with her old classmates.)

Louise is in her school uniform: a blue-and-white striped dress with the school emblem. Her cousin, Katasi, is wearing a blue dress and her hair is tied in a short ponytail. Her face is glowing and she smiles a lot.

Two years ago, Katasi moved to Randolph, Massachusetts, with her mother and brother to join other relatives already living there. She spends her summers with her father, who stayed in Kampala—a city that sits magnificently on the banks of beautiful Lake Victoria. It is exactly on the equator, but its high altitude keeps temperatures mild. Once called the "Pearl of Africa," Kampala is breathtakingly beautiful with its red-clay earth, lush, green vegetation, and beautiful hilltop vistas.

We consider what to order for lunch. Nando's offers us all kinds of choices: pizzas and Italian pastas, burgers and fries, sandwiches, ice creams, and all kinds of other sweets. Katasi and I order cheeseburgers and fries and Louise orders a pizza, which she shares with Beverley. We sit down to eat, and our conversation is soon punctuated by the girls' giggles and laughs.

If I Could Be...
by Katasi

When I grow up I would like to be a lawyer. To be this, I would have to go to school longer and study and memorize the whole English dictionary. If I could become a lawyer I would have to study three more years after my college education. This will not be a problem for me because this is really what I want to do.

I would like to be a children's lawyer because, since I am a kid now I know what amount of pressure can be put on a child by their peers. For example, a child might be forced to do something that may hurt them or another person, physically or emotionally.

The duties that I would have as a children's lawyer would be to defend the child in court, for example, if the child got in trouble. If I had a child's case on my hands, I would talk to the child and ask him or her what tempted them to do what

Katasi: Future lawyer!

they did. Then I would talk to any witnesses. After that I would talk to the family of the person who was hurt and find out where they were at the time. Then I would investigate where the crime took place and gather together clues to help my client's case.

Another reason why I want to be a lawyer is that people say I talk a lot and when I tell them that I want to be a lawyer, they tell me that I would make a good one.

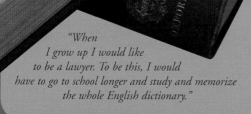

"When I grow up I would like to be a lawyer. To be this, I would have to go to school longer and study and memorize the whole English dictionary."

"I would like to be a children's lawyer because, since I am a kid now I know what amount of pressure can be put on a child by their peers."

Growing Up
a creative essay by Katasi

A few years back, a girl named Katasi was on her way to school when she spotted her friend across the street. Her friend had changed physically and seemed to have a lot of self-confidence.

Although Katasi had also matured physically, she was not emotionally ready for junior high school. Her friend also spotted her and said hello.

When they got together, they talked about what would be happening that year. Then they promised to be friends forever. When they entered the classroom, they found many of their old friends. Everyone had all matured. Katasi was still the same, and yet, felt different.000

Oh, why can't I be the same?

> "If I were a famous leader of my country, I would be remembered and respected like Nelson Mandela..."

"Then they promised to be friends forever."

I Won a Gold Medal at the Olympics
a creative essay by Louise

The race would start and I would win the race. I would pinch myself because all I ever wanted was to win the gold medal. I would like to race with Marion Jones and other record holders like Cathy Freeman. Uganda has not won a gold medal for a long time. If I won a gold medal at the Olympics, I would represent Uganda, or Africa at large.

In the history of Ugandan Athletics, few have won gold medals, but they all won these medals in long distance. (My best races are long distance.) John Akiibua represented Uganda in the 1992 Olympics and then there is my favorite Ugandan runner, Boican Inzikduru. I would also want to be like Grace Birungi, who has represented

Uganda on a number of occasions.

One advantage of winning a gold medal is that gold is a valuable mineral. Everybody likes the way gold glitters, except for the proverb, "All that glitters is not gold." But as soon as one wins a gold medal one shouldn't let oneself down. What I mean is that if you are number one, you have to ensure that you stay number one.

Another advantage of winning a gold medal is that you can be famous. If one is running at the Olympics, what has taken them there is the possibility of winning a gold medal and becoming famous.

In 1999, when I was in P4 [fourth grade], I became famous in school after I won a medal on Sports Day. I was declared the best runner in the girls' group in the WHOLE of the Primary Section. I had a feeling that I could do this.

During my training, some people threatened me that even though I had been beating them in training sessions, they would beat me in the finals.

I want to conclude that if God had not been there, I would not have won the medal at school. Next time, I think I will win the gold medal worldwide.

If I Could Be...
by Louise

If I could be elected the leader of my country, I would first have to think about the villages. Why? When we are talking about how Uganda is an underdeveloped country, we must first look at the villages.

In the villages, there are many poor people. Most of them are hungry and don't have money to pay school fees for their children. That's why they take their children to the UPE [Universal Primary Education: a new national education program in Uganda]. In the villages, there are also epidemic diseases that can lead to the loss of lives.

If I were the leader, I would like to attend different conferences in the world, especially in places like France, United Kingdom, USA, and Australia. In the conference, I would lead the discussion on the topic, "How to make the world a global village."

Another reason why I would like to be elected as the leader of my country is to be famous and try to teach the world how to have communal prayers. If I were a famous leader of my country, I would be remembered and respected like Nelson Mandela, who tried to stop the apartheid policy in South Africa.

And the day I came to power and the day I left power would be declared public holidays.

"If I were the leader, I would like to attend different conferences in the world, especially in places like France, United Kingdom, USA, and Australia."

SCHOOL DAYS: Louise

Louise is in seventh grade, which, in Kampala, is the final year of primary school. Louise's school day is very long. The students arrive at school at 7:30 in the morning for an 8:00 a.m. start and classes don't end until 6:00 in the evening! Each class is 40 minutes long. The students stay in the same classroom throughout the day, while the teachers change classrooms for each lesson.

Louise's classes are: English Grammar, Comprehension and Composition, Science (Agriculture and Electricity), Social Studies, Civics, Geography, History, Mathematics, and Gym. Mathematics is Louise's favorite subject and she recently participated in a mathematics competition. She is also interested in current events and enjoys her nightly homework assignment of reading daily newspapers and summarizing the main articles.

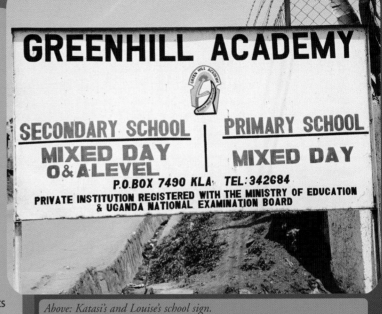

Above: Katasi's and Louise's school sign.
Below: Other students at Greenhill Academy.

SCHOOL DAYS: Katasi

In Massachusetts, Katasi attends an international school. She will be entering junior high this coming fall. Last year, her classes included Mathematics, Science, English, History, World Cultures, French, Music, Computers, Current Events, Arts and Crafts, and Library. Her favorite subject is Science, and in particular, the study of Earth and outer space. Katasi does not wear a uniform at school in Massachusetts like she did at her school in Kampala. She prefers the uniform, because, as she says, it was easier to get ready in the morning.

I ask Katasi whether school was more difficult in Uganda or in the United States. She says that school was more difficult in Uganda because the teachers were stricter and there was more home-work. She does mention, however, that there is more peer pressure at her new school in the USA.

Did You Know?

- Uganda, located in East Africa, is mostly rural and very fertile. Kampala, the capital city and business center, is its only major city. A number of African ethnic groups live in Uganda, with the Ganda, being the largest. The Ganda people speak Lugandan (a Bantu language), like Louise and Katasi, but English is the official language in Uganda.

- Kampala is the largest city in Uganda. Actually, Kampala and areas around Lake Victoria are the only heavily populated areas. More than 90 percent of the population live in rural areas.

- Ugandan history is marred by political upheaval, but its beautiful natural landscapes and wildlife remain a source of pride for the Ugandan people. Uganda has magnificent mountains, which are the world's last remaining natural habitat for mountain gorillas.

- Yoweri Museveni, president of Uganda since 1986, has overseen significant improvements to Ugandan society. Kampala is now prospering again. But things are still difficult in northern Uganda, where Ugandan rebels, intent on overthrowing Museveni's government, have been waging a bloody insurgency for more than 15 years.

Ugandan Flag

- Although Louise leads a harmonious life in Kampala, many children in Uganda are suffering a great deal due to poverty, illness, and lack of education. The UPE that Louise mentions in her essay stands for Universal Primary Education. This is a new government initiative aimed at providing at least primary school education to all Ugandan children. It is not very effective, though, because there are no proper learning facilities, so children study under trees. There is also no money for textbooks or other supplies.

Ugandan Currency

- More than one-third of the population in Uganda are Christians, with Catholics outnumbering Protestants. In fact, European missionaries in Uganda were an important part in education development and reform.

- Each of the ethnic tribes has its own monarchical system, where the head of the tribe is either a chief or king. Many of these royal lines span centuries.

Some words in Lugandan
Hi = Ki kati
Good morning = Wasuze otya nno?
Good night = Sula bulungi
See you later = Tunaalabagana
My name is = Erinnya lyange nze
Friend = Mukwano gwange
Thank you = Weebale

A hillside view of Uganda with Lake Victoria in the background.

Uganda

Sudan

Zaire

Kenya

Kampala

Lake Victoria

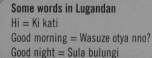
Katasi's and Louise's hometown

Rachel Johannesburg, South Africa

Rachel

Nationality: South African

Religion: Jewish (orthodox)

Languages: English

Brothers and Sisters: Two brothers Nathan and David

Pets: Two dogs, Gus (Border collie) and Harry (we're not quite sure what she is. Perhaps an Alsatian and something else!)

Hobbies: I enjoy reading, dancing, eating, and sleeping.

Talents: I have been reading since I was four and I do well at school (sorry if I sound big-headed). I do well in ballet. I am also artistic.

Favorite Sport: I am not the sporty type; I can't run or swim very well, but I do ballet, and I am on the netball team at school.

Favorite Books: At the moment I like the Louise Rennings series (particularly *Dancing in My Nuddy-Pants*); *Abhorsen* by Garth Nix; and *All-American Girl* by Meg Cabot

Favorite Food: I don't have one. I love almost any food.

Least Favorite Food: Liver of any kind

Whom do you most admire? I admire a lady named Andy Sostak, who risked her life to save kids. While doing this, she lost the ability to walk and was paralyzed from her waist down. She has been through a bad time and now as a single mother looks after her two sons. She is not world famous but to me she is admirable.

Favorite Possession: I have a blanket that was my father's, which my grandmother covered and gave to my cousin, who then gave it to me.

Do you help with chores at home? Not really. I clean my room and my brothers and I take turns clearing the table. I sometimes help my Mom help my brother with his homework.

Do you use the Internet? Yes I do. I love www.bubblegum club.com. I use the Internet to do all my school projects.

Do you have your own telephone or computer? I have my own cell phone.

Where would you most want to travel? America

What comes to mind when you think of the United States? Superstars

...and France? Fashion

...and China? Markets

...and Kenya? Game reserves

What do you talk about with friends? We just talk about what is happening in our lives at the moment or the first thing that comes to our minds.

What do you want to know about other girls your age? I would like to know how they live their lives.

Dancing in My Nuddy-Pants by Louise Rennings; one of Rachel's favorite books.

About Me

"I have always wanted a sister since I am the only girl."

Hi my name is Rachel. Did you know that more people are killed by donkeys than by plane crashes in a year? There. That was some useless info you will never need to know that I used for my introduction since my mind has gone blank.

I was born in Johannesburg, which is a city in South Africa. Johannesburg is the largest city in South Africa, but it is not the capital. The capital of South Africa is Pretoria.

I am short with brown hair, brown eyes, and I wear glasses or contact lenses. I live with my mother my father and my two younger brothers. I have always wanted a sister since I am the only girl.

I have three grandparents. I am very close to my grandparents and they are a very important part of my life. So family is a very big part of my life. My aunts, uncles, and cousins are very close to us. We spend many happy hours together especially sitting around the dinner table!

My family is Jewish. Practicing Judaism is part of our everyday lives. My family celebrates religious festivals together. In South Africa the dominant religion is Christianity, and there are also a large number of people who belong to the Muslim faith. In South Africa it is easy to practice any religion you want. We have many different religions and cultures.

Being Jewish, I attend a religious Jewish school. I wake up at half past six in the morning and get collected for school by a lift club. That's with a few families that live close by. One of our parents takes us to school. School starts at twenty to eight and every day we start off with prayers and then carry on with our regular studies. I enjoy school work. I like most of the subjects we do at school. At times though school can get a bit stressful. We sometimes get a lot of work. Most days I have to study after school and we often have projects to complete in our spare time. This does not leave time for spending time with friends during the week.

I also do ballet. I have been doing ballet for seven years and have passed my Grade 5 exams. I have just gone on to point shoes. I go to ballet lessons in the afternoons. So things can really get busy around here especially if I have a ballet exam or a concert. I also play netball. It's a ball game similar to basketball except you do not bounce the ball. I am on the school team. It's usually fun, apart from last week when I broke my wrist playing a match! I also do art after school. I love art, especially painting. I paint with oils and am learning sketch techniques.

My weekends are spent with my friends. We usually spend time at a friend's house and sometimes we go to movies on Saturday nights. I am friendly with a group of girls. These are the kids that I spend most of my time with. I also enjoy just being at home and reading. On the weekends I love to stay in my pajamas and read the whole day. It's my way of taking time out. I spend a lot of my time reading. I hate running out of books to read. I even read in the bath!

In South Africa we do not have a good public transport system so kids cannot

"My experience as a white kid is really different than that of many black kids. I have (because of our political history) had a lot of chances that perhaps black children did not have..."

catch buses. We don't have an underground train system either (there are plans to build one soon in Johannesburg!). So our parents have to take and fetch us where ever we go. Unfortunately, we also cannot really walk around much. This is because our crime rate is high and it's not really safe for kids to walk

A lion catches an afternoon rest from the hot sun.

around by themselves. So in some ways our lives are a bit restricted. I often envy children who live in other countries that are able to walk to the shops and friends houses.

My friends are those kids that are at my school. In South Africa over the last 15 years many people have emigrated to other countries. I think people were not sure of South Africa. I have lost quite a few good friends. This has been hard particularly with two of my very best friends leaving to live in Australia.

South Africa is a beautiful country and we have an interesting history. In many ways this has affected my life and the lives of many other children of my age. South Africa, because of its political history, was a country divided along race lines. So before 1994 (when the Apartheid government was still in power) black and white children were not allowed to go to the same schools or use the same public places.

But since 1994 things have changed and my experience of living in South Africa is different to my parents'. Black and white people were not allowed to live in the same areas and were not even allowed to get married. My experience as a white kid is really different than that of many black kids. I have

"I have been doing ballet for seven years."

(because of our political history) had a lot of chances that perhaps black children did not have and so their situations are different today. It's hard to think that if all of the people who are my parents' age had equal opportunities then there would be more black kids in similar positions as me. So things have changed and I am lucky to be living in a country that is very different and much freer than it had been in the past.

South Africa is a beautiful country. Traveling in South Africa and other African countries has been a big part of my life. My family holidays are spent at the beach in the south of the country. We are also lucky to have some of the most beautiful game reserves. Imagine being surrounded by 400 elephants with no escape or not being able to breathe because a pack of lions may jump on your open air vehicle.

So my life is like a kaleidoscope, it's made up of different facets. My family, my religion, my African history and, of course, my friends. I think I am a lucky girl. I have a lot of opportunities in this world. I am privileged to have things that other children do not have and I suppose I have to keep remembering those people that are not as fortunate as I am.

I love my country and what it gives me and what it allows me to do. Being a girl of my age is exciting, and, I suppose, a little scary at times as well…but I am looking forward to the adventure.

My Best Day

The best day if my life...well it's difficult to describe just one, so I have decided to describe a few. I suppose best days for me are when I achieve something and feel good about myself. My best days are when I feel happy about my world around me. So some of these days are:

Getting an A in my ballet exam: This was the greatest day for me....

Actually it begins the year before when I was diagnosed with a benign tumor in my big toe! My toe had been sore for weeks. I had gone to doctors but they could not find anything. Eventually one very clever doctor picked up the real problem. I had surgery.

Four years later I am perfect and have never had any more problems. So back to my story. Obviously after my operation I was not allowed to do ballet for many months. I was really upset. I was enjoying my ballet. My friends in my class were getting ahead, dancing in competitions, and I was not allowed to.

Eventually I started my ballet again and over the next two years I did okay. My teacher kept telling my Mom that my very average results were because of the delay from my operation. I, however, secretly was getting despondent because I knew that I was good and a bit better than just average!

So two years later it was yet another examination and I was determined to show everyone that I was good!

Everyone prepared me for disappointment and reminded me of the time when I missed so many months of lessons (I thought—boring, boring!).

Anyway I felt good after the ballet examination, but not as good as I felt the day the results came out. Yes, this is a feel-good story! I got an A; that's a distinction. Days often don't get better than this!

Another great day was the birth of my youngest brother. The day he was born was also one of my best days. When my middle brother was born, I was only 22 months old, so I did not really know what was going on. But, I will never forget when my youngest brother was born, even though I was 5 years old—that good feeling when our baby was brought home.

So these are my best days. I could actually go on and on....

Did You Know?

• Apartheid (which means "separateness" in Afrikaans) was the policy of racial segregation in South Africa from 1948 to the early 1990s. Social contact between white and nonwhite races was forbidden, and there were even segregated public facilities. Enforcement of these strict laws turned South Africa into a police state.

• Nelson Mandela was the first black president of South Africa, and winner of the Nobel Peace Prize for his social activism during South Africa's apartheid era. Born in Umtata, South Africa, Mandela was the son of a Xhosa-speaking Thembu chief.

• Johannesburg is the provincial capital of Gauteng, a densely populated province in South Africa. It is a modern city with a population of over three million people.

Some words in Afrikaans

Girl = Meisie

Dance = Dans

Please = Asseblief

Thank you = Dankie

Excuse me = Verskoon my

Book = bestel

Art = Kuns

South Africa

Namibia

Botswana

Swaziland

South Atlantic Ocean

Johannesburg

Lesotho

Rachel's home city

Cape Town

Indian Ocean

Ilke Cape Town, South Africa

Ilke

Nationality: South African

Religion: Anglican

Languages: English; Afrikaans

Brothers and Sisters: My brother, Oliver

Pets: None

Hobbies: Dancing; singing; going out and being with my friends; listening to music

Talents: Singing; dancing; acting

Favorite Sport: Gymnastics

Favorite Books: *Harry Potter* (all of them) by J.K. Rowling; *The Secret Heart* by David Almond; and works by William Shakespeare

Favorite Food: Curry (a spicy type of sauce usually eaten with rice or vegetables)

Least Favorite Food: (No response)

Whom do you most admire? My brother

Favorite Possession: My cell phone

Do you help with chores at home? Yes, washing dishes and cleaning the rooms

Do you use the Internet? Yes. My favorite website is www.horoscopes.com.

Do you have your own telephone or computer? Cell phone; computer

Where would you most want to travel? Europe

What comes to mind when you think of the United States? Celebrities

...and France? Love

...and China? Karate

...and Kenya? ??????????

What do you talk about with friends? Lots of things but mostly boys at this stage!!!!!!!!

What do you want to know about other girls your age? What they like to talk about and what they do in their free time

Ilke and her brother.

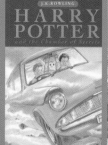

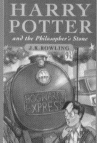

Some of Ilke's favorite books.

About Me

Ilke and her family.

What can I say, I'm just plain Ilke, and many people can agree with that.

I am as ordinary as any other person. I can sometimes be very loud. I think that I am fun to be with. I am one for making jokes (but I always laugh alone). I love going out and being with my friends. Most of the my friends say I'm crazy, but they say that's a good thing.

I have a lot of things that I like, but the one thing I like at this moment is my Drama and Music. I'm at New Orleans secondary school.

At our school we can choose the subjects that we want to do. One of my subjects is Drama and that, along with Accounting, is my favorite subject.

I love Drama because in the Drama class I can be myself and I don't have to worry about what other people think of me. Another reason is because my dream is to become an actress and my Drama class is going help me reach my goal. Our Drama teacher is Ms. Celeste Loriston. She is the best teacher because she is on our teenage level. She unfortunately can't be with us for a couple of months because she went to Hawaii.

I'm addicted to my cell phone. I can't do or go anywhere without my cell phone. I always feel lost without it. Once my phone broke so I had to wait six months before I could get another phone.

I love going out and enjoying myself. I'm actually a very soft person. I'm a person that will always laugh with everyone, but I will also tell people if they are being annoying. One thing that I'm trying to change is that I always say what's on my mind. I'm a person that will always make somebody else feel welcome. I take pride in everything I do.

One thing you should know is that I have the utmost respect for my brother (Oliver), and my friends, Ryno and Nicole. My friends say that if my brother were to ask me to jump, I would reply with, "How high?"

But there's one other important thing and that is that my friends play a very important part in my life, especially my cousin and best friend, Meghan, and my other best friend, Meagan.

Meghan and Meagan are the people that make me feel good about myself. We are always there for one another. When one of us cries, all of us cry. The reason why they are so important in my life is because they make me feel complete.

So as you can see, I'm just Ilke.

> "I love drama because in the drama class I can be myself and I don't have to worry about what other people think of me."

Ilke (left) with a friend.

"... it almost felt like I was in a fairytale."

My Best Day

People who know me will agree when I say that I like to have a good time. I love looking good and being told that I look good. To get to the best day I ever had. This is how it all started:

One Saturday, I went to the Junior Town Councils (JTC) Ball. I was elected as one of the representatives of my school on the JTC. This is an elected position that lasts for two years. The boy who accompanied me was Jody. I was looking forward to that ball since last year. Then finally the day came. My parents were not at home as they were enjoying themselves in Europe at the time. To be honest I was very, very nervous because this was kind of like a big day for me.

I was dressed in a black boob-tube dress with dainty sandals. My brother's girlfriend, Nicole, did my makeup.

Jody was dressed in a black pants with a white shirt and white suit-jacket.

When we arrived at the town hall it was beautifully decorated in black and white. The tables were set perfectly and everything looked stunning. The food was okay and the music was TIGHT (cool). It started at 20:00 and ended at 00:00, but we left at 23:00 [Starla's note: In South Africa they keep time on a 24-hour clock. 20:00 is the same as 8:00 p.m. on a 12-hour clock; 00:00 is 12:00 a.m.; and 23:00 is 11:00 p.m.].

Afterwards we went to a friend's house to have the after-party. We all just sat there and enjoyed each other's company. We had a barbecue, but the food wasn't that okay. It was actually disgusting. We sat there until 00:30 [12:30 a.m.] and we all went home.

Everything that happened was just so nice and it almost felt like I was in a fairy tale. I wouldn't mind having such a day again, but that will have to wait until next year when the next ball takes place.

South African harbor with Table Mountain in the distance.

If I Could Be...

I'd prefer to become a movie star because that is what I'm striving for.

I'm starting to make my dream a reality by doing, in my view, the most important subject at school, which is Drama.

In Drama class, you learn how to be yourself and to be satisfied with who you are. Drama is a practical subject, which means that it entails applying things that you learned, and not just the theory.

The reasons why I strive to become an actress are because I've always seen myself on stage or on TV. To tell you the truth, I always wanted to be in the "LIME LIGHT." I always saw myself studying a script for a scene.

The reasons why I did not choose one of the other topics suggested above are because I don't have any interest in them. I maybe have some interest in being a pop star because I love singing, but who says singing is for me? Maybe when I've reached my goal, I can start singing, but for now, I know that acting is what I want to do.

Another reason why I like acting is because of the vocal warm-ups we do, and playing around with words.

Like for example:

Tilm, Talm, Telm, Tolm
Silm, Salm, Selm, Solm
Gilm, Galm, Gelm, Golm

Most of the exercises we do are in Afrikaans because there are more different sounds in Afrikaans than there are in English. So I'll get back to striving for my dream.

Did You Know?

- South Africa is the southernmost country on the African continent and is divided into nine provinces. It has three capitals: Cape Town is the legislative capital; Pretoria, the executive capital; and Bloemfontein, the judicial capital.

- The Nguni People (including the Zulu, Xhosa, and Swazi tribes), make up two-thirds of the population in South Africa. Other groups include: the Sotho-Tswana people, the Tsonga, the Venda, the Afrikaners (of Dutch Origin), and the English. South Africa has more than ten official languages, and most South Africans are multilingual. English is widely spoken, especially in the major cities.

South African Flag

South African Currency

- Cape Town was the first European settlement in South Africa (founded in 1652). With a population of approximately three million people, Cape Town is a major port

today, and a center of culture and industry. Cape Town residents enjoy a Mediterranean climate characterized by warm, dry summers and cool, wet winters.

- Afrikaans is an official language of South Africa, spoken by more than eight million people. It is derived from the Dutch spoken by the Boers (or Afrikaners), who emigrated from the Netherlands in the 17th century. It is the only African language that is of European origin.

South Africa

Namibia
Botswana
Pretoria ◉
Swaziland
Lesotho
South Atlantic Ocean
Cape Town ◉
Indian Ocean

Ilke's home city

Some words in Afrikaans

Hello = Dag
Goodbye = Tot siens
Good morning = Goeiemôre

Good night = Goeienag
How are you? = Hoe gaan dit met u
Yes = Ja
No = Nee

Hadil* Gharbia, Egypt

Hadil

Nationality: Egyptian
Languages: I speak Arabic and study English and French.
Religion: Islam
Brothers and Sisters: A brother named Ahmad
Pets: A cat called Tiger
Hobbies: Singing; drawing; and playing the accordion
Talents: [Starla's note: Hadil did not respond to this question, but her mother tells me Hadil is a talented artist and is particularly good at drawing pictures of nature.]
Favorite Sport: Jogging
Favorite Books: The Adventures of Huckleberry Finn and The Adventures of Tom Sawyer by Mark Twain; and a book called Ancient Egypt.
Favorite Food: Mouloukheyya: a green vegetable prepared with garlic and soup
Least Favorite Food: Fasolia (beans); a vegetable cooked with onions, tomatoes, and butter, which is accompanied by rice
Whom do you most admire? My father, who is my highest example in every respect
Favorite Possession: The camera my uncle gave me
Do you help with chores at home? I used to help my mother in the kitchen.
Do you have your own telephone or computer? No
Do you use the Internet? I use the Internet with the help of my father, and sometimes with my friends.
Where would you most want to travel? Paris
What comes to mind when you think of the United States? The country of freedom
...and France? The country of fashion
...and China? The country of activity and vitality
...and Kenya? The country of forests
What do you talk about with friends? We talk about nice clothes, accessories, and weaving we own. Further topics: the places that we have visited, school, and study.
What do you want to know about other girls your age? I would like to know their concerns, the matters in their lives, and their state of mind. I also want to know their opinions in order to check whether they fit with mine.

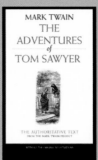 

Hadil's favorite books.

* Hadil and her family moved to the Kingdom of Saudi Arabia temporarily during the making of Girl, 13.

Cats in Egypt

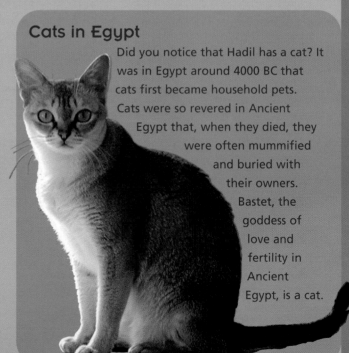

Did you notice that Hadil has a cat? It was in Egypt around 4000 BC that cats first became household pets. Cats were so revered in Ancient Egypt that, when they died, they were often mummified and buried with their owners. Bastet, the goddess of love and fertility in Ancient Egypt, is a cat.

My Best Day

translated from Arabic

Hadil's school portrait.

My best day was the day I passed the elementary school exam with a 95 percent score. A party in honor of the winners was organized by the physicians' union, of which my father is a member.

When I got up in the morning, I felt like all the members of my family were treating me like I was a queen. I prepared my new clothes and started thinking of the way that the celebration would take place.

In the afternoon, we went to the party in our new car. The honoring ceremony went very nicely, and my whole body was shaking with fear and happiness before I was given the prize.

When I came down off the stage, I felt a very strong desire to go on with my success. My father took some pictures and then he invited us to have dinner at the Kentucky Chicken restaurant [Kentucky Fried Chicken]. Afterwards, I went to visit my grandmother and grandfather and I showed them my prize.

Meeting Hadil

by Starla

Hadil posing for the camera.

Hadil, whose name means "little bird's voice" in Arabic, was born in Egypt and spent most of her life near the city of Tanta in the Gharbia (Western) Governorate of Egypt. Gharbia is northwest of Cairo, Egypt's capital, and Tanta sits along the River Nile. In fact, in Egypt, nearly every town and city sits along the Nile. Perhaps the river culture in Egypt influenced Hadil's appreciation for the stories of American author, Mark Twain, about life alongside another large river on the other side of the world, the Mississippi.

At home in Egypt, Hadil lives in a multistory house, with different parts of her extended family living on different floors. A set of grandparents lives on the second floor, her uncles and their families live on the first and fourth floors, and Hadil lives with her mother, father, brother, and her cat, Tiger, on the third floor.

Recently, however, Hadil and her immediate family left Egypt temporarily for Riyadh in the Kingdom of Saudi Arabia (KSA) for her father's work. Hadil has enjoyed being close with her immediate family in KSA, but misses her friends, grandparents, and other family members who are still in Egypt. One of the biggest changes for Hadil when she moved from Egypt to KSA was her school clothing. In Egypt, the girls wore school uniforms similar to those worn by students in European schools. In Saudi Arabia, Hadil must wear Islamic dress to school. All women and girls in Saudi Arabia are expected to wear Islamic dress when in public. This dress called an abaya consists of a black cloak-type garment that is worn over day clothes, and a headscarf called a shayla hijab.

Fashion aside, Hadil's life revolves around four main priorities: family, friends, studies, and religion. At present, her first passion is her studies. Partly because of the example of her parents, who are both accomplished scientists, and partly because of her own desires and the traditions of her culture, Hadil is determined to enter the world of medical research and make an impact. Therefore, school and studying is of the utmost importance to Hadil. Not surprisingly, Hadil is considered a very good student.

When not studying, Hadil enjoys time with her friends and family. With friends, she sometimes plays on the computer, takes walks, and, talks about clothing and the latest fashion trends. (Even though the girls are covered in public, they still love fashion like most girls do everywhere else in the world.) On weekends, Hadil helps her family

Hadil in her burqa.

Islamic Dress

The requirement for girls to wear Islamic dress (as Meera must also do in the UAE) derives from a line in the Koran, which encourages girls and women to dress "modestly" in public. The actual type of covering, which ranges from the burqas of Afghanistan that cover the entire body from head to toe with just a small netting over the eyes, to the simple hijab, that cover only the head, is as much a cultural as a religious tradition.

with the chores and often they will go together to one of the beautiful shopping centers in Riyadh. Because KSA has so much oil, it is a very wealthy country with modern buildings, shopping centers, and parks. By the way, women are not allowed to drive in Saudi Arabia, so Hadil will have to wait until she returns to Egypt to get her driver's license (when she is a little older, of course!).

Islam is part of Hadil's everyday life in a way that is different than for other girls throughout the world. Even before moving to the KSA, where it is the state religion, Islam was important to Hadil as a result of her upbringing. Although Egypt is a secular state, where religion does not officially mix with government, Islamic law strongly influences business, law, and social customs. It determines dress, dietery, and prayer codes. It is not surprising that Hadil's choices for her future are taken with consideration of her religion in mind.

What I Most Want The World To Know
translated from Arabic

I want the world to know that I am studying and making my best effort to be successful. I want to be like all the girls of my age, to keep my religion, my manners, and my friends. I try to reach people's hearts thanks to my friendship and my good manners.

Hadil outside her home.

SCHOOL DAYS

In both Egypt and Saudi Arabia, Hadil has attended all-girls schools since the age of six. In fact, all of the schools in Saudi Arabia are split into separate establishments for girls and boys, and most public schools in Egypt also separate boys and girls.

In Saudi Arabia, Hadil currently studies Arabic, English, French, Science, Mathematics, History, Geography, and Arts. Her favorite classes are her Science classes, and she is less enthusiastic about Mathematics. School runs from Saturday to Thursday, as Friday is a holiday in Muslim countries.

Every night, Hadil has an enormous amount of homework—much more than is customary in schools in the United States or Western Europe. Since Hadil is intent on learning everything and getting the best marks on her exams, she sometimes stays up studying until 2:00 in the morning!

If I Could Be...

translated from Arabic

I would like to be a scientist specializing in medical analysis, like my mother and my father and I would like to discover characteristics of complex diseases so that I would qualify to receive the Nobel Prize when I am older.

I did not choose the other possibilities because exploring outer space would be dangerous. Being the leader of the country could be painful and exhausting. I do not want to be a pop star or movie star because I want to stick to my religion. And, although it could be nice to win an Olympic Gold medal, it would require much training, which would distract me from my studies, which are my first priority.

MEDICINE IN ANCIENT EGYPT

The ancient Egyptians were the first people on earth to have a specialized medical profession. This has even been described in Homer's epic poem the Odyssey. It is also believed that doctors in ancient Egypt had specializations, like eye-doctors, and head-doctors. It even appears from these that there was a sort of "Minister of Health" overseeing the various physicians and establishing a hierarchy within the profession.

Did You Know?

- Ancient Egypt was one of the world's great civilizations, with a history going back to 4000 BC. Under the rule of the Pharaohs, Egyptian civilization contributed many advances in technology, science, and the arts.

- The pyramids, sphinxes, ancient temples, the Great Library of Alexandria (which is being rebuilt), the Coptic churches, the Citadel, the Suez Canal, and the diverse languages, food and people are all testaments to Egypt's past. Egypt is also a very modern and cosmopolitan place.

- The Nile, the world's longest river at 4,160 miles long, is actually two rivers, the Blue Nile and the White Nile. The Nile has made Egypt an oasis in an otherwise harsh desert.

Egyptian Flag

- Islam began when the Prophet Muhammad received revelations from God while in Mecca (present-day Saudi Arabia) during the sixth century. The Koran is the holy text of Islam. The Muslim (Islamic) faith contains five main pillars: 1) belief in one God (Allah) and Muhammad as God's messenger; 2) daily prayers; 3) giving to the poor; 4) fasting during the month of Ramadan; and 5) pilgrimage (or hajj) to Mecca.

Egyptian Currency

Some words in Arabic
Hello = Ahalan
Yes = Na'am
No = laa

Nice to meet you = Sorirart Biro'aitak
Thank you = Shokran
Good morning = Saba'a AlKair

Egypt's rich history is present throughout the land.

Egypt

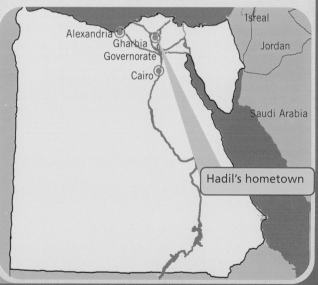

Isreal

Alexandria
Gharbia Governorate
Cairo

Jordan

Saudi Arabia

Hadil's hometown

Shani Golan, Israel

Shani

Nationality: Israeli

Religion: Jewish

Languages: Hebrew and English

Brothers and Sisters: Three brothers, Itamat, Eitan, Matya, and two sisters, Meitav and Naama

Pets: Dogs and fish

Hobbies: Hiking; basketball; TV; reading

Talents: Drama

Favorite Sport: Basketball

Favorite Books: The *Harry Potter* books by J.K. Rowling; *Charlie and the Chocolate Factory* by Roald Dahl; and my photo album!!

Favorite Food: Tuna fish salad and mashed potatoes

Favorite Possession: A picture with a small, square, green frame. In the middle there is a rabbit. My brother and my sister-in-law brought me this picture for my tenth birthday. On the back of the picture, there is a short poem written and a blessing. Because I love my oldest brother a lot, I see in this picture love and a lot of importance.

Do you help with chores at home? Yes

Do you have your own telephone or computer? I have my own telephone. I recently received a cell phone because I study in a school far from home. The computer belongs to everyone in the family.

Do you use the Internet? Yes, but not much.

Where would you most want to travel? I want to travel all over the world. But the country that attracts me the most is Kenya because I love animals a lot, although I am afraid of snakes. Actually, it doesn't matter where I will travel because anywhere I will be, I will always love my native country, Israel, the most.

What comes to mind when you think of the United States? The White House and rich people

… and France? Baguettes and mustaches

… and China? Rice

… and Kenya? Heat and safari

What do you talk about with friends? Life in general

What do you want to know about other girls your age? How do they perceive Israel and Israelis

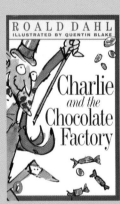

Shani's favorite books.

"In the moshav, life is very tranquil and sometimes too much so."

About Me
translated from Hebrew

"I want to be somebody that won't be forgotten so fast, like Einstein, Napoleon, and Shakespeare."

My name is Shani and I am 13 years old. In my immediate family, we are six children: three boys and three girls. I am the youngest daughter. My mother has three brothers and my father has two brothers. I am the youngest grandchild; therefore, I have no cousins my age and sometimes that is annoying. My family is scattered around Israel and abroad: Jerusalem, Petah Tikva, Tel Aviv, Hong Kong, London, etc. My father's family immigrated to Israel from Transylvania in 1950, two years after the independence of Israel as a result of the *Shoa* in Europe.

My mother, her youngest sister, and her parents immigrated to Israel in 1964 from London because they were Zionists and they always dreamed of living in Israel.

I live in an agricultural *moshav* in Golan. There are 100 families in this *moshav*. Everybody is a friend to everybody else: the eldest as well as the youngest. In the *moshav*, life is very tranquil and sometimes too much so. But it is so great. The animals walk around freely and there is almost no traffic on the road, and the *moshav* is so small we don't need to go far to get where we want to go. Most of the people in the *moshav* deal with agriculture and with animals. We

Hebrew Words from Shani's Essay

Shani uses some words in her essay that some of you may not be familiar with. Here is a list of their meanings:

Shoa (or Shoah): Another term for the Holocaust, which was the Nazi policy aimed at systematically exterminating the Jewish population in Europe during World War II.

Moshav: A kind of cooperative similar to a kibbutz. In a moshav, people are more independent than in a kibbutz. Also, in a moshav, children live at home, rather than in a special children's quarters common as they do in the kibbutz.

The Torah: The Jewish religious text.

Succoth: A Jewish holiday that occurs every year in September or October, depending on the Jewish calendar. The four fruits of Succoth are myrtle, lulab (palm branch), willow, and ethrog (a kind of lemon).

Bat Mitzvah

In the Jewish religion, the important coming of age ceremony for girls is the *Bat Mitzvah* (for boys it is called a *Bar Mitzvah*). Girls celebrate their Bat Mitzvah when they turn 12, boys when they turn 13. The ceremony marks a moment in a child's life when she earns her own identity within the religious community, the right to lead services, and participate in various ways in the community. Today, the *Bar* or *Bat Mitzvah* is usually marked with a big party that follows a religious ceremony during which the child reads a portion of the *Torah* (recites a *Haftorah*), leads a part of the service at the synagogue, and makes a speech. Girls of the very Orthodox Jewish religion do not have a *Bat Mitzvah*.

have a lot of cowsheds for the milk and sheep pens for the wool. There are also fields of myrtle, which is one of the four fruits of *Succoth*.

In Golan, there is a magnificent landscape, a lot of rivers, and waterfalls. In my opinion, Golan is the most beautiful place in Israel. We also have a youth movement in the *moshav* called "Bnei Akiva," which has as its motto "Torah and Work." This is a religious group that meets every Sabbath afternoon and also in the middle of the week. There is a group for each age from fourth grade to ninth grade. Usually, the activities deal with Israel and having good manners. During the year, we have camps with all the children of our age from around Israel.

I have a lot of friends, but I have four best friends. We do everything together. We go to town, we go for walks, and we just stay at each other's homes. My father is a farmer. He cultivates fruits and vegetables. Behind the house we have a green-

"I have four best friends. We do everything together. We go to town, we go for walks, and we just stay at each other's homes."

house where he cultivates seedlings.

We also have a big field outside the *moshav*. We have Arab-Israeli workers who are not like the Arab Palestinians. The Palestinians want their own country, but we don't agree with their conditions and that is why we have a lot of bomb attacks and casualties.

It is very hard to wake up every morning to find out that more Israelis died. I don't understand a lot about politics, but I know that it is very hard for the citizens of the country. Therefore, our politicians try to make peace with the Palestinians.

Our *moshav* is very close to the borders with Syria—around two kilometers. A few weeks ago, a terrorist destroyed the security fence, which secures the border, and it was scary. But it is said that Golan is the safest place in Israel.

I wish for all the children in the world to live a safe and happy life and that there will be peace in the world and especially in Israel and in the Middle East.

If I Could Be...

translated from Hebrew

I am hesitating between prime minister or traveling to outer space.

Prime Minister: I want to change and add to the country so that it is perfect.

Traveling in space: I dream of being in space. It sounds so great and interesting to discover things, such as is there life in space; or how outer space can help human beings.

Movie star: I wouldn't want to be

a movie star. There is no privacy. People always investigate private things about you. You can't do anything without people knowing it.

Gold medal in the Olympics: I would be very happy to represent my country. This would be a source of great pride for me. But I don't think it is really useful except to know that you are better than the others in a sport.

I want to be somebody that won't be forgotten so fast, like Einstein, Napoleon, and Shakespeare, etc....

My Best Day

translated from Hebrew

It was the second day of school, and I had a course on *The Mishna* [religious texts]. I hated the teacher, so I caused her a lot of trouble. When this happened, she would always send me out of the classroom. Therefore, I would go to the drawing room, which is a basement used for art class. I remember I was drawing something and then the school secretary, who is also a good friend of my mother, came to me and told me my father was waiting for me. We started going up the stairs and I said to myself that Adina, my sister-in law, might have given birth. I asked Hannah (the secretary), "Adina? Yes?"

"Yes!"

"Yah!!!!!!!!!!"

I screamed like a crazy girl. I ran crying to my father. I remember he was sitting near a desk and speaking to somebody. I ran to him and hugged him. He started laughing and told me, "Girl," and I asked him "When?" (I almost couldn't speak) and he told me, "This morning at seven."

I was so happy. I can't describe this feeling because it is such a special and strong feeling. I was especially happy because I am the youngest in the family and I have always wanted baby brothers or sisters. My friends always complained about having to look after their little brothers, and I got angry because they should have said thank you to God for having young brothers.

After my father had left, I wanted so much to tell my friends. I started knocking at the doors of their classes in order to tell them, but none of the teachers agreed to let them out in the middle of class. Therefore, I waited until the break. When I told them about the birth of my niece, everybody was happy and congratulated me. I was so happy that finally I was congratulated.

My niece is called Amit and she is one year old AND I LOVE HER SO MUCH!

Did You Know?

- Shani mentions in her essay that her mother's family moved to Israel from England in the 1960's because they were Zionists. Zionism is the movement that inspired the creation of the state of Israel as a nation-state for the Jewish people.

Israeli Flag

- Israel is the only democracy in the Middle East. It is a parliamentary democracy with a prime minister who leads the country.

- As Shani points out, the Israelis and Palestinian Arabs have yet to find a peaceful solution to their dispute over "occupied territories," which Israel had taken control of in 1967.

Israeli Currency

- The Dead Sea in Israel is located at the lowest point on Earth, 1,349 feet/411 meters below sea level. It has such a high concentration of salt minerals that you can float on its surface with no effort!

Some words in Hebrew

Hello = Shalom
Goodbye = Shalom
Yes = Ken

No = Lo
Please = Be'vakasha
Thank you = Toda
Friend = Chaver (m), chavera (f)

Israel

Golan

Mediterranean Sea

Syria

Jordan

Egypt

Shani's hometown

Meera Abu Dhabi, UAE

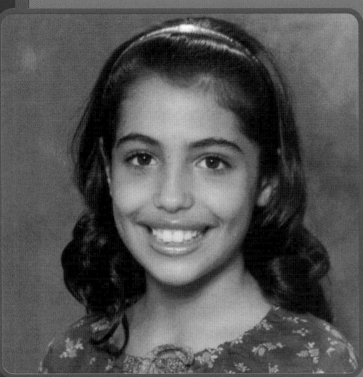

Meera

Nationality: Emirati (United Arab Emirates)
Religion: Muslim
Lanuages: English; Arabic
Brothers and Sisters: One brother, one sister
Pets: None
Hobbies: Hanging out with friends at the mall/our houses/the beach; chatting on MSN; talking on the phone; messaging friends on my cell phone; shopping
Talents: Meera was too modest to list her talents. Her mother says: "Meera's talent is definitely meeting people and making friends. She is a very social girl and is always a leader in any group."
Favorite Sport: Basketball
Favorite Books: *Dreamland* and *This Lullaby* by Sarah Dessen; *Second Helpings* by Megan McCafferty
Favorite Food: *Janarek*, a small green fruit that resembles an apple, sometimes sweet, sometimes sour
Least Favorite Food: Eggplant
Whom do you most admire: My 15-year-old cousin. She is extremely popular with everyone, parents, teachers, and all the other students. She's fun, nice, caring, etc. Even though a lot of her friends drink and smoke, she has enough will power not to, and she still hangs out with them. Everyone admires her for that. If you need advice, she's the person you should go to. She's a sister to everyone.
Favorite Possession: My cell
Do you help with chores at home? No

The little jewels on this cell phone from the UAE light up when it rings!

One of Meera's favorite authors is Sarah Dessen.

Do you use the Internet? Yes, and www.firehotquotes.com is my favorite site.
Do you have your own telephone or computer? My cell and computer
Where would you most want to travel? New York or London
What comes to mind when you think of the United States? Chilling in New York City
...and France? Good shopping (Paris)
...and China? Chinese food!
...and Kenya? I don't usually think of Kenya.
What do you talk about with friends? Boys
What do you want to know about other girls your age? What they do during free time

My Best Day

translated from Arabic

The best day I have had in the past two years is the day I went to Kuwait for the Middle School Sports Festival with my team. Only about five of us were close friends at the beginning. But, after the trip, the whole team knew each other really well. Anyway, so we got on the bus all dressed up because the coaches wanted us to give a good reputation for our school. While we were on the bus my friends and I stayed in our little group since we didn't know the other people on the team. Once we were at the airport waiting for our boarding passes, the whole team talked, but in that polite kind of way you talk to someone that you do not know that well. Then we got into the airport and we were allowed to walk around. We bonded even more. So basically after only one or two hours a whole group of people that barely knew each others' names were hanging out and laughing and having fun together. Then it was time to board the airplane and we were all sitting together making fun of the bad food, laughing at Chris imitating the flight attendant, listening to each others' music, laughing at Simone who had to sit next to a really old man with a long beard, stealing food from the trays, making up our own little songs, getting shouted at by our coach because of our screaming and shouting, laughing about Thomas and his little imaginary friend Roy, and then finally, after we were all worn out, just talking and telling stories. It doesn't really seem like that great of a day, but for me it was; that day the whole team bonded and became friends, making it easier for us at the tournament. Our team probably cooperated with each other the most compared to all the other teams because we were such great friends.

If I Could...

translated from Arabic

I would prefer to travel the world with all my friends. I don't want to explore outer space because I have never really been a fan of the planets and stars and stuff, also I'm not an adventurous or exploring kind of person.

Being elected leader of my country would be a really hard job with many responsibilities and it doesn't really seem like you have that much fun. Also I don't have the character traits you need to be a leader.

I don't want to be a pop star or a movie star. First, because I don't have the skills; and, second, pop stars and movie stars get whatever they want whenever they want it and they live the picture-perfect life. I would kind of miss living a normal life.

I really never want to win a gold medal in the Olympics and I don't even watch the Olympics. I mean, I am good at sports and everything, but I am not that skilled or motivated to even go to the Olympics.

Did You Know?

- Abu Dhabi is the name of both the city and emirate (or state) in which Meera lives. It is one of seven emirates that form the Federation of the United Arab Emirates, (UAE for short), established in 1971.

UAE Flag

- Abu Dhabi is a very wealthy country, thanks to its oil resources. The government spends a great deal of its budget on education, which is required through primary school, and free at all levels. Schoolbooks, uniforms, equipment, and transportation are all free (paid for by the state).

- In Islamic countries, the faithful are called to prayer five times a day by a beautiful and haunting sound, known as the Muezzin's call.

United Arab Emirates

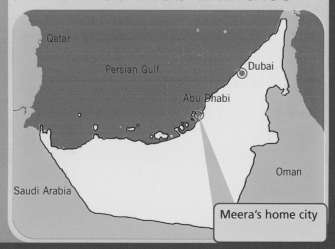

Qatar · Persian Gulf · Dubai · Abu Dhabi · Saudi Arabia · Oman

Meera's home city

Naz Izmit, Turkey*

Melodi Naz ("Naz")

Nationality: Turkish
Religion: Muslim
Languages: Turkish, and I am learning English.
Brothers and Sisters: I have two brothers.
Pets: None
Hobbies: Listening to music; painting; reading
Talents: Singing and writing
Favorite Sport: Basketball
Favorite Books: *Martilar* (*Seagulls*); *Calikusu*; the *Lassie* books

Favorite Food: *Patlican oturtma*—eggplant with minced meat
Least Favorite Food: Black beans
Whom do you most admire? A Turkish singer named Sertab Erener
Favorite Possession: Our computer
Do you help with chores at home? Setting the table
Do you have your own telephone or computer? Only a computer
Do you use the Internet? No
Where would you most want to travel? Canada
What comes to mind when you think of the United States? Movies and skyscrapers
…and France? Eiffel tower and museums
…and China? Chopsticks and the Great Wall of China
…and Kenya? Elephants; natural parks; wildlife; safari
What do you talk about with friends? Soccer
What do you want to know about other girls your age? How and where do they live, and about their relations with their families and friends

* Turkey: Middle Eastern or European?

We have included Naz in our "Africa & Middle East" section because Turkey borders Middle Eastern countries like Syria, Iraq, and Iran. Geographically, Turkey is, in fact, located at the southeastern corner of Europe and the southwestern corner of Asia. Politically, Turkey is moving closer and closer to Europe, as it may very well join the European Union in the future.

About Me
translated from Turkish

My family is what you could call a teachers' family. My mom, my grandmother, my mom's aunt, and my great grandmother are all teachers. My great grandmother is the person who opened up Izmit's first primary school and the first specialized school in the city.

My grandfather is a construction engineer. My grandfather built a part of Ulugazi Primary School, the Izmit Police Department building, our house, and many other houses in Izmit.

I have two uncles. My older uncle is Ersin and the younger one is Ugur. My uncle Ersin works at Arcelik in

Istanbul. (Arcelik is one of the biggest appliance manufacturers in Turkey.) My uncle Ugur is a computer programmer in Toronto, Canada.

And, I have two brothers. My oldest brother is 18 years old and his name is Cem. Cem is studying at Sabanci Anatolian Technical High School. He is now in his last year at high school. My younger brother is 15 years old and his name is Arda. He just started high school.

I will be in my second year at secondary school this semester. I am studying at Ulugazi School. My mom is a teacher at my school. She teaches third graders in the primary school section.

My uncle Ugur and my two brothers all play the

The train station at Istanbul.

"My family is a teachers' family."

guitar. UNICEF [United Nations Children's Fund] built Uzunciftlik Youth Center where my brothers are members of a theater group. UNICEF also produced the Uzunciftlik *August* newspaper, where both Cem and Arda are teenage correspondents.

My oldest brother, Cem, also took first-aid and search-and-rescue lessons at the Youth Center and took part in various search-and-rescue teams after the earthquake, which hit Izmit a few years ago and killed many lives.

When my brothers Cem and Arda play their guitars at home, I sing along with them. I studied singing at the conservatory for a year. I am starting theater acting this year, too.

Earthquake

Two catastrophic earthquakes hit Turkey during 1999. The first struck the heavily populated city of Izmit, where Naz lives, in August. It left 17,000 people dead and thousands homeless. The second earthquake struck a few months later in November, 100 kilometers/ 62 miles from Izmit in Duzce, Turkey. The death toll was reported as 450 with thousands injured.

Turkey has a long history of earthquakes because it sits on the North Anatolian faults, one of the world's best-studied fault lines. The North Anatolian is very similar to the San Andreas faults in California, and scientists from Turkey and the US have been working together to understand earthquakes.

Did You Know?

- Izmit is the capital of the Kocaeli Province in northwestern Turkey. It is between major cities, Istanbul and Ankara, and is heavily industrialized, producing about half of all the paper used in Turkey.

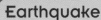
Turkish Flag

- Turkey, uniquely located between Europe and Asia, has been a bridge between these two very distinct regions throughout history. Because of this, it has acquired its own unique identity.

- Istanbul sits on both the European and Asian continents separated by the Bosphorus River. Therefore, it's possible to eat dinner in Asia and see a movie in Europe, just by crossing a bridge.

Turkey

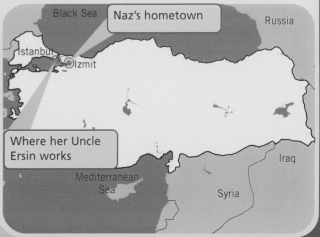

Black Sea

Naz's hometown

Russia

Istanbul

Izmit

Where her Uncle Ersin works

Mediterranean Sea

Iraq

Syria

North America & the Caribbean

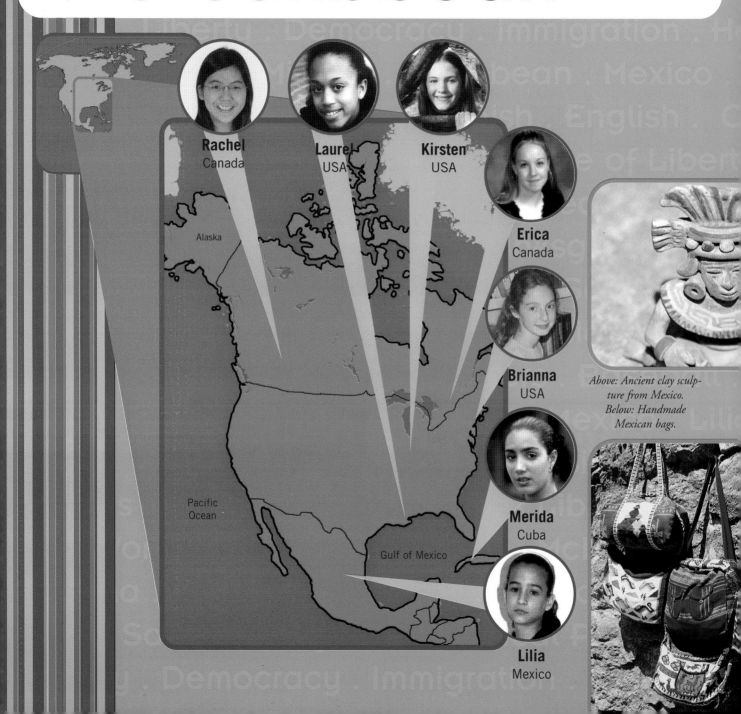

Rachel
Canada

Laurel
USA

Kirsten
USA

Erica
Canada

Brianna
USA

Merida
Cuba

Lilia
Mexico

Alaska

Pacific Ocean

Gulf of Mexico

Above: Ancient clay sculpture from Mexico.
Below: Handmade Mexican bags.

Grazing moose in Canada.

Above: The Golden Gate Bridge in San Francisco, California.
Below: Palm trees and golden sand in the Caribbean.

Above: Mardi Gras beads in New Orleans.
Below: The Statue of Liberty overlooking New York City.

Laurel Louisiana, USA

Laurel Elizabeth

Nationality: African American

Religion: Catholic

Languages: English and French

Brothers and Sisters: I have a brother, Mason, and a sister, Jessica, who is away at college.

Pets: I have a dog that is a Jack Russell Terrier—named Jack!

Hobbies: Playing soccer and music

Talents: Playing piano by ear

Favorite Sport: Soccer

Favorite Books: The Giving Tree by Shel Silverstein; Silent to the Bone by E.L. Konigsburg; and To Kill a Mockingbird by Harper Lee

Favorite Food: Chocolate-chip cookie-dough ice cream, ice cream with chunks of cookie dough and chocolate chips.

Least Favorite Food: Any kind of cooked fish or raw fish. I just can't stand the taste.

Whom do you most admire? I admire my grandfather the most because, even though he is over 80 years old, he still does everything, like pick us up after school, and play ball in the park, and he is always in a good mood.

Laurel's grandfather is always in a good mood!

Favorite Possession: My dog, Jack

Do you help with chores at home? I help clean up my dog's mess because he is five months old and not fully housetrained.

Do you have your own telephone or computer? I have my own computer and phone, but I don't have my own telephone line.

Do you use the Internet? Yes

Where would you most want to travel? I would want to travel to Australia.

What comes to mind when you think of the United States? Freedom and diversity

... and France? Fancy hotels

... and China? Architectural buildings

... and Kenya? People, weather

What do you talk about with friends? People is one topic that dominates the conversations that I have with my friends, but not in a bad way.

What do you want to know about other girls your age? I would want to know what their homes are like. I would also want to know what type of person they are.

Jack

About Me

Laurel

My personality is very outgoing. I enjoy meeting new people and making new friends. I am fun loving and very easy to get to know. I am very friendly, but like everyone else, I have my bad days. I have many friends who care about me and I care about them. I would put them at top priority in a dangerous situation.

One of my best days is when I met a lot of my relatives for the first time. These relatives, who live as far away, came to New Orleans to celebrate the 60th anniversary of the day that my my grandfather's sister, Sister Bertand, took her vows to become a nun. It was so exciting to meet family that I have never met. I love little babies so I was excited when my sister and I got to hold our little cousins.

I love traveling to new places. I have traveled to other cities in Louisiana, and to Florida, Mississippi, and Alabama with my soccer team. Try-outs for the team are held every year. This fall, I will begin my fourth year on the team. I play full back. I hope to travel to even more places with the team this year.

Although I am very athletic and I love sports, I can be very girlish. I love shopping. I also love animals. Three weeks ago, my family got a puppy, a Jack Russell Terrier. Our puppy's name is Jack.

I try to do my best at everything. When I put my mind to something I never stop until I accomplish it. I have a very busy schedule year round, and I try to do my best to never complain about it, because I know that in the end it will all add up to something great.

What I Most Want The World To Know

I want people around the world to know that I do everything with an exclamation point! I like excitement!

I would like people in other countries to know that I live in a beautiful country, a country of freedom. In the United States, you can be any religion and you have the right to speak. The country that I live in is full of diverse people and places. My home has respect for people who are different.

If I Could Be...

If I were given a choice between exploring outer space, holding elective office, being a movie or pop star, or winning an Olympic gold medal, I would choose to explore outer space.

Having an opportunity to explore a place where very few people have traveled and to be able to increase our understanding of the universe would be truly an honor.

It would also be a challenge. Explorers in space must take everything that they need to survive in space with them: oxygen in tanks, water, and special space food. There would also be many sacrifices. In space, I would not be able to see my friends, play soccer, or do any of the other things that I like to do. I believe, however, that the sacrifices would be worth the honor of exploring space.

I think exploring outer space would be the best experience because there are many things in space that are waiting to be discovered. You never know when you may be surprised at the results of your exploration. Being in and exploring a whole new world is something that I dream of doing.

Meeting Laurel by Starla

Laurel and I meet at her big, brick house in New Orleans, Louisiana on a warm, January day. It is Saturday afternoon and her brother has a soccer match. Laurel and her mother are home by themselves until the boys (brother, father, and grandfather) come home after the match. Laurel, a tall, slim 13-year-old with black hair pulled up in a half-ponytail and curled under at her shoulders, answers the door. She has very big, brown eyes and is quick to smile.

Starla and Laurel.

On another day, it might have been Laurel playing soccer with her school team, but today I see the artistic, rather than the athletic, side of Laurel. Although she doesn't mention anything about it, Laurel is an extremely talented painter. Nearly every room in the house has a piece of artwork that stands out, and each time, it is one of Laurel's paintings or pastels.

Laurel's other talent is playing the piano, by ear. She discovered this talent by accident. Already an accomplished pianist who can read music, one day Laurel wanted to play a song that she really liked, but she couldn't find the sheet music for it. Determined, she began trying to figure out the notes by ear. She could play the song in minutes!

Laurel has grown up in New Orleans, Louisiana and loves it. She loves the heavy, tropical rain that falls in buckets in bursts of minutes or for days at a time. She loves the variety of people who make up New Orleans and the varied cultural influences. She loves the shop-

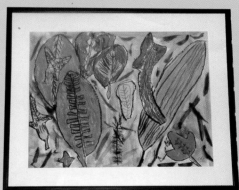
One of Laurel's paintings.

ping, especially in the quaint shops of New Orleans' French Quarter. And she loves the food—gumbo, jambalaya, crawfish, and bouillabaisse!

She is very active in New Orleans' city life through a community service group called Jack and Jill. This group helps less fortunate people by making Thanksgiving gift baskets, buying Christmas presents, sponsoring car washes to raise money, and throwing parties.

Laurel also spends time with her family. She supports her brother's soccer team and attends his matches whenever possible, and she loves playing ball with her grandfather, her most admired person!

SCHOOL DAYS

Laurel attends a private school in New Orleans for boys and girls. School begins at 8:00 in the morning and ends at 3:10. Laurel's classes are French, English, Math, and Science five days a week, plus Art three days a week, and Computers two days a week. Her favorite subject is English. Because Laurel is on the school soccer team, which practices every day after school, she is not required to take Gym.

Mardi Gras

Mardi Gras, which means "Fat Tuesday" in French, is a big celebration in Louisiana, and in particular, in Laurel's hometown of New Orleans. Originally a pagan celebration of spring in Roman times, Mardi Gras is celebrated on the last day before Ash Wednesday, which begins the season of Lent for Catholics. Mardi Gras or Carnival is celebrated throughout the world, but in New Orleans it's extra special! Here are some of the ways that the people of New Orleans celebrate:

Parade watchers yell, "Throw me something, Mister!"

Krewes: Krewes are secret societies. On Mardi Gras, they organize parades and host huge parties and balls. There are literally hundreds of Krewes with names like Bacchus, Endymion, Dionysius, Rex, and Cleopatra. (There are also funny Krewes, like the Krewe of "Barkus", which hosts a special parade of dressed up dogs!)

Throws: During the parades, people admire the floats and scramble for "throws." Throws are usually beaded necklaces, varying in quality from intricate and beautiful to cheap and silly. Parade watchers yell to the masked people on the beautiful floats asking them to "throw me something, Mister!"

King Cakes: King Cakes are the special cakes eaten during Mardi Gras. They are usually round like a large donut with a hole in the middle—delicious, sugary and highly colorful cakes not unlike a large Danish pastry.

Mardi Gras in New Orleans is so unique it is really beyond description!

Did You Know?

- The territory of Louisiana first belonged to the French and is named for France's King Louis XIV. France sold the territory of Louisiana to the United States in a transaction negotiated by Thomas Jefferson in 1803. It was the 18th state to join the Union.

US Flag

- New Orleans sits at the mouth of the Mississippi River where it flows into the Gulf of Mexico. Its geographic location made it an important city for river commerce since its beginnings. But because the land was also low and swampy, it also made it difficult for the early colonial settlers.

US Currency

- Cajuns and Creoles have contributed to the unique culture of Louisiana and New Orleans: the Cajun people (originally called Acadians) descend from French Canadians; and the Creole people descend from original French and Spanish settlers in Louisiana (who also were regarded as New Orleans original high society).

- New Orleans is the birthplace of jazz music. Jazz developed at the end of the 1800s when classically-trained Creole musicians began to mix with African-American Blues musicians in a section of the city called Storyville. Jazz greats "Jelly Roll" Morton and Louis Armstrong both hail from New Orleans.

United States of America

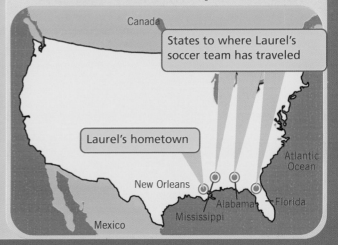

Canada

States to where Laurel's soccer team has traveled

Laurel's hometown

New Orleans

Atlantic Ocean

Alabama   Florida

Mississippi

Mexico

Some words in Creole
Slow stream = Bayou
Sidewalk = Banquett
About to = Fixin to

Witchcraft = Voodoo
Hello, how are you = Where Yat?
The French Quarter = Vieux Carre
My Love = Cher

Kirsten Indiana, USA

Kirsten Lynderup ("Kirsten")

Nationality: American

Religion: Lutheran

Languages: English, and I am just starting to study Spanish in school.

Brothers and Sisters: I have an older half-brother.

Pets: Yes, we have a beagle, Casey, a cat, Houdini (named for his unbelievable ability to escape), and a goldfish, Goldie.

Hobbies: Singing; riding my scooter; and doing artwork. I like to ski, but we only go once or twice in the winter.

Talents: Singing and acting

Favorite Sport: Volleyball and skiing

Favorite Books: *Number the Stars* by Lois Lowry; *Are You There God? Its Me, Margaret*, by Judy Blume; and the *Harry Potter* series, by J.K. Rowling

Favorite Food: Spaghettios (O-shaped noodles in tomato sauce that comes in a can)

Least Favorite Food: Liver (I think, anyway, I've never really tried it.)

Whom do you most admire? My mom, because she puts me first no matter what.

Favorite Possession: Our computer; it keeps me connected to my friends and family wherever they are.

Kirsten and her mother, Starla's sister.

Do you help with chores at home? A little; I pick rotten apples off the ground in the summer so my dad can mow the lawn.

Do you have your own telephone or computer? I have my own telephone in my room and my family shares one computer.

Spagetti-O's.

Do you use the Internet? Yes, I use the Internet a lot. My favorite website is the familychannel.com.

Where would you most want to travel? France

What comes to mind when you think of the United States? The stars and stripes of the American flag

...and France? The Eiffel Tower

...and China? Rice

...and Kenya? Safari

What do you talk about with friends? Shopping

What do you want to know about other girls your age? I would like to know what a typical day is like for them.

About Me

My name is Kirsten, and I was born in our nation's capital, Washington, DC. When I was six-months old, my parents and I moved to Fort Wayne, a medium-sized city in Indiana. I have lived here pretty much my whole life, and I would not move for anything. Fort Wayne has everything to offer that a big city does, but on a smaller scale. We have theater, ballet, and symphony for people who like the arts.

For sports fans, we have hockey and baseball teams. We have lots of activities for kids, including the zoo, a hands-on science activity center, roller-skating and ice-skating rinks, and much more. What my friends and I most enjoy, though, are the movies and the shopping mall!

"...keeping busy prepares me for life."

I live in a house on two acres of land with my mom, dad, dog, cat, and goldfish. I go to middle school with about 600 other students. At my middle school, there are three grades: sixth, seventh, and eighth. I am in the seventh grade. My school doesn't require us to wear uniforms, but the dress code doesn't allow us to wear belly shirts, T-shirts that advertise drugs, or shorts that are shorter than the length or our thumb tips when we put our hands straight down at our sides.

On a typical day, I ride the bus to school where I meet my friends in the cafeteria. We usually finish any leftover homework from the day before. When the bell rings, we head to our first period class. The next time we meet is during lunch. That is when we talk the most. We talk about who has a crush on who, what kind of homework we have in each class, and how mean the assistant principal is for splitting up our group and making us sit at different tables. When the dismissal bell rings at 3:08 p.m.,

I rush to get a good seat on the bus for the ride back home. As soon as I get home, I usually get online to check my e-mail and chat with my friends.

On Mondays and Wednesdays, I have choir practice. I have been in the Fort Wayne Children's Choir for four years. We have been to sing at festivals in England, Germany, and Canada, as well as all over the USA. Choir is fun for me because I have a great director, and I sing with many other talented kids who have become close friends.

Singing is such an important part of my life, and I am lucky to have such an awesome opportunity. We sing songs in different languages and different styles. Just recently we recorded a CD. The profits from the CD are going toward a scholarship fund for the children of New York firefighters who died in the attacks on September 11, 2001.

After choir, I do my homework and take a shower. If I have time, I watch some TV before I go to bed. Every day is very busy for me, but I think that keeping busy prepares me for life.

> "The dress code doesn't allow us to wear belly shirts, or shorts that are shorter than the length of our thumb tips when we put our hands straight down at our sides."

Meeting Kirsten by Starla

Kirsten

Kirsten is my niece and we are seeing each other for the first time in a year. My family is gathering at my father's home in Indiana for Thanksgiving. Thanksgiving is celebrated annually on the third Thursday of November all over the United States.

When Kirsten and her family arrive at the house, she rushes inside in a whirl of blue fluff. Dressed in flared jeans, a trendy sweater, hoop-earrings, and a light blue fluffy fur coat, Kirsten is at least five inches taller than I remember her being. Has it been that long since we've seen each other? Then I see the shoes. Ah ha! Very big soles! Her thick reddish-brown hair is long and straight, her fingernails are painted bright red, and I think that I can detect a little mascara and lip-gloss! Thirteen-year-old Kirsten is no longer the young girl I saw last fall. It's almost like meeting her all over again!

The day is unseasonably warm and sunny. Kirsten trades in her fashionable shoes for an old pair of sneakers, strips off the fur, and begins to look more familiar. We head out to the woods where she and her cousin start climbing a tree. Kirsten's mom—my sister—runs after us, shouting, "Kirsten, don't mess up those clothes!" Kirsten and I exchange a "look," but she happily responds, "Don't worry mom, I won't!" Kirsten always seems to be in a good mood, never wants to upset anyone, always wants to help…and she even does her homework everyday without being asked! Strange, huh?

Inside, it is time for our Thanksgiving feast. A typical Thanksgiving dinner includes turkey, mashed potatoes, sweet potatoes, corn, cranberries, and dressing. This meal represents the first feast the Native Americans shared with the Pilgrims. We have all this and more, with Kirsten's choir's CD playing in the background. Kirsten quietly harmonizes with it. She has been singing for quite a while. What is new is her recent foray into modeling. This happened unexpectedly when Kirsten and her mom were at the mall. They signed Kirsten up for a talent competition just for fun, and next thing you know, Kirsten had a contract with a children's talent agent in Chicago!

My Best Day

My best day was the day of my photo shoot. It started with my hair and makeup appointment at the beauty salon. All beauty shops smell alike. Fruit and flowers mix with bitter ammonia, but the combination isn't unpleasant. In fact, it's a really good smell. My hairdresser's name was Lori. Usually my hair is straight or a little wavy, but Lori put some curl enhancer in and used a special hair dryer to make it really, really curly. Then she pulled some front pieces in a little ponytail and sprayed my hair stiff. That was a good thing because it was very windy and rainy outside.

Kirsten modeling one of her outfits.

Next was makeup. When Lori was finished, I looked more like sixteen than twelve! Finally, we headed downtown to the Hilton Hotel where the photographer was waiting in one of the conference rooms on the second level. A stylist introduced herself as Inga. I showed Inga my outfits, and she decided that the blue blouse I was wearing was better than the one I brought for my headshot.

When it was my turn for pictures, I met the photographer, Andrew. For my headshot, he sat me on a stool and had me do a lot of different poses. Sometimes I smiled and other times I tried to look serious. Next, I changed into my first outfit: a red plaid skirt, white T-shirt, white tights, and a denim jacket. I wore my hair back in a headband and looked very much like a schoolgirl. My other outfit was a pair of white Capri pants, a navy sweater with the American flag on the front, and some white lacy tennis shoes. My hair was in low piggy tails for a more casual look.

The rain continued throughout the day. Because Andrew likes to take pictures outside whenever he can, his assistant kept watching the weather. Whenever there was a break in the rain, we would rush outside to get a few shots. Once, some people walked by and said, "Look,

it's a model." Another group waited and watched for a while, afraid to come across. "This looked pretty important; we didn't want to interrupt," they said. Hearing them say these things made me feel really beautiful, proud, and special.

When the photo shoot was over, my family and I went to my favorite restaurant for dinner. I was hungry and exhausted. I knew that I would remember everything about this day for the rest of my life.

If I Could Be...

If I could choose between exploring outer space, being elected the leader of my country, becoming a pop star or a movie star, or winning a gold medal in the Olympics, I would choose to be a movie star.

First of all, my talents are acting and singing. I would love to have a job that allows me to do the things I do best. As a movie star, I could be a role model for other girls. I know that most girls my age in

America know more about movie stars than they do about politicians, astronauts, and athletes. I would get to pick roles that I wanted to play. I would be careful not to take roles that made girls seem stupid or weak.

As a movie star, I would have a bodyguard to protect me from crazy fans. A personal hairdresser would be on call for me whenever I needed her. People would recognize me on the streets. I would have enough money to travel and help people less fortunate than I am.

Did You Know?

• Indiana means the "Land of the Indians." Fort Wayne, where Kirsten is from, is Indiana's second largest city and was named for an American Revolutionary War commander named "Mad" Anthony Wayne.

• Fort Wayne became the home of many great inventors of modern consumer products. Baking powder, the first self-contained washing machine, the Bowser Pump (gasoline pump), and the Jenny Arc Light (used for outdoor lighting) were all invented in Fort Wayne.

• The Fort Wayne Daisies was the nation's first female baseball team. During World War II, baseball teams were depleted because men were fighting in the war. A women's baseball league was formed by Chicago Cub's owner Philip Wrigley (owner of Wrigley Stadium and Wrigley's chewing gum).

• The movie star Carole Lombard, the television star Shelly Long, and the fashion designer Bill Blass all come from Fort Wayne, Indiana.

• Fort Wayne was French territory in colonial times. Its location on the intersection of three rivers was important for French fur traders. The river junction was called the "Portage," which in French means "the carrying place." It linked France's Canadian territories to Louisiana.

United States of America

Canada

Fort Wayne

Atlantic Ocean

Kirsten's hometown

Los Angeles, and America's movie industry

Mexico

Brianna New York, USA

Brianna

Nationality: American

Religion: Jewish

Languages: English and French

Brothers and Sisters: I have an older brother, who is in university.

Pets: No, but I hope to get a dog soon. Preferably a big one!

Hobbies: Playing the piano and violin; making pottery; and reading

Talents: Music; languages; and math

Favorite Sport: Skiing and water skiing

Favorite Books: *The Phantom Tollbooth* by Norton Juster; *Many Waters* by Madeleine L'Engle; and *Little Women* by Louisa May Alcott

Favorite Food: Spaghetti Carbonara (spaghetti in a cream sauce with bacon chunks)

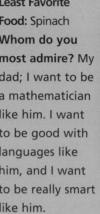

One of Brianna's favorite books.

Least Favorite Food: Spinach

Whom do you most admire? My dad; I want to be a mathematician like him. I want to be good with languages like him, and I want to be really smart like him.

Brianna with her father.

Favorite Possession: I like all the things I own.

Do you help with chores at home? I make my bed, clean my room, tidy up after meals, sometimes take out the garbage, and clean up after myself.

Cabs are a big part of life in NYC.

Do you have your own telephone or computer? I have my own computer.

Do you use the Internet? Yes. My favorite website is Neopets.com.

Where would you most want to travel? Spain, and all over Europe

What comes to mind when you think of the United States? New York

...and France? My second home

...and China? The Great Wall

...and Kenya? Safari

What do you talk about with friends? I talk about anything under the sun.

What do you want to know about other girls your age? What they are like; what they do; and what goes on in their life

About Me

Hi. My name is Brianna and I live in New York City. To be specific, the Upper West Side of Manhattan. Every morning I wake up to the sound of screeching tires and honking horns. Not too pleasant, but you get used to it after a while. My first day of school is coming up, and I don't know half the girls in my class. As you can imagine, there are a lot of "whats" going through my head. What to wear? What to expect? What to wear? What to do? What to wear? Oh yeah, and what to wear?

   "Brianna, hurry up, you're late!" "Calm down," I say, still trying to finish the chapter of my book. "I'm not late yet and I've already got my backpack together." 5 minutes later. "Brianna! Now you're really late!" Ahh, mornings, mornings were a bad invention.

At least school is fun:
   "Brianna, put the book down and start paying attention." "OK, sure, but hold on, let me finish this page." "Brianna, if you don't put that book down this instant, I'm going to have to ask you to leave the room." The book goes in my desk, but 10 minutes later, "Right, that's it! I warned you! Give me the book and go sit outside. Now!" Everyone tells me that I read too much.

   My whole day is like this. I can never wait for the bell to ring at the end of the day, announcing proudly that school is out. When I get home, I wonder why I wanted to leave school in the first place, if it means coming home to hectic land. The afternoons at home are almost as bad as the mornings. "Brianna, did you do your homework?" It's going to be another long and tiring afternoon, and I'm quite sure it won't be too tragic to say, "Good night."

If I Could Be...

I would like to become a famous writer. I've always loved to read, and so I want to give the gift of good books to other kids when I grow up. Also, I love to write, and that's that. I would write kids' books, not baby books, but books for older children and teenagers.

   My teachers are a big part of what made me want to write. I want to influence kids to read more, and, better yet, to write. I want to do what my teachers did for me, but do it through books. For instance, I admire J.K. Rowling (the author of the *Harry Potter* series) because she has a wonderful talent for writing.

   I also want to be known, but not quite famous. I want people to see a book of mine and say, "Oh, Brianna! I've read one of her books and it was really good! I wonder if this one is good too," or something like that. I think it would definitely be a thrill to become a writer.

Did You Know?

• Today, New York City, also known as the Big Apple, is the most populous city in the USA.

• Millions of immigrants came to America through Ellis Island, just off of Manhattan. Seventeen-million immigrants came in the early 1900s alone: Irish fleeing the potato famine, Eastern European Jews fleeing pogroms, Italians seeking a better life, and countless others. New York City and the Statue of Liberty have been a beacon of hope to millions of people seeking the promise of a new life.

• New York City is known for its ethnic diversity, its tolerance, and as a center for the arts and commerce.

United States of America

Canada

New York City

Los Angeles

Washington D.C.

Pacific Ocean

Mexico

Brianna's home city

Rachel Vancouver, Canada

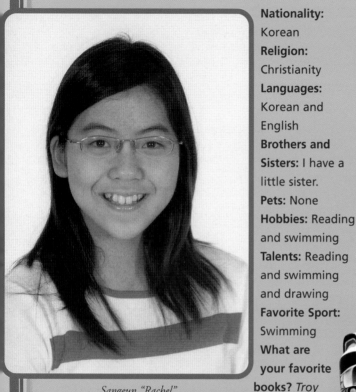

Sangeun "Rachel"

Nationality: Korean
Religion: Christianity
Languages: Korean and English
Brothers and Sisters: I have a little sister.
Pets: None
Hobbies: Reading and swimming
Talents: Reading and swimming and drawing
Favorite Sport: Swimming
What are your favorite books? *Troy* by Adele Geras; the *Gossip Girl* series by Cecily von Ziegesar; and *Life of Pi* by Yann Martel. Because I read quite a lot of books, I do have more favorites.
Favorite Food: Tortellini, the one that my mom makes, AND sushi!
Least Favorite Food: Raw ginger...smells and tastes horrible
Whom do you most admire? My dad, for his humor, patience, and understanding
Favorite Possession: My room. It's a beautiful room my mom decorated for me, plus she cleans and organizes it with me, too. I've grown very attached to it, the way it keeps my stuff and belongings. If somebody takes it away from me, I'll cry very hard.

Also another thing is my model of my favorite car, the HUMMER, a yellow model H1.
Do you help with chores at home? Yes. I run errands that my parents wish and I do a little cleaning.
Do you have your own telephone or computer? I have my own cell phone.
Do you use the Internet? Yes, of course! Hmm. I have a few: 1. www.google.ca; 2. www.vpl.ca; 3. www.addictinggames.com
Where would you most want to travel? All over Europe: England, France, Germany, Spain, Italy, Portugal, Switzerland, Austria, Denmark, and Norway. But now, I really want to go to Korea and visit my relatives.
What comes to mind when you think of the United States? New York and Disney amusement parks
...and France? Paris (Eiffel Tower) and Monarchy (history)
...and China? The Great Wall of China and the pronunciation of Chinese
...and Kenya? The map of Africa and African drums
What do you talk about with your friends? Clothes; makeup; parties; and gossip
What do you want to know about other girls your age? What they think is cool and their point of view around the world

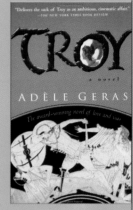

Two of Rachel's favorite books: Troy and Because I'm Worth It, a Gossip Girl book.

Vancouver has many totem poles, like the one on the left, that now serve as prized remnants of the indigenous population.

About Me

"I try not to go close to serious gossip, but sometimes you have to know what is going on."

Hey there! My name is Rachel and I live in Vancouver, British Columbia, Canada. I am 13 years old, as you might expect, and I was born in Seoul, South Korea. I immigrated to Canada four years ago. Anyway, both of my parents are from Korea. I lived in Korea for eight-and-a-half years, and the memories are fantastic!

Some don't know very much about Korea and its potential. It has character, a great, interesting, long history, high technology, and fabulous nature! Korea might have similarities to China and Japan, as they have affected each other throughout history, but it's not the same. They are each individual countries that can be distinguishable from one another.

When I was in Korea, I visited different places, big cities, and small country towns. My aunt once lived near big mountains, because my uncle was an army doctor. When my family and I visited the mountains, we walked up a trail to a famous waterfall, and the streams and the trees along the trail were so welcoming. It always smelled of fresh air, and the view from the trail was so enchanting. The path was filled with the rocks and the streams assembled between different shades of green-leafed trees. The water that came from the mountain and flowed to the valley was so clear, and the deep places were the color of jade. Because of this, there is a legend that fairies came from the sky to bathe there.

However, in the big city, Seoul, there are lots of tall buildings that are equipped with high-tech materials. Korea has the most wireless Internet connections. It also specializes in excellent cell-phone technology. I believe that Korea is an incredible country that hasn't showed its top self, which is yet to come. The world saw some of it in the 2002 FIFA World Cup, but it is far greater than that. For me, just as I am proud to be a Canadian, I am proud to be a Korean, too!

I think immigrating to Canada was a great choice for my family. I love Vancouver and I think there is no doubt why people call it the city just below heaven. Since our move here, the city has grown, but I hope it won't anymore. Vancouver is a place where many cultures come together, especially in the neighborhood where I live. There are a lot of Chinese, Koreans, and Japanese, too. Nobody becomes racist in this kind of community. I love my neighborhood and my school. My friends are the best, and everybody knows everybody, and they know how to help.

My life is filled with school, parties, extracurricular activities, and free time I spend with my family and friends. I enjoy going to school. Of course, I don't enjoy homework, but I love meeting my friends, and doing what I can in the activities at school. This past year, I had joined cross-country, volleyball, basketball, and track-and-field. I attended games, where we competed against other schools in the district.

I was also involved in the student council of my

> "If there is one thing I've learned in my 13-year lifetime, it's to never say that 'I can't do something.'"

school as a chairman for two years. I organized events at school, such as dances and theme days. Two of our successful theme days were Crazy Hair Day, and the classic Pajama Day. It was so much fun making it work and seeing it happen, the whole school participating in the theme days. Being in student council isn't nerdish; it's an opportunity you don't want to miss.

Recess and lunch hours were the best times at my school. I really got around with my friends and played a wild game or sat around to talk and

"I really consider myself lucky because I have fantabulous friends...."

eat. We usually talked about clothes, makeup, parties, gossips, and sometimes boys. Last year, and the year before, we just talked about schoolwork, and other topics like movies or singers. But, this year, a lot of things changed as we turned into the graduation group. Girls and boys got closer together, but none as in a relationship, then people started to gossip. I try not to go close to serious gossip, but sometimes you have to know what is going on.

Rachel with her father at the community pool.

Also, I love parties; sometimes because they give you break from school stuff, but usually because I get to hang with my friends for a long time. Recently I had my 13th birthday party, and it was a very special day for me. My parents rented the whole community pool for my friends and me. We just hung around with loud music on, and played Marco-Polo at the end. Then we had the best birthday party dinner prepared by my mom. Everyone had second helpings, and it was so much fun swimming, eat-

ing, and opening presents. My favorite part of the party was the cutting and eating of the Dairy Queen ice cream cake, which had a print of a yellow HUMMER on it, my favorite car in the entire universe! It was one of my best days during the past year.

Swimming is the sport I picked to work on, and I swim six times a week. I can't stop swimming. I love it, and I want to get much better at it. One of my goals is to get a gold medal from the Olympics. I believe that if I work hard enough, I will be able to because as soon as you say it, you can't. But if you have a goal, and you are positive, you will end up doing it.

These days, I really consider myself lucky because I have fantabulous friends who invite me to their gatherings and parties. Also lucky, because I have people who support my swimming, and lucky that I got into the high school I wanted to attend. I'm the luckiest girl because I have the best family in the world, too! My mom is famous for being the mom with endless food, but nowadays she is also the "paparazzi" with her new digital camera. She takes pictures of everyone, everywhere she goes!

SCHOOL DAYS

This past school year was Rachel's last at elementary before starting secondary school, and for this, she is moving on to a private school. Her new school is a "mini" school with a very small student body. To get in to this school, Rachel had to pass some examinations and interviews. She is very excited about it, but sad to leave her great friends from elementary. She is not sure what she will be studying at her new school, but in grade seven at elementary, which she just completed, she studied Mathematics, Language Arts (English), Social Studies, Science, French, Art, Physical Education, Music, and Personal Planning.

The amount of homework Rachel has on any evening depends on the time of year. On average, Rachel will spend one to three hours doing homework, although she may stay up all night to perfect a project. It has paid off making her a straight-A student.

Meeting Rachel
by Starla

Rachel is always smiling. She doesn't wear braces, although she wishes that she did! She wears glasses, though, and is usually dressed in casual clothing—a tank top or T-shirt and Capri's or long board shorts (or on cold days, jeans). She likes to wear her shiny black hair pulled back in a Lululemon headband (usually white). (Lululemon is Vancouver's own brand-name yoga clothing line that is also popular among people who don't do yoga). At the moment (it's summer time), she has a very noticeable swimsuit tan on her back that everybody seems to comment on, and she always wears her Nike sports watch on her left wrist. She doesn't wear much makeup—just lip-gloss when she feels like it, unless it is a very special occasion.

When Rachel goes out, she always has a bag with her. She used to carry a red Kipling bag that could hold two books and more. But for summer she has a new pink, fuzzy bag. It is smaller and therefore only holds one book (but it is much more stylish). It also holds her wallet (with library and bank debit-cards) and her cell phone.

Rachel stands out in a crowd (although she is not very tall, but not too short either) because she is a positive thinker and one of a kind. She is also very talented in a number of areas—sports, school, and music. But if you really want to know what Rachel is like, a key chain that her best friend gave her sums it up perfectly. It says:

"I'm not weird, I'm gifted!"

Rachel playing the flute.

Rachel is Korean-Canadian, and feels at home in both countries. Her family (mother, father, and little sister, Alicia) moved to Vancouver, Canada from Korea when she was eight years old. Rachel's Korean name is Sangeun. The Chinese character for Sang means "exalting/revering" and the character for Eun means "grace." Although she really seems 100-percent Canadian now, and is very active in her school and community, her family still speaks Korean at home, and she still has wonderful memories of her childhood and family trips back to Korea. When I asked her if she felt more Korean or Canadian, she responded that she felt both quite equally, although perhaps the Korean was a tiny bit stronger. This is just a gut feeling she has because, as she explains, although she doesn't like when Americans and Canadians make jokes about one another, she doesn't really mind and is not sensitive to them. But when Koreans are compared to the Japanese, for example, "I have a little flicker of something inside me."

Rachel's family decided to emigrate from Korea to Canada even though they did not have family members in North America already and it was a bit of a gamble. Rachel was quite scared and nervous about this momentous change, especially on the plane. Once the family arrived in Vancouver with their heavy bags in tow, however, everything felt fine. One of Rachel's first memories in Canada is being given the choice of which house the family should live in—the house they now live in or another—by her parents. They are all still delighted with Rachel's choice: a townhouse in a beautiful garden setting. The house is a small two-story, and according to Rachel, "just good enough for my family."

Rachel is an avid swimmer and hopes to qualify for the Olympics one day. Six days a week she is at swimming practice by 5:45 in the morning (even on Saturdays)! Afterwards, she either has school, or if it

A totem pole in Vancouver.

is Saturday, she enjoys a healthy and delicious brunch of Chinese dim sum and tea followed by a short nap. Afterwards, she does her homework or sees her friends. Even Sundays are active in Rachel's home with church, a family lunch, then grocery shopping, or riding bikes, or playing tennis.

My introduction to Rachel wouldn't be complete without mentioning her obsession with the Hummer. Yes,

Rachel's ultimate, ultimate dream is to have a Hummer! A Hummer, as in a large, ominous-looking, jeep-type vehicle that is currently the vehicle of choice for the US military! But Rachel doesn't want just any Hummer, she wants a yellow, model H1 Hummer. If she owned this yellow, model H1 Hummer, as Rachel says, "even though I don't have a driver's license, I could sleep with it, hug it, wash it and yes, polish it!" Ah well, a girl can dream!

My Best Day

So many events happened in my life in the past two years, especially exciting events. There were a lot of days that made me feel like I was on cloud nine. However, the best day I had from two years ago is during my visit to my home country, South Korea.

It was my second visit to Korea since I immigrated to Canada. My family and I had not gone back for about three years, and it was thrilling to even realize that we were going for a visit. Even though my relatives all came and spent time with us, going to them all the way in Korea was different than waiting for them to arrive. When my family arrived at Taejeon, and met my aunts and my cousins, I had lost my words. I did manage to say "I missed you," "Oh my God," and "I love you," but it was so exhilarating. However, as soon as I got to my grandparent's place, where my family was staying, I immediately flopped onto the bed.

Arriving in Korea was exciting, but was not the best day. The New Year's Eve was far more entertaining than the tedious, tiring arrival day. First of all, it was all of the relatives gathered at my grandparent's place, including all my aunts, uncles, and cousins from my mom's side. It was

Rachel's family portrait.

not just some people, but all of us. We all dressed up, and my cousins and I had our time together. We played cards and computer games, watched TV, and talked about Canada. During our time together, the older cousins and I went to a shop beside our grandparent's place. It was a stationary shop, and it looked very familiar to me, like Korean stationary shops in Canada. There were so many quality items with cheap prices crammed into the small, dim shop. I helped one of my cousins pick out a wallet, and the other to pick out some pens and notebooks. It was special to go to a little neighborhood place with my cousins, whom I hadn't seen for three years, because I was personally talking to them alone, without any adults around. They wanted advice from me, and they listened to what I said. They were also people I spent a lot of my time with when I was a baby.

When we came back, the whole family had an enormous, grand meal, prepared by my grandmother, my aunts, and my mom. It was a Korean dinner, one I couldn't have in Canada. There were food I vaguely remembered from my childhood in Korea, and some similar to what I had in Canada. I remember the different kinds of *kimchi*,

"I was born in South Korea...I immigrated to Canada four years ago."

and soups that only my grandmother can make. The food tasted unbelievable, and I was overcome with joy! It made me feel like I was home, as in my home country. It was a feast with so many servings of the finest food.

After dinner, everybody played the traditional Korean New Year's Eve game, called "Yut." It is a type of a board game, but somewhat different from other games. You play it with four wooden sticks, and you throw them onto the mat. Each way they fall has a meaning to the game. However, we edited the game to play it a different way, so everyone would be involved.

After the game, we had the bowing ceremony for the New Year. Bowing is a way of showing a lot of respect to the elders. There are different ways to bow for the man

and the woman. However, the simple way is that you kneel to the floor, and then you fully bring your upper half of your body down to the ground with your hands in front of your face. The uncles bowed to the grandparents first, and then the aunts bowed. My cousins and I bowed to the elders. We each got money, too, as a New Year present. It was a serious, respectful event, but my cousins and I had a lot of fun during bowing. It only happens once a year, and I had missed doing it for three years!

Before saying our goodbyes for the night, we had a family talk and service to God. We mostly talked about my family and our life in Canada, and how my little sister and I grew up to be fine children. I was dazed by then, didn't really listen carefully to what was going on, except some little questions my grandparents and aunts asked. At the end, we wished everybody a Happy New Year, and prepared to go to sleep. That day was a memorable, exceptional day.

South Korea

The Republic of Korea (commonly known as South Korea) covers the southern half of the Korean peninsula in East Asia. Originally, Korea was one unified country, and there was no division between North and South. But in 1910 Japan took control of Korea, establishing itself as a colonial power. This occupation lasted until the end of World War II in 1945. Afterwards, the Soviet Union occupied the Northern portion, and the United States occupied the Southern portion. In 1948, the 38th parallel was established as the dividing line between communist North Korea and democratic South Korea. Although the division was intended to be temporary only, attempts at reunification of the two countries have yet to be successful.

The capital city of South Korea is Seoul, which has over ten million inhabitants. It is one of the largest and most populated cities in the world. Overwhelmingly modern, Seoul is also one of the most "digitally-wired" cities, as Rachel mentioned, comparable to Tokyo and

New York. The youth in Seoul usually spend their free time by watching movies, shopping, singing at Karoke rooms, and meeting friends at cafes.

Millions of South Koreans have settled in countries outside of the Korean peninsula. The United States ranks first in Korean population with over two million, followed by China, then Japan.

A busy street in Seoul.

Credit: Tim Kang

If I Could Be...

"When I first started swimming, I thought that the Olympics were far off, but nowadays...it doesn't seem as far as before."

When I grow up, I want to win a gold medal in the Olympics. I'll qualify in swimming, because I know that if I don't stop training, I can go to the Olympics. I already love swimming, and it's a lot of fun. When I first started swimming, I thought that Olympics were far off, but nowadays, even though I'm not the best swimmer, it doesn't seem as far as before.

I want to win a gold medal in 100m butterfly. If I do, I might try in 200m and 50m butterfly, too. Currently, 100m fly is my best and favorite event in swimming. Once, sometime in May, some swimmers from my swim club and I went to watch the Mel Zajac Jr. Swim Meet at UBC (University of British Columbia). In that meet, there were great swimmers, including national-ranking swim-

mers, and world-ranking swimmers. During the meet, my friend, Samantha, told me that Mike Mintenko was going to swim next in 50m fly. She also supplied me with more details, such as that Mintenko holds the Canadian national record in 50m fly. She made me watch the race with her, and when I did watch it, I said to myself that I could do that. Sam, as if reading my thoughts, told me that if I tried hard enough, I might be able to swim like Mintenko, and that I would be fast. I told her that I would.

I really want to get that medal, because I think it will be a lifetime opportunity. To get into the Olympics will be another hill, getting better times each meet, and getting higher and higher in the level of swimming. When I look around, there are people who have gone and come back all happy and proud of themselves. Some as young as 15 in my swim club are going to Pan Pacific Games, and other international meets! I want to be a part of that group.

There are more extreme experiences and careers that I can do in my future, for instance, exploring the outer

Rachel (center) with her swim team.

Rachel has swim practice six times a week. Here she is competing at a meet.

space, or being a pop star or a movie star. However I'm afraid to leave Earth, and worried about the media's affect on my life. I've been asked if I want to be a doctor or a lawyer, and I've always said that I wasn't sure yet. I really don't have a reason to not want to be one, or a reason to want to be one. I wouldn't mind trying, even though they seem to work twenty-four-seven. They are always the clean, well-mannered type in society. It would be a good, respectable role. I have thought that qualifying for Olympics is more important, and professional occupations can wait until I am older.

For now, I am determined to win a gold medal at the Olympics in swimming. I don't care when I will, I just will. I believe that I can and will swim like Mike Mintenko if I try and push myself. Just like Samantha and I said, I am capable; it's just a matter of time, and my effort.

Did You Know?

- Canada is one of the few countries that still have significant immigration programs. It accepts people from nearly every other country in the world. The country's estimated population in 2004 was 32,507,874.

Canadian Flag

- South Koreans are the single largest foreign-student group in Canada. They travel to Canada from South Korea to attend university for graduate as well as postgraduate degrees.

Canadian Currency

- Olympic contender, Mike Mintenko is one of Canada's biggest and most consistent international swimmers, and he holds the Canadian national record for the 50-meter butterfly—24.15 seconds. Mike began swimming when he was eight years old, but he only started to train rigorously in high school.

- Vancouver is a peninsula-city located in the southwest corner of Canada in the province of British Columbia. It is the largest city in the province, and the third largest in Canada.

Some words in Korean
Yes = Ne
No = A-ni-yo
Please = Je-bal

Thank you = Gam-sa-ham-ni-da
Hello = An-nyong ha-se-yo
Goodbye = An-nyong-hi ga-ship-sio
Friend = Chin-gu

- Vancouver, known by some as "Hollywood North," has a thriving film industry and many Hollywood films and TV shows are made there.

Canada

Alaska

Greenland

Vancouver

Edmonton

Rachel's home city

Ottawa

United States of America

Erica Ottawa, Canada

Erica

Nationality: My Nationality is Canadian.

Religion: Protestant (United Church of Canada)

Languages: English and French

Brothers and Sisters: I have two brothers, Bryan, 20, and Andrew, 18.

Pets: One dog, Carmen, a Wheaten Terrier covered in curly, golden fur and one cat, Snuggles, a gray, white, and black Persian

Hobbies: Family activities; reading; synchronized swimming; flute; violin; sports; and shopping

Talents: Mathematics; science; reading and writing; music; and swimming.

Favorite Sport: Synchronized swimming

Favorite Books: The *Guests of War Trilogy* by Kit Pearson, the first and second books particularly because they taught me about war and because the characters are varied and 3-dimensional (they are believable, complex people); *Harry Potter and the Prisoner of Azkaban* by J.K. Rowling because it opens up your imagination; and a childhood favorite, *Out and About* by Shirley Hughes, a book of fun, little poems.

Favorite Food: Cheesecake; a soft, rich dessert made from cream cheese, sugar, and graham cracker crumbs as the crust. It is usually topped with luscious blueberries, strawberries, or cherries. Eat and enjoy.

Least Favorite Food: Mushrooms; slimy, rubbery, little plants that grow from the ground

Whom do you most admire? Someone who has goals and dreams and is not afraid to pursue their dreams. They are driven and dedicated to achieving their goals. They have perseverance but are not afraid to have fun along the way.

Favorite Possession: The gold medal from the Ontario Winter Games I won recently for synchronized swimming

Erica and and her team won the gold medal in synchronized swimming at the Ontario Winter Games.

Do you help with chores at home? Yes, I help do my laundry; wash, dry, or put away the dishes; set the table; bake (supper, snacks, food); and clean (dusting, washing floors).

Do you have your own telephone or computer? No

Do you use the Internet? I only use the Internet for school assignments. I find that it is too complicated and not specific enough.

Where would you most want to travel? All around the world, including Holland to see the windmills; Hawaii to see the palm trees; and to see all Seven Wonders of the World

What comes to mind when you think of the United States? New York City and its night lights

...and France? Little shops with balconies and umbrellas, which are open along the street

...and China? Great Wall of China and many smiling faces

...and Kenya? Green savannah with lots of exotic animals

What do you talk about with friends? Here are a few subjects we discuss: venting about a problem (or person); telling stories or interesting things that happened recently; any exciting news and upcoming events; movies; and boys, once in a while.

What do you want to know about other girls your age? I want to know what they would most want to change about their lives, communities, or living (experiences) surroundings.

If I Could Be...

What do I want to be when I grow up? I could be an astronaut. I would travel light years through space and discover unknown galaxies. My crew and I would find disposal areas where we would desert all the unwanted pollution we produce on earth and save life as we know it from the danger of the hole in the ozone layer. I would search and track comets and meteorites and save the earth from destruction.

Or, I could be a doctor. I would work for years to discover unknown cures for harmful diseases. Thousands of needy people across the globe would be healed and would be very grateful. People worldwide would turn to me for my aid and answers to their medical questions. I would work in third-world countries to help prevent horrible diseases. I would donate my money to buying vaccinations for the underprivileged. I would live on the satisfaction of saving others' lives every day.

Or, I could be a super-star athlete. I would run, jump, swim, and sprint. I would push myself to the maximum of my physical and mental ability. I would have the opportunity to participate in the Olympics. I would tour around the world and tell children that you can do anything you want to, as long as you believe in yourself and train hard. I would have a chance to set world records across the globe for other tremendous athletes to fulfill.

I could accomplish anything. But right now I think I'll concentrate on dreaming. I might as well be a kid while I have the chance. I have the rest of my life to figure out what I want to do, and I'll take all the time I have.

> **"...right now I think I'll concentrate on dreaming."**

Did You Know?

- Canada is a parliamentary democracy, with elected federal and provincial legislatures. The Parliament, which meets in Ottawa, is made up of the House of Commons, whose members are elected, and the Senate, whose members are appointed.

- Ottawa, where Erica lives, is the capital city of Canada and is in the province of Ontario. It is the home of Canada's government organizations, such as the Government of Canada, Parliament, the Senate, and the Supreme Court of Canada.

- With a population of over 1.2 million, Ottawa is the fourth-largest city in Canada. Over a third of the population are native French speakers. Both French and English are the official languages in Canada.

Canada

Greenland

Erica's home city

United States of America

Ottawa Montréal

Atlantic Ocean

Lilia Nuevo León, Mexico

Lilia Yobana Villareal ("Lilia")

Nationality: Mexican
Religion: Catholic
Languages: Spanish, and I am studying English.
Brothers and Sisters: One brother
Pets: I have two parrots, a turtle, and three fish.
Hobbies: Collecting coins
Talents: Studying and sports
Favorite Sport: Tae Kwon Do

Favorite Books: The Harry Potter books and Moby Dick by Herman Melville
Favorite Food: Fillet of fish empanizado [breaded]
Least Favorite Food: Entomatadas. These are rolled tortillas with cheese inside, soaked in spicy tomato salsa.
Whom do you most admire? I admire Victor Estrada because he is a very persistent sportsman who yields to nothing, and is a very responsible and well known, not only for excelling in sports, but also in his personal and professional life.
Favorite Possession: My coin collection
Do you help with chores at home? Yes, I make my bed, clean my room, wash or dry the dishes after dinner, and sometimes I sweep the patio.
Do you use the Internet? Yes, but I don't have a favorite website.
Do you have your own telephone or computer? No
Where would you most want to travel? The beaches of Cancun
What comes to mind when you think of the United States? Terrorism
...and France? The Eiffel Tower
...and China? The Great Wall of China
...and Kenya? Malnutrition
What do you talk about with friends? Music
What do you want to know about other girls your age? What do they think about; what do they like to do?

My Best Day
translated from Spanish

It all began when I was 12 years old and entered, for the first time, the State Selection for Tae Kwon Do in the state of Nuevo Leon. I was a black belt, and I loved to compete. When this great day, which I had so longed for, finally arrived, I woke up early so as not to arrive late. When I arrived at the gymnasium, I encountered many people that I didn't know, but I was with a friend from my Tae Kwon Do school where I train. She had already been in the Selection and knew many people who were in the competition. My friend introduced me to everyone she knew. After talking for a while, we went to warm up before the fights began. All of the competitors were weighed. I was placed in the weight range 30 to 35 kilograms. [Starla's note: for every kilogram, it is 2.2 pounds. So Lilia's weight range is about 66 to 77 pounds!] in the female children's category.

When all of the competitors had been weighed, they posted the names of the competitors and who each would be fighting in her weight class. I found my name all alone. I didn't have anyone against whom to fight! I called my coach to tell him and he said, "How lucky! You don't have to fight!" I was annoyed, because I like to fight, but it was okay because I knew that I would still qualify for the Selection.

As I had been selected, I learned that I was going to have to be coached three times a week in the city of Monterrey. However, I could not go three times a week because I had other school activities. Then my professor spoke to my coach and it was arranged that I would go on Thursdays and Saturdays for training.

At my first training, I stayed very separate from everyone because I didn't know anyone and I am very serious. I barely spoke to anyone and just practiced. But when we started doing tests and demonstrations, my companions began to ask me things. Everyone could throw me very well, but there was one who could throw the best. Her name was Andrea. During the training sessions we were always put together.

OLIMPIADA NACIONAL INFANTIL-JUVENIL
ETAPA REGIONAL
COAHUILA 2003   SALTILLO

"I did everything I could to win, but sometimes things do not work out so well, and one must know how to lose."

After one month of training, we arrived at the regional event. We managed to pass the regional phase and continue on to the National Olympics. I could not believe it! I was very excited to go to the Olympics!

When the time finally came to go to the National Olympics, I was very nervous, but I tried to forget my nervousness and concentrate on my fight. Luckily I was chosen to fight on the first day. I entered the battle area with my coach who gave me final instructions. This fight I won in the first half. Then it was time for my second fight, which I unfortunately lost. I did everything I could to win, but sometimes things do not work out so well, and one must know how to lose.

My parents, Mario and Sanjuanita, and my brother, Mario, were there supporting me the whole time and giving me encouragement. They went with me to all of the competitions. The other person who gave me all of his support was my Tae Kwon Do teacher. That was one of the most important and happiest moments of my life. I met many people and plan to continue to compete until I have won a gold medal, not just at the National Olympics, but in the international Olympics, as well.

Did You Know?

- Mexico is the largest Spanish-speaking country, and the second largest Roman Catholic country in the world. It is divided into 31 states. Lilia lives in the state of Nuevo Leon. Monterrey City is its capital.

Mexican Flag

- Mexico was the home of the ancient Mayan, Toltec, and Aztec empires. The Aztecs were the last Native American ruling empire in Mexico before the arrival of Spanish conquerors in the 1500s. Mexican society today is the cultural combination between the Native Americans and the Spanish.

- Tae Kwon Do is a Korean martial art focusing on self-defense instincts.

Mexico

United States of America

Lilia's hometown

General Terán,
Nuevo León

Gulf of Mexico

Pacific Ocean

Mexico City

Guatemala

Merida Guanajay, Cuba

Merida

Nationality: Cuban
Religion: Catholic
Languages: Spanish and English
Brothers and Sisters: I have a brother.
Pets: Yes, a cocker spaniel
Hobbies: Singing; dancing; mathematics; and playing piano
Talents: Painting; writing tales; and inventing stories
Favorite Sport: Football (soccer)
Favorite Books: Corazón (Heart) by Edmundo De Amicis; El Pequeño Principe (The Little Prince) by Antoine de Saint Exupéry; and La Edad de Oro (The Year of Gold) by José Martí
Favorite Food: Rice; black beans; pork; and French fries
Least Favorite Food? Calamari (fried squid)

Whom do you most admire? My aunt
Favorite Possession: My cuddly toy
Do you help with chores at home? Yes, I clean and dust the furniture.
Do you have your own telephone or computer? No
Do you use the Internet? No
Where would you most want to travel? The capital city of my country, Havana
What comes to mind when you think of the United States? Racial discrimination
...and France? The Eiffel Tower
...and China? The Great Wall of China
...and Kenya? Poverty
What do you talk about with friends? Different themes: pop music; things that happen in our daily lives; our future aspirations
What do you want to know about other girls your age? Their concerns about things that happen to them

Merida's dog is a Cocker Spaniel, like this one.

If I Could Be...
translated from Spanish

It would most appeal to me to be a movie star or pop star so that all of the people in the world would know me. I would be famous for my talent and be part of the world of action. Becoming a pop star like Madonna would be fantastic. I am passionately fond of the stage, bright lights, and a large audience applauding.

To win a gold medal in the Olympic Games is not something that interests me because I am not a big sports fan. When I was little, I took ballet classes, but they never really held my attention. But I do admire great sportsmen like Maradona [Diego Armando Maradona, a famous Italian soccer player].

To explore outer space would be interesting, but I am afraid to fly in a spaceship, and, besides, my passion is art. I would not like to be the leader of my country because there are many duties and I would not have time for things like music.

"I am passionately fond of the stage..."

My Best Day
translated from Spanish

The best day that I have had was during my holidays. I was at my aunt's home when the news came that we could go to a house at Guanabo Beach. At first, I was very enthusiastic, but upon arriving, it seemed very boring and I did not want to stay. But, there was nothing to be done. We were already there.

That day we went to swim at the beach. There, we were asked to join in various games. At first, it was difficult and annoying to play. But then I realized that everyone there felt the same as me. We were laughing the whole time. While eating, we all told funny stories. At night, we went to a party and walked along the side of the beach. And, thus, we shared many ideas, all together.

That day was important for me because I got to know new places and new people and I shared true friendship with them. I

"Among us was a boy..."

also realized that older people could share experiences and spend time with adolescents. And I realized that I could be an independent person if I needed to be. The following day after we ate breakfast together, we walked to where we knew that there was a hotel that we could not enter. We made up a story that we were a group of explorers interested in exploring that area and that is how we ended up there. As my aunt was with us, we said that she was the Professor and our guide, and this is how we learned about this hotel called "Itabo."

After learning so much, I became tired, and started to get bored again until I realized that among us was a boy who was attracting my attention.

He asked me to accompany him playing cards. The tiredness and boredom never arrived. I thought that I would never see him again, but there still remains something. We call each other on the phone and write each other letters.

> "I realized that older people could share experiences and spend time with adolescents ...and that I could be an independent person..."

Did You Know?

- Cuba is an island nation in the American Caribbean governed by a Communist regime led by Fidel Castro. Havana is the capital of Cuba and Spanish is the official language.

- Cubans value their education and Cuba has a 97 percent literacy rate, virtually equal between males and females. This matches the literacy rate of the US.

- Cuban music is internationally famous and includes Mambo, Rumba, Latin-jazz, Afro-Cuban beats, and Salsa. All these different styles are completely unique to the people of Cuba.

Cuban Flag

Cuba

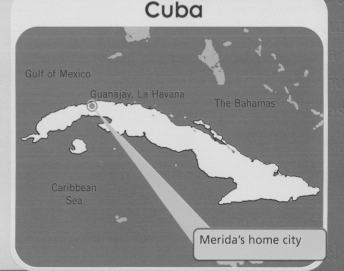

Gulf of Mexico

Guanajay, La Havana

The Bahamas

Caribbean Sea

Merida's home city

South America

Panama
Venezuela
Guyana
Ecuador
Peru
Bolivia
Paraguay
Pacific
Ocean
Chile
Uruguay
Atlantic
Ocean
Falkland
Islands

Manuela
Colombia

Nathalie
Brazil

Sofia
Argentina

The colorful architecture of Buenos Aires, Argentina.

The "Corcovado" Statue of Christ in Brazil.

Pineapples grown in the high plateaus of central South America.

The crowded Valparalso Beach in Chile.

Cool, blue, Peruvian balcony.

Tropical bird in the Amazon.

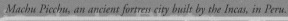

Machu Picchu, an ancient fortress city built by the Incas, in Peru.

Above: The exotic fruits of South America.
Below: The tranquil Gulf of Honduras.

Manuela Bogotá, Colombia

Manuela

Talents: My talents are to write songs, books, poetry, playing sports, but most of all playing instruments, singing AND dancing.

Favorite Sport: My favorite sport is basketball.

Favorite Books: *Harry Potter and the Goblet of Fire*, *Harry Potter and the Prisoner of Azkaban*, by J.K. Rowling; *Sixth Grade Secrets*, by Louis Sachar.

Favorite Food: *Ajiaco*, a thick soup with corn, potato avocado, chicken, sour cream, capers, and bread.

Least Favorite Food: Spinach, a green vegetable that can be a topping in any salad or soup (except *ajiaco*).

Whom do you most admire? I most admire Shakira, a great Colombian singer. She likes to help people in every way that is possible, and she is really beautiful in personality and physical features. Her name has two meanings. I personally know only one, which is "Goddess of Light."

Manuela also plays the violin.

Favorite Possession: My *Harry Potter* books

Do you help with chores at home? Yes, yes I do help with chores in my home. I help in making my bed and organizing my room on Sundays, and sometimes feeding our dogs.

Do you have your own telephone or computer? Yes, I have my own cell phone and computer.

Do you use the Internet? Yes, yes I do use the Internet frequently and my favorite website is hotmail.com, because I can send my friends any messages and also receive messages from my contacts.

Nationality: Colombian

Religion: Catholic

Languages: Spanish is my first language. I'm studying English and French in school.

Brothers and Sisters: I have two brothers and one sister: Santiago (the oldest of my siblings), Ana Maria (the second of my siblings), Alejandro (my other older brother).

Pets: Yes I do have pets. I have three dogs. Two Rhodesian ridgebacks and a Golden Retriever.

Hobbies: My hobbies are to read, write, chat on the net, talk about boys, bother friends and family (just a little bit), sing, dance, play instruments, party, watch TV or movies, play basketball, football, volleyball, kickball, tennis, horseback riding, and swimming.

Maneula has three dogs.

Where would you most want to travel? I would love to go to New York City, England, and Paris. New York is where I want to study at the Julliard School of Music, for I want to be a singer, dancer, and song writer. England is where I would love to write, because most of my favorite writers are from England. Paris would be the place where I would find my inner soul, my romance could come true, and I could go to the Eiffel Tower and feel "On the Top of the World."

What comes to mind when you think of the United States? Excitement

...and France? Romance and passion

...and China? People and integrity

Manuela's eldest brother, Santiago, and her "darling sister," Ana.

...and Kenya? The past and life

What do you talk about with friends? With the gals, we talk about boys. With the guys, we talk about sports and our likes and dislikes. But with guys and gals, we talk about everything.

What do you want to know about other girls your age? What is it they like to do? Do they judge others as geeks or popular people? What do they talk about on the phone? What do they think about themselves? What would they like to do with their talents? Do their parents respect their space in life? Are their fathers acting strange when they know we are growing up?

About Me

My name is Manuela. I am 13 years old, I live in Bogotá, Colombia, and I live with my mother, father, two brothers, and my darling sister.

I am not one of those girls that don't fight for what they want. Yes you may say I might be a little spoiled, but that is not the only thing I have in my personality. Personality is not only based on what you are, but it is also based on what you feel. THAT is what I want to tell the world about myself.

I hope this story will get you interested, and teach you a whole lot about what girls feel at my age when things become confusing. Well here it goes:

When we girls are born, we tend to be daddy's little girl. But don't take this the wrong way, we adore our mothers but it's mostly about dad.

We start to grow up. All of our family loves us just the way we are. We always get top grades, we are the best

Manuela in front of one of the murals she painted.

in the class, we're beautiful according to our family, but then we turn ten years old.

This is one of the hardest ages both for the parents

"Girls feel confused. The only thing they want is for their first kiss to be romantic, but our parents wouldn't agree."

and the gals. Why, you may ask? This is because we start to grow a little bit faster. In a way this scares our parents. But our parents don't understand that we are afraid of growing up and getting our menstruation.

After this fear has passed, we just can't wait to get to our teenage years, for we want our parents to give us more space than they were given. We start to think that you mothers don't remember what it was like to be told you are pretty, and not to have any success with the guys. Because the boys are afraid to talk to us; they go for us but then they turn out to be frauds, and we start feeling horrible.

To take this anger out of us we start ignoring your advice, start using bad words at school; if you say "no" to something we want to do we start answering very rudely. If we want to go to the mall with our friends, you say we are young women growing up, and that you are afraid that some guys may come near us, you say that our brother should come with us. Then we fight over the fact that we girls are not children any more and that you don't trust us, but after the argument, you say there is no going to the mall if our brother doesn't go with us. We start feeling miserable and finally agree just for the sake of shopping.

This brief story gives us a couple of conclusions. Parents don't get that one of the most important things for a girl of this age is a boyfriend, but they don't let her have a boyfriend, so conflicts happen at home. Girls feel con-

fused. The only thing they want is for their first kiss to be romantic, but our parents wouldn't agree with that so we don't even bother telling them who we have a crush on or what our ambitions are. In other words, fights take place every five minutes at least, any time, anywhere.

This little story is sort of my history of life shortened and only giving the facts of the relationships I have with my parents and family.

Another conclusion to my story might be that we girls turn out to become rebels, but this is not because we want to. This is because our parents, teachers, siblings, or friends turn us into rebels, making us mad, making us as rude as possible with anyone who is in our way.

I have never blamed my parents for what I've become. I blame myself for everything that happens at home. I feel as if I grow any more, or faster, more conflicts will happen. Even if we twelve and thirteen-year-old girls start blaming our parents for everything, it is because we are blaming ourselves for ever being born. For we feel that change is never good, and that our parents don't pay attention to us anymore.

It is because of these feelings that we start acting

Manuela with her father and brother, Alejandro.

strangely, so basically apart from needing our space, we also need attention. Everybody's life is complicated, and if you want attention from anybody, just tell them to give you advice, and to comfort you. They are not going to do it unless you gals tell them! So gals, I know how you feel, I'm your age, too. But you have got to communicate with the people that you love most.

We girls have ambitions that we want to fulfill. My ambitions are to get out of Bogotá, get a good education for writing poems, books, and songs in England, go to the Julliard School of Music, and become the greatest celebrity in the world. I know my ambitions are too obvious to be said by a girl my age, but this has been my dream since my voice was noticed in the first grade.

COFFEE

Colombia is known to most of us for its mild arabica coffee beans, which is the country's main crop. Coffee export is important for Colombia's economy. It produces 12 percent of the world's coffee, many of them gourmet varieties. Coffee is grown about 900 to 1,800 m (3,000 and 6,000 feet) above sea level.

The secret to a good cup of coffee is the roasting of the coffee beans. Developing the aroma and flavor of coffee is determined by length of time, as well as temperature of the roast.

Meeting Maneula
by Starla

The first question you must ask yourself when you meet Manuela is, "How does she speak English so well?" You would be forgiven for thinking she spent time living in the United States. Some of her English teachers believe she has! But as Manuela says, "Don't think so guys!" Manuela is an example of how at-home language immersion really works. She learned English and now speaks almost like a native, thanks to the efforts of her family, who, from when Manuela was about three years old, decided to speak only English in the house. A little awkward at times, no doubt, but it worked!

Bilingual Manuela, who read all of the *Harry Potter* books in their original English, is also, in many ways, a typical Colombian girl, growing up in Bogotá. On weekends you will see her dressed in a T-shirt, jacket, and in low-cut, flared jeans going to the movies or walking around the shopping mall at the Centro Andino with her friends. Or she may be having an ice cream or lunch with her friends or family, or watching scary movies (sometimes with guys!) at a friend's house.

But then again, Manuela is also a little different than your average Colombian girl, in the sense that she must climb 92 steps to get to her bedroom. As Manuela says, "It's good exercise."

In and after school, Manuela enjoys playing musical instruments. For the moment, she plays the flute, piano, and violin, but who knows what she may try next. And she loves the singer, Shakira, a Colombian who recently broke onto the international stage. If you ask Manuela whether she prefers when Shakira sings in Spanish or

English, Manuela will respond without hesitation that she much prefers the Spanish songs. Manuela also likes dancing and sporting activities. After school, if she has time in light of her heavy school load, she plays basketball, volleyball, and football. And, sometimes, as you'll see, she falls in the mud (it rains a lot in Colombia), but that doesn't sway her determination!

Manuela has dreams to study abroad and travel the world. So far, she has been to Argentina, Chile, the US, and Colombia. But, she really loves her native country. According to Manuela, the culture in Colombia is very beautiful. There is wonderful music, and a beautiful dance called the *Cumbia*. Bogotá, Colombia's capital, is especially lovely in the autumn, Manuela's favorite time of year. The leaves turn orange, and the weather cools slightly.

Colombia still has some problems, however, as it is still a developing country. Undeterred by the problems, Manuela has many plans for improving life for her fellow-countrymen and women, which she would implement if she could become the leader of Colombia.

The lasting impression of Manuela is that she is very mature for her age. This may be because she expresses herself so well in English (and my Spanish is not very good, so I am very grateful), or because she has older siblings, with whom she gets along very well (usually!). Nevertheless, meeting Manuela has changed my perception of Colombia, and converted me into a faithful Shakira fan!

My Best Day

The best day I've ever had in the last two years is... WOW! I just figured I haven't had the best day in my life.

I guess this is because my life hasn't been very interesting in the past two years of my life. I don't even consider the day I first kissed with my crush to be the best day of my life.

The reason I didn't or don't consider that day to be the best in the past two years is because I had fought for a long time with my crush, and it had only been that day that we had forgiven each other, and my crush said "EWW!" when we had finished the kiss! Either way when I told the person I most trust in the whole wide world (my aunt Maria Consuelo) she said "That wasn't what a first kiss was supposed to be". Even if she was a little hard on me I didn't care, for she was completely right.

But in the past two years the other reason why I haven't had the best day in my life is because, I've felt enormous despair a couple of times. You see since I was little girl, I have always wanted to be a singer, but none of

"When I started fifth grade, boys started to notice me..."

my teachers would notice me until I got to first grade. When my music teacher left, another teacher came to my school. I didn't like her very much. Actually, I didn't like her at all! She noticed me, but she never picked me to be a solo. When I passed to fifth grade, I got noticed again, but it wasn't anything like before, but still I had to be thankful for what had happened.

Also, when I started fifth grade boys started to notice me a little bit more at least (finally!!!), and even my English teacher told my parents I was a wonderful and beautiful young lady with a lot of potential!

It was since my English teacher talked to me that I started swimming again (I had left it a long time ago), I started getting better grades (since I hadn't cared for grades before, as I thought I knew everything), and I started to get serious with my life. But that didn't stop the misery I started to have since the beginning of the year.

I didn't know what the cause of the misery was, I still don't, but I did know that I had or have my whole life ahead of me, and that I should live every day as if it were the last day of my life, enjoying every little moment that has happened.

I suppose I speak for every twelve or thirteen-year-old girl by saying that our lives have never been simple and they never will be. But even though our lives will never be simple we will always feel as if we've loved, hated, liked, or detested at least one or two moments throughout being raised by our wonderful parents and family.

"Our lives will never be simple."

Sometimes we've been embarrassed by our friends, family, or people we don't like, but we shouldn't care for the things that people say or do. For example: Once, a couple of days ago I was replacing a girl from fifth grade on her football team [in most countries other than the USA, soccer is called "football"]. The football field was extremely wet, because the night before and that morning it had rained without a pause.

So a girl of seventh grade on the other team had the ball, and I wanted to stop her from kicking the ball hard because my team mates were a little bit scared... OK, I'll be honest. My friends were extremely afraid of the ball, and were not capable of kicking it hard. Anyway, I rushed to take the ball away from the seventh-grade girl, and as I was taking it away from her, I slid, without noticing that I was in front of the whole crowd, and that there was a puddle beside the player. I fell all over the puddle, and the WHOLE CROWD started laughing at me, and calling me names as if I were the stupidest girl in the whole wide world! But still, I continued playing even though I fell over AGAIN! I didn't want the crowd to think that I would stop playing and go off crying for just falling!! I knew that I was trying to help the team and that I made the right decision by going for the run even

though the uniform was white and I ended up like a black Labrador Retriever, or even if I ended up like Scooby-Doo! I continued having one of the greatest times of my life! I got muddy! I helped the team! And I didn't look like the type of girl who would stop playing for just falling over!

I gained respect for being strong and good at sports! So if embarrassment is what you're worried about, just tell your parents not to embarrass you in front of your friends, and tell your friends not to tell your embarrassing moments, unless you want people to know how funny things can be and that you don't care what most people think about you.

Don't take this the wrong way. I'm not saying that popularity is not good. Don't even pretend I'm saying that! On the whole contrary, if you're popular GREAT! Enjoy! You just have to be nice to people, so that people can be nice to you.

> "I didn't know what the cause of the misery was, I still don't, but I did know that I had or have my whole life ahead of me, and that I should live every day as if it were the last day of my life... "

SCHOOL DAYS

When Manuela is not enjoying her weekends, she is being a very good student in school. Manuela attends a coed school in Bogotá, where the boys and girls all get along very well. Classes start at 7:00 a.m., (sharp!) and end at 2:15. She studies Mathematics, Humanities (History and Geography), Combined Science, Spanish, French, English, Art, Music, Numeracy (an advanced Mathematics class), Drama, ECL (Estudios Colombiano y Latinoamericanos, which is Latin American Social Studies), DT (Design technology and computers), PE, ATL (Approaches to Learning) and PSHE (Personal, Social and Health Education). That seems like a lot of subjects, doesn't it? That is why Manuela has a lot of homework in the evenings, except during exam periods when it is just reviewing. Manuela's favorite subjects are Music and English. She hates ECL, French, Mathematics and Science, which makes the days difficult at times.

Manuela (center) and her school friends.

If I Could Be...

I would choose to be the leader of my country, because I have a thousand ideas to help my country and the people of my country. Such as: Working on the economy to fix the problem of poverty, unemployment, piracy, and all of the other specific problems that are involved with the economy. I would make this possible by creating a product that everybody would like so I could make enough money to help this economy and unemployment problem.

After making the product, and making enough money to improve the education of my country so that the people without any education at all could get the education and get on with their lives working and letting other people work as well. I would give the poor a home and some money so that they could organize themselves and be healthy.

After helping the poor I would start forbidding piracy (selling second-hand, fake, and illegal things), so that people can have useful and good things.

I chose this possibility because this is the thing that

"We will have the freedom to scream 'VICTORY!' and have criminals in prison and have a country with peace around it."

helps start the development of good people and actions in this world. I also chose it because if this good action starts in one country it will start spreading all over the world.

If that happens there would be peace in the world and there would be no EXTREME wars. Maybe disagreement will happen and the terrorist groups will still exist, but if we continue to fight against them and don't give up until they surrender, we will have the freedom to scream "VICTORY!" and have criminals in prison and have a country with peace around it.

This may take time, but it is worth having the patience to make this great cause possible.

What I Most Want The World To Know

I want them to know the real me. The passionate, intelligent, romantic, aggressive, respectful, be-careful-who-you're-talking-to, think-before-you-talk-to-me type of gal that I am. I also want them to know what life is like for a twelve or thirteen-year-old-girl. I want to tell the world what goes on in our minds, when our parents start acting weird around us, and when fathers become over-protective over us gals.

Did You Know?

- Colombia is located in the Northwestern corner of South America. Its capital city, Santa Fe de Bogotá, where Manuela lives, is in the middle of the country. The famous Andes Mountains are in the West, while the lowlands are in the East. Spanish is the official Colombian language.

Colombian Flag

Colombian Currency

- *Cumbia* is a form of Colombian music and dance. It combines African rhythms with both Spanish and Native American harmonies.

- Colombia lies in the "Pacific Ring of Fire," an area of earthshaking unpredictabiliy characterized by frequent volcanoes and earthquakes.

Some words in Spanish

Girl = Ella	Brother = Hermano
School = Escuela	Sister = Hermana
Dog = Perro	Soccer = Fútbol
	Coffee = Café

Colombia

Caribbean Sea

Panama

North Pacific Ocean

Venezuela

Bogotá

Ecuador

Peru

Brazil

Manuela's home city

Sofia Buenos Aires, Argentina

Sofia "Sofy"

Nationality: Argentine (My parents are from Italy.)
Religion: Catholic
Languages: Spanish; Italian; and English
Brothers and Sisters: I have a brother.
Pets: A dog named Dany
Hobbies: Listening to music and dancing
Talents: Rhythmic gymnastics
Favorite Sport: Handball and volleyball
Favorite Books: Short stories by Oscar Wilde; the *Harry Potter* books by J.K. Rowling; and *Cartas a un Gnomo* (*Letters to a Gnome*) by Margarita Maine

Sofia's puppy, Dany.

Favorite Food: Veal Milanese with mashed potatoes
Least Favorite Food: Broccoli
Whom do you most admire? My mom
Favorite Possession: A cuddly toy called Pépé
Do you help with chores at home? A little
Do you have your own telephone or computer? Yes
Do you use the Internet? Yes, ICQ is my favorite website.
Where would you most want to travel? To Patagonia
What comes to mind when you think of the United States? Large commercial empire
…and France? Paris, the city of love
…and China? Big producer
…and Kenya? I don't know about it
What do you talk about with friends? Boys
What do you want to know about other girls your age? What their lives are like

A church in Buenos Aires.

Sofia's favorite possession, Pépé.

My Best Day

translated from Spanish

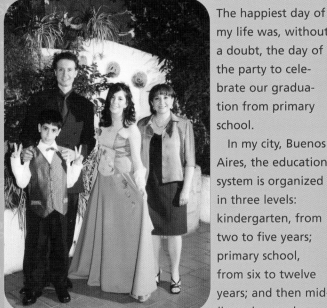

Sofia and her family.

Tomar Mate

Tomar Mate means "Drinking Mate," a kind of bitter tea (its full name is *Yerba Mate*, pronounced yare-ba mah-tay). Drinking Mate is a tradition in Argentina, which Sofia enjoys with her family every Friday evening. *Yerba Mate* is a product of the Guarani Indians of South America who come from Paraguay and Argentina. The tea-like drink contains many properties that provide energy and mental alertness, optimize the immune system, and assist in weight loss. There is a ritual to drinking mate where families and close friends often share one large wooden cup of mate, which is passed around and drunk from a straw called a *bombilla*.

The happiest day of my life was, without a doubt, the day of the party to celebrate our graduation from primary school.

In my city, Buenos Aires, the education system is organized in three levels: kindergarten, from two to five years; primary school, from six to twelve years; and then middle and secondary school from thirteen to seventeen years.

When I was two and three years old, I attended a small and cute kindergarten called La Casa de la Campana (The House of the Bell) because there was an enormous bell on the patio. Anyway, it seemed enormous to me! But the last two years of kindergarten until the last year of primary school (seventh grade), I attended the School Tomàs Devoto (Devout Thomas)—no less than nine years of my life! Now I am in the first year of secondary school at a different school, Nicolàs Avellaneda. For these reasons, that party meant a lot to me and I consider it the happiest day of my life, or the most important. I thought that day would be the last day that I would see my friends for so many years. It was a very special moment that I shared with my friends.

Everything was thoroughly planned to the very last detail, from what we would eat to what we would wear. One week before the party, we went with my mom to Urquiza, a neighborhood in Buenos Aires with many clothing shops, to see what we might find that was pretty but not expensive. After looking and looking, we decided on a red skirt with black stripes, a black sweater that had triangle points at the bottom, and black sandals with high platform heels, which was good because I am not very tall. When we got home, my mother tried to make my dad think that we had spent a fortune (which would not have been very nice since the money issue in my country is now very serious because there is very little work).

The parents of the graduates met for months before the party in order to agree on the location for the party and the food. Finally, they decided on a *boliche*. Here, this is what we call a place that is used only for dancing, and for kids much older than us. The place was called Bella Roma, and it was very exciting because, for nearly all of us, it was the first time we had gone to a *boliche*. It was all ready, the place, the buffet, and a special dance that my friends and I had prepared to perform for everyone at the party.

The great day arrived. We were all outside the *boliche* wearing our elegant clothes. It was the first time we had seen each other dressed in formal clothing because we attended a private school and wore school uniforms. In

"...with the music playing in the background, we glamorously descended the stairs as though we were all professional models."

fact, we rarely saw each other dressed casually, let alone all dressed up for a party. We were all waiting to enter.

First the parents were let in. Then we were let in 30 minutes later through another door that entered onto the first floor. We waited on the first floor for a couple of minutes. Then, with the music playing in the background, we glamorously descended the stairs as though we were all professional models.

The dancing started...the club was decorated in Roman style with statues, as its name, Bella Roma, would suggest. It was beautiful with a catwalk that crossed the dance floor in the middle and continued up the stairs, with chairs set up on either side.

At one moment during the party, they showed a video with photos of the graduates, meaning us, from when we were little children up until the present, along with our nicknames, in my case, "Sofy." It was the most emotional moment of the party.

In the middle of the party they played the song that my friends and I were all waiting for since we had pre-pared the dance. The moment we heard the song the five of us went to the center of the walkway and began our dance. It was impressive, everyone watching us, filming us, and taking photos as though we were real stars.

More towards the end of the party, a group of parents, already half drunk, began to sing and dance to the songs of a well-known group in Argentina because one of the parents looked like the lead singer in the group. When the daughter of this man saw him, she went to the loudspeakers to tell him to stop the foolishness. That was the funniest moment!!!

Little by little, midnight was approaching, and with it, the end of the party. Like all parties typical in Buenos Aires, this one ended with everyone singing songs of friendship. This caused a collective crying that accompanied the end of the party.

And thus, ended the best day of my life, for now. Because I know that I will share perhaps with different people, or in another time, other equally unforgettable moments.

Quinceañera

Quinceañera is the name of the coming-of-age ceremony in Latin America, celebrated on a girl's birthday. Similar to a sweet sixteen party in parts of the United States, the *Quinceañera* is celebrated by Latinas throughout Latin America from Mexico to Argentina. The celebration has its roots in a time when teenage girls were separated from their younger siblings and taught the skills necessary to become a good wife, mother, and member of the community. The mother and women from the community would give thanks to the Gods for the new young woman, while she vowed to serve her family and the community faithfully. Later, a Christian aspect was added to the celebration. Today, several traditions accompany the *Quinceañera* celebration. Following a church blessing, a big party, almost like a wedding, is held. The *Quinceañera*, as the girl is called, is accompanied by escorts; the number of escorts represent the previous years of her life. If she has a younger sister, she gives her a gift of a porcelain doll to mark her graduation from childhood. She changes from flat shoes to heels, to reflect her advancement to womanhood, and dances the first dance of the party with her father. After the *Quinceañera*, the girl is treated by her parents more as an adult than a child.

Here is glamorous Sofia attending a Quinceañera.

Meeting Sofia
by Starla

At just 13 years old, Sofia has had a hard lesson in reality that many other girls her age have not had. She has been an eyewitness to and an unwilling participant in a terrible reversal of fortune—really an economic and political meltdown—in her country, Argentina.

Before this economic reversal, Argentina was

Plaza de Mayo, Buenos Aires, Argentina.

home to the wealthiest, most educated and cultured people of Latin America. Argentina's capital and Sofia's home, Buenos Aires, which rises from the banks of the enormous Rio de La Plata, was the premiere cultural, political, and economic center in the region, drawing people and investments from the United States and Europe. By all cultural and economic measures, Argentina was like a little piece of Europe in the New World. Then it began to fall apart. You wouldn't think that a young teenager would necessarily be aware of these things, but in the case of Argentina's economic difficulties, no one, not even those among the country's youth, has been left unaffected.

In this background of struggle that has seen thousands of people protesting on the streets of Buenos Aires, hundreds of people losing their jobs, and many others their homes, Sofia and other kids her age are still trying to make the most of their youth. Dressed in her jeans, sweater, beret, and colored stockings, funky Sofia, budding actress and political activist, and potential spokesperson for the Internet-generation, starts every Monday with high spirits that she hopes will last all seven days of the week, even if it rarely happens. Part of Sofia's blossoming political consciousness has come from attending secondary school. In Buenos Aires, secondary school starts when you turn 13. Sofia's parents decided that she should attend a public high school, rather than a private school. She had to pass an entrance exam to enter, as it is one of the better public schools in Buenos Aires. As Sofia herself says, the private schools may be more demanding, but the state schools provide benefits that the private schools do not: "They show you the realities of the country, what is occurring around us, and the students learn to fight for their rights. I believe that my school has opened my eyes and my mind to things I didn't see before."

After school, Sofia takes private English classes on Mondays and Thursday evenings. She takes advanced Italian classes on Wednesday evenings, and is on a handball team that practices on Tuesday afternoons. On Thursdays, she teaches volleyball at the local church. "This," Sofia says, "is my small contribution to the community." Sofia's volunteering translates into food for Caritas, an organization for people who live on the streets. Instead of paying for the volleyball lessons, the girls bring food for Caritas, because, as Sofia says, "my country is very poor and unfortunately there are many hungry and homeless people."

But her favorite afterschool activity takes place every Tuesday evening. This is when Sofia attends a Musical Comedy course at the local arts club called "Buenas Artes." According to Sofia, there are really great professors at this club, which she adds, is strange, because usually the good

professors are only at the very expensive clubs, and this one is not too expensive. First, Sofia has two hours of drama. "This is what I want to do with my life!" Then one hour of dance and one hour of singing. It is always great fun, and she is always wishing that Tuesday would hurry up and get here. The only bad thing is that she does not get home until 10:40 p.m. This group, the most advanced in the club, is usually for kids older than Sofia.

Friday kicks off the weekend, and is the only day that Sofia is not running off to some evening class. She only has handball practice and gets home at 2:30 in the afternoon. After doing her homework and finishing any chores in order to free up her Saturday, Sofia and her family tomar mate (drink mate) on Friday evening with her family, as is the custom for families in Argentina.

Then Friday nights are for telephone conversations with her best friend "Mica" (with whom Sofia went to kindergarten and primary school), and cruising the Internet. Sending e-mails, and conversing in chat rooms is a huge pastime for Argentine youth. As Sofia explains, it is common in Buenos Aires for young people to be connected to the Internet throughout the day, but especially at night. And many kids are introduced to one another through the Internet, and end up meeting up at concerts or other events...Sofia has met many other kids this way.

Saturday is the day to sleep in and maybe visit her grandparents. After lunch, either at home or with her

Caminitas la Boca District, Buenos Aires, Argentina.

grandparents, Sofia sees her friends. They will usually meet up at one person's home, tomar mate with the family, and then go dancing, to a movie, to a theatre, or just stay in, order a pizza, rent a film, and chat all night long—Sofia's favorite activity. In Argentina, everyone goes out on Saturday nights, and everyone loves to dance, especially the young people. Now that they can go to boliche (dance clubs), previously the domain of the older kids, Sofia and her friends are often there. Sofia says that there are many different boliche, with each playing different kinds of music that cater to a specific type of crowd. Sofia hates Sundays because they are too routine. The family goes out and buys the Sunday newspaper. Then, they do chores for the upcoming week, and afterwards, they go for a family walk. The only good thing about Sundays is that she can use the Internet because the tariffs are lower. Otherwise, it is a time for reading and imagination.

As a young girl, Sofia traveled with her parents to neighboring countries like Brazil, Uruguay, and Chile, but she does not remember them very well. More recently, however, Sofia and her family had the opportunity to travel a little in Europe, a long plane ride away from home. This is because Sofia's mother was sent to Trier, in Germany, to work for a month, and she missed her family so much they all flew over to spend time with her. Sofia visited Germany, Belgium, and Luxembourg, and saw a ton of interesting and historical places. But what really caught her attention was that just outside of her mother's apartment in Trier was the "Porta Nigra." Sofia explains, "This was built for the Roman emperor Constantine in the fourth century, and the people just walked under it as if it were any old modern gateway."

This vibrant, tropical flower, Heliconia, grows in Argentina.

If I Could Be...

translated from Spanish

I would choose to be a pop star or actress because that is the option that most attracts me since I love to sing and dance.

I would not choose to be the leader of my country because Argentina is in such a delicate situation. I think that any wrong move might cause us to fall into a well with no escape. I would not be the right person to move the country forward.

My second option would be to win a gold medal at the Olympic games because I adore sports and am good at them.

Getting back to my first choice: I think becoming a pop star or actress would be fantastic. I imagine giving concerts, making films, giving interviews, signing autographs, filming music videos, and recording albums. All of this is what I would love to do.

"Public schools in Argentina show you the realities of the country...my school has opened my eyes and my mind to things I didn't see before."

I am from Rio de La Plata

translated from Spanish

This is a creative story invented by Sofia during a moment of reverie, to describe a little what it is like to be from Buenos Aires on the Rio de La Plata, an estuary that opens into the South Atlantic Ocean near Buenos Aires. Aside from being an important asset for the development of Buenos Aires throughout history, Rio de la Plata is the home of a particular species of dolphin, called La Plata River dolphins that swim into the estuary from the Atlantic Ocean.

I am from Rio de La Plata

It was my birthday, and like every other year, my family gave me a gift of a trip with anyone I chose. So, without a doubt, my cousin Veronica would be the one to accompany me to Colonia, a small city in Uruguay, which you can reach from Buenos Aires by crossing the Rio de la Plata. For those who don't know, this is the widest river in the world. The trip by ship takes about three hours.

The morning of our departure, unfortunately for us, was cold and wet. The clouds reflected in the brown waves that the ship formed in its wake. We were on the ship's deck looking out at the landscape that surrounded us. We could see the imposing coast of Buenos Aires. Its tall buildings looked like giant mirrors in which the flirting stars could see themselves at night; other small buildings painted in many colors could be seen in the area called La Boca (the Mouth) where the Italian immigrants of the 20th century settled upon reaching this great city. As the ship moved along, the horizon began to change. Each moment there were fewer buildings, and green appeared on all sides. The horizon extended without limit; it appeared endless.

Colonia, which got its name from being a colony of Spain, and then of Portugal, has conserved its style of the 16th and 17th centuries and is considered a Cultural Heritage Site by UNESCO. [The United Nations Educational, Scientific, and Cultural Organization.] There we were, with my cousin Vero, so far yet so close to Buenos Aires. Evening fell and the ship left to return to our city. Not perfect, but ours.

A breathtaking view of the Iguazu Falls in Argentina.

SCHOOL DAYS

During the school week, Monday through Friday, Sofia is up at 6:15 a.m., earlier if she has an exam that day. Her mother prepares a breakfast of coffee and toast with low-fat cheese because, as Sofia says, "In my society, adolescents are expected to be as thin as models on TV," and then she takes a bus for 40 minutes to school. There she studies Mathematics, History, Geography, Sciences, and Foreign Languages. Her favorite subjects are History and Geography, and this year she is studying the history of her country and the geography of the continent of South America. She is very excited to learn these subjects. Biology, Physics, and Chemistry, on the other hand, are her least favorite subjects: "It is trying for me to imagine what an atom or molecule is, whereas it is easy for me to imagine how people of different eras thought and how they were organized."

School starts promptly at 8:00 a.m. with the flag-raising ceremony, and ends at 12:55 p.m. It seems like a short school day, but Sofia's days never end there. Usually she goes home and joins her father for lunch, and then she is off to one of her many afterschool activities.

Did You Know?

- Originally a Spanish colony, Argentina gained its independence in 1816. Buenos Aires is its capital and Spanish is its official language.

Argentine Flag

- Argentina is the eighth largest country in the world and takes up nearly all of the southern half of South America. The northern part of Argentina is subtropical, while the southern part reaches near Antarctica.

Argentine Currency

- Italians, like Sofia's family, are the single largest immigrant group in Argentina.

- Beef, wool, and grain are stable Argentine agricultural exports. In fact, it is possible to eat Argentine beef almost anywhere in the world.

- The Tango, a famous but difficult dance in two-four time, is the Argentine national dance.

- Maria Eva Duarte de Peron, better known as "Evita," is a famous Argentine, and her life was the inspiration for both a musical and a feature film. Born in 1919 in a small, poor village, she left for Buenos Aires to pursue her acting career, and eventually found success as a radio soap opera actress. She married Juan Domingo Peron in 1945, who became president the following year. As First Lady, Eva was active and passionate about social causes. She became the second most influential person in Argentina, and even sought the vice presidency in 1951.

Some words in Spanish
Hello = Hóla
Goodbye = Adiós
Good morning = Buenos días
Good night = Buenas noches
How are you? = ¿Como estás?
Please = Por favor
Thank You = Gracias

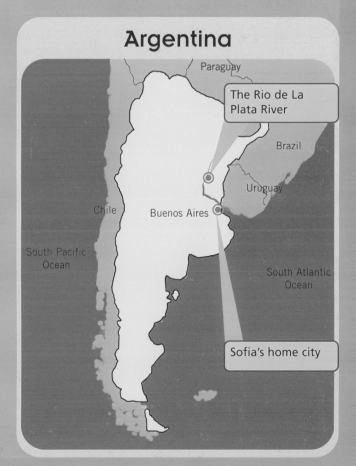

Argentina

Paraguay

The Rio de La Plata River

Brazil

Uruguay

Chile

Buenos Aires

South Pacific Ocean

South Atlantic Ocean

Sofia's home city

Nathalie Rio de Janeiro, Brazil

Nathalie

Nationality: Brazilian

Religion: I am Jewish and I go to a Jewish school, but I do not practice.

Languages: Portuguese, and I study English, French, and Hebrew.

Brothers and Sisters: An older brother and a little sister

Pets: I used to have a bird, but it died.

Hobbies: Listening to music

Talents: I can act well; I like the stage.

Favorite Sport: Surfing

Favorite Books: The *Harry Potter* books by J.K. Rowling

Favorite Food: *Brigadeiro*, a Brazilian sweet made of one can of condensed milk and two spoons of cocoa stirred in a casserole until thick and eaten when cold with a spoon or in little rolls

Least Favorite Food: Banana and papaya

Whom do you most admire? My parents because of what they have done for me

Favorite Possession: A clown my great-grandfather gave me when I was born and a teddy bear my uncle gave me when I was a little girl

Do you help with chores at home? Yes, I make my bed, I clear the table, and sometimes wash the dishes.

Do you have your own telephone or computer? I have my own cell phone and use my father's or my mother's computer.

Do you use the Internet? Yes, my favorite websites are ICQ and KAZAA.

Where would you most want to travel? Egypt; Israel; and New Zealand

What comes to mind when you think of the United States? Economy/Shopping

...and France? Ancient, medieval cities

...and China? A huge country

...and Kenya? Poverty

What do you talk about with friends? We talk about boys and we recall funny things that happened to us.

What do you want to know about other girls your age? How they relate to their family and other people

Nathalie with a friend.

About Me
translated from Portuguese

I live in Ipanema in Rio de Janeiro. This town is between the beach and a small inner lake. On this lake, there is a tiny island with a club where my parents are a member. It is a ten-minute-walk from home and I often go there in the afternoon or weekends to swim and have fun. Ipanema Beach is also a ten-minute-walk from home, and it is where I take surfing classes twice a week. This is my first year and I really enjoy it.

My school is far—a half-hour drive away—and I arrive back home at 2:00 p.m. The rest of the day is dedicated to surfing, swimming, or taking extra classes on subjects that I need for school.

On weekends I go out with my friends to the movies or to the beach. I also enjoy when my family meets for a meal. I just love them.

Nathalie at the beach.

If I Could Be...
translated from Portuguese

I would like to be a movie star or rock star, or rather both. The reason why is that I enjoy performing on stage, which is something I have always been able to do, in spite of being shy. I also like music, especially rock music, and would like to play the electric guitar and the drums. Next year, I intend to learn how to play the guitar first because it is the basis for the electric guitar. I like to sing, play, and perform, so this would be a wonderful life for me.

If not a movie star, I would like to win a medal in surfing and why not become a professional surfer, winning medals everywhere? I am taking surfing classes on the beach nearby, and I just love the beach and love surfing. So it would be nice to have both in my life.

I would not complain about going to outer space as a tourist, but have this as my regular activity? No. And, I do not see myself as the leader of my country because Brazil has big problems that I would not be able to handle. I have to learn how to solve my own before trying to face such big questions.

Did You Know?

- Portuguese is the official language in Brazil. Brazil is the only country in all of Latin America where Spanish is the not official language. This is because Brazil was a Portuguese colony for 300 years. It became independent in 1822.

Brazilian Flag

- Rio de Janeiro has 45 miles of white-sand beaches, including the Copacabana beach, and Ipanema, where Nathalie is learning to surf.

- The Amazonian rainforest, the world's largest, covers nearly one-half of Brazil. The rainforest is home to several hundred mammals, reptiles, and birds. It is also home to an astounding variety of plants and insects, some of which have yet to be discovered. Medical researchers hope the Amazon's unique plant life might hold cures to some of today's most troubling diseases.

Brazil

Nathalie's home city

Europe

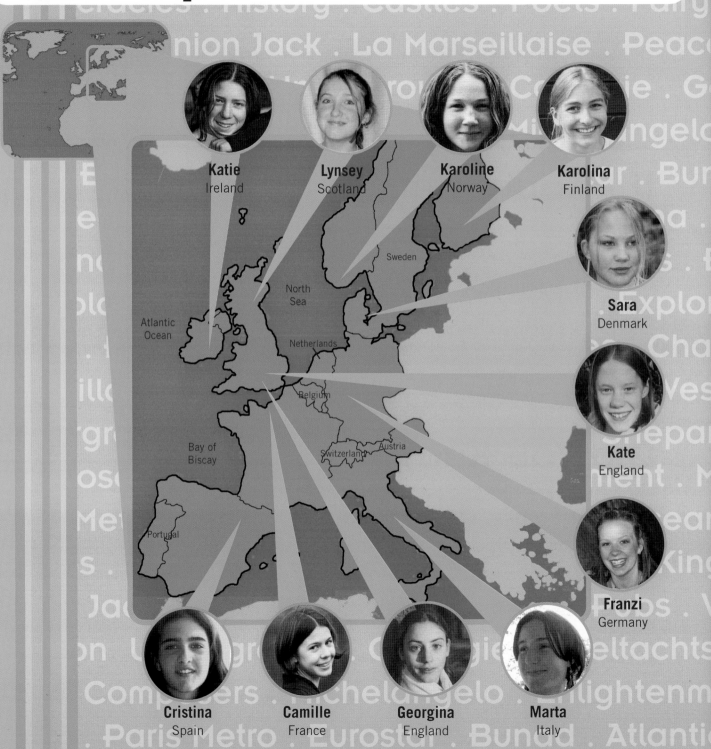

Katie
Ireland

Lynsey
Scotland

Karoline
Norway

Karolina
Finland

Sara
Denmark

Kate
England

Franzi
Germany

Cristina
Spain

Camille
France

Georgina
England

Marta
Italy

Sweden

North Sea

Atlantic Ocean

Netherlands

Belgium

Bay of Biscay

Switzerland

Austria

Portugal

Palace guards in London, England.

The Coliseum in Rome, Italy.

Parade in Oslo, Norway.

Above: The Eiffel Tower in Paris, France.
Below: Dutch windmills in the Netherlands.

The port of Helsinki, the largest in Finland.

Georgina and Kate

Georgina Frances ("Georgina")

Nationality: British

Religion: Protestant (Church of England)

Languages: English, and I am learning French at school.

Brothers and Sisters: One brother, Richard

Pets: A dog called Galaxy. She is two years old and we got her as a puppy from an animal rescue place called Battersea Dogs Home.

Hobbies: Trampoline-jumping; drama (I belong to the drama club at school); ballet; and dance (modern, jazz, and tap)

Talents: Mathematics and Science

Favorite Sport: Gymnastics and trampoline-jumping

Favorite Books: The Harry Potter books by J.K. Rowling; His Dark Materials trilogy by Philip Pullman; Lord of the Rings trilogy and The Hobbit by J.R.R. Tolkien

Favorite Food: Fresh anchovies fried and eaten whole. I eat them when I am on holiday in Spain where they are called boquerones.

Least Favorite Food: Octopus cooked in its own ink

Whom do you most admire? Nelson Mandela, because he believed in something and stuck with the consequences

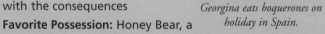

Georgina eats boquerones on holiday in Spain.

Favorite Possession: Honey Bear, a cuddly toy that I have had since I was born

Do you help with chores at home? In the kitchen, I like to help with the cooking, especially baking cakes, and I keep my room tidy.

Do you have your own telephone or computer? I use a laptop computer at school for my work.

Do you use the Internet? Not often

Where would you most want to travel? To Australia because it is completely the other side of the world and I have never been there

What comes to mind when you think of the United States? My dad, who grew up there, and school friends because some of them are American

… and France? Skiing holidays

… and China? Chopsticks

… and Kenya? Wild animals

What do you talk about with friends? Things that have happened to us and things we want to do in the future

What do you want to know about other girls your age? What their everyday lifestyle is like

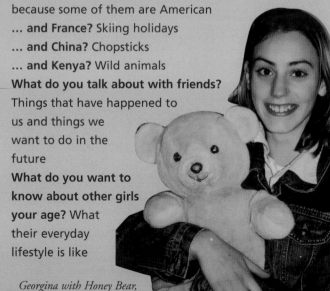

Georgina with Honey Bear, her favorite possession.

Friends in London, England

Nationality: British

Religion: Protestant (Church of England)

Languages: English, and I am learning French at school.

Brothers and Sisters: A younger sister named Lizzie

Pets: Two cats called Elsie and Patch; a parrot called Percy; a gerbil called Tingo; and two fish called Bubbles and Bellyflop

Hobbies: Trampoline-jumping and drama

Talents: Science; French; and sports games

Favorite Sport: Tennis

Favorite Books: The Harry Potter books by J.K. Rowling; Double Act and Bad Girls by Jacqueline Wilson

Favorite Food: Pasta

Least Favorite Food: Lamb

Whom do you most admire? My parents

Favorite possession: Polar, my special cuddly toy

Do you help with chores at home? Hardly, but I keep my room tidy.

Do you have your own telephone or computer? I have my own cell phone.

Do you use the Internet? Yes. Neopets.com is my favorite website. There, you have virtual pets that you do things for like buy food using virtual money.

Where would you most want to travel? Greece sounds like a nice place to go and I have friends who have been there and had a good time.

What comes to mind when you think of the United States? My American relatives (my mother is American)

... and France? The Loire Valley

... and China? Noodles

... and Kenya? Safari

What do you talk about with friends? Things that have happened to us

What do you want to know about other girls your age? What their environment is like

The Harry Potter series is at the top of Kate's booklist.

Katherine Anne ("Kate")

SCHOOL DAYS: Kate

Kate attends an all-girls school in London. She arrives at school everyday at 8:30 for a 9:00 start and has eight classes a day: Latin, French, English, Mathematics, Art, Gym, Drama, Geography, History, Religious Studies, or Science, depending on the day. School ends at 3:45. After school, Kate is involved in clubs and activities like Drama and Sports clubs. She rarely gets home before 5:15 or 5:30. Then she usually has about two hours of homework a night. She adds that attending an all-girls school is "OK," but there is a lot of fighting over silly things and some of the girls are "catty."

Meeting Georgina and Kate by Starla

Georgina, Kate, and Barbarita.

Georgina's home in west London is abuzz with people and activity. Georgina, often called "George," is looking on as her cousin from Spain, Barbarita, fixes her best friend Kate's hair. Georgina's grandmother is sitting on the leather couch expressing mild disapproval of the music

Georgina and her father.

videos playing on the TV. Georgina's brother, Richard, and his friend are sitting at the family dining table, a big wooden picnic table, discussing what movie to go to, and her other cousin, Ingrid, also from Spain, is on the phone. Galaxy, the dog, is contributing to the commotion by bouncing up and down in front of the back door.

It is an unusually sunny day in London. At the house, the teenagers' attention is turned to what to do next. 13-year-old Georgina is dressed in flared jeans, a T-shirt, and a denim jacket. Her chestnut-colored hair is pulled up on the sides and she carries herself with a uniquely British sense of cool. It is all very bohemian chic, especially the henna tattoo around her belly button that Barbarita has painted on. Kate, Georgina's best friend, has golden-red-dish, shoulder-length hair, deep, blue eyes, and porcelain, white skin. She is dressed in maroon corduroys, a pink, long-sleeved T-shirt, and a pink GAP sweatshirt. She looks cool, too, but in a more American way, probably because Kate's mother is American.

Georgina and Kate spend most of their time talking and hanging out in Georgina's bedroom, which they describe as "very vibrant." When I follow them into Georgina's room, I see that it is vibrant indeed! Each of the walls and the ceiling of the room are painted a bright primary color, plus

A royal guard outside Buckingham Palace.

green and orange. The armoire is coordinated to match the walls, and the white dresser (the only white in the room) has a large purple flower spray-painted on it, which, combined with the lava lamp on top of the armoire and the animal patterned chair and multicolored rug, is all very psychedelic.

But that's not all. Every wall is painted with small silver stars that Georgina has applied everywhere using star stencils. The overall effect is, well, vibrant! An enormous pyramid of cuddly toys sits on top of another dresser, topped by the famous Honey Bear. Kate is currently adding to the decor by painting hearts and flowers on the windows. They assure me the paint washes off with water. The CD player is blasting in the background. As Georgina and Kate discuss favorite songs, some differences emerge, but the girls agree on most things, including where they like to vacation (Turkey!) and their great ambition (to fly!).

At the end of the day, Kate's father stops by to take her home. At Georgina's, the remaining kids must finalize their evening plans. The girls are watching music videos—they get five different music channels—and dissecting each one. They flip from good to bad at a breathtaking speed. I slip out without any fanfare just as the new Lionel Ritchie video is being booted off the TV. "Change it, quick!" Click!

English vs. American

The English spoken in England and the English spoken in America differ more than just in the way the words are pronounced. Some words are used in completely different ways. So much so that the Harry Potter books (and others) were published in two different English versions, one for the UK and other "English"-speaking markets, and one for the readers in the United States and other "American"-speaking markets. Not all words were changed; only those that would create confusion because they have distinctly different meanings in

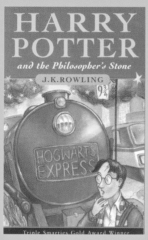
The UK edition.

The US edition.

the US and UK. Nevertheless, in the first Harry Potter book, Harry Potter and the Philosopher's Stone (The Sorcerer's Stone in America), 78 changes were made to the book! Here are some examples of basic differences in

American	English
Dessert	Pudding
Elevator	Lift
Truck	Lorry
Flashlight	Torch
Band-aid	Plaster
Apartment	Flat
Trashcan	Dustbin
Bangs	Fringe
Sweater	Jumper
Soccer	Football
Sneakers	Trainers
Stand in line	Queue
Restroom	Loo
Field	Pitch
Merry Christmas!	Happy Christmas!
Closet	Wardrobe
Two weeks	Fortnight
Studying	Revising
Trunk (of a car)	Boot
Cookies	Biscuits
Sidewalk	Footpath

If I Could Fly...

by Georgina

I have always wished to fly, fly like a bird as high as possible. One of the other things I have always wanted to do is to jump into thin air from a great height with nothing to stop me from falling and falling. The closest thing to these two things is to jump from 10–15,000 feet off an airplane with a parachute.

The reason I want to do this is that when you are falling there is a huge thrill of exaltation and adrenaline rushing through your body. There is also an eminent sense of being free and able to do whatever you wish because nothing can stop you from falling. You may get a slight sense of this on a roller coaster, but it is just not enough. I want to be truly free with no worries as I am falling through the air.

"I want to be truly free with no worries as I am falling through the air."

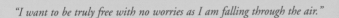

If I Could Fly...

by Kate

I have always wanted to fly and see everything below from up above. It would be amazing to just fly through the air freely. Unfortunately, I don't have wings. I would love to go microlighting (a microlight is a one-person flying machine) because it would be very close to flying and I would be able to look down, controlling the microlight as high or as low as I wanted.

I would be able to see small towns and villages and all the tiny people walking around. I would be able to fly over the sea and watch all the boats sailing and maybe, if I'm very lucky, also see a dolphin. All the people would be sitting on the beaches and looking up at me and waving. I could wave back. I'd feel the breeze brushing past me. It would be a glorious feeling.

"I would be able to fly over the sea and watch all the boats sailing and maybe, if I'm very lucky, also see a dolphin."

My Best Day

by Georgina

We were on holiday in Turkey (Kalkan), and my mother and father took us out on a boat to go S.C.U.B.A. diving. As I lifted the enormous air tank on to my back, I felt like collapsing. As soon as I jumped off the boat and into the water the weight was lifted off of me and I started to test breathing under the sea.

At first the ability to breath under the water without coming up was confusing and hard to get used to. As I started to get used to it I started to go under, but when I was about halfway down, my ears became excruciatingly painful. So I came up to the top and started to complain.

My parents said that all I had to do was squeeze my nose and breathe. I started to go down and as the pain arose I tried squeezing my nose like they said and it worked. Finally after much confusion I got to the bottom.

When I was at the bottom I started to swim back and forth along the bay, staring at and admiring some of the wondrous and peculiar fish and rocks. As it neared the end of our dive, a very strange sight appeared; a school of baby barracuda started to circle us. Their teeth and shiny bodies were quite beautiful with the rays of light shining through the water.

"I held onto the bottom of their fins and they started racing back to the platform."

My Best Day

by Kate

I was on holiday in Turkey and my mom and dad arranged for my sister and me to go swimming with dolphins. I was really excited because I had always wanted to swim with dolphins. Once we arrived in the town of Cas, we watched half an hour of the dolphin show. Then, during the half-hour break, we went over to the platform and climbed into the water. It was very fishy. I went straight to the dolphins and started stroking their wet, rubbery skin.

Next, we swam to the other side of the arena and the dolphins came, too. I held onto the bottom of their fins and they started racing back to the platform. I was clinging on to one dolphin and trying to grab hold of the other dolphin's fin, which wasn't easy. I loved it. I did it about five times and then the lady gave us a small fish to feed to the dolphins. I didn't want to touch the fish at first, but I was going to feed it to the dolphins so I didn't mind.

A few minutes later we had to get out so the other people could have a go. I stroked the dolphins one last time and got out. It was my dream come true.

Alone in the Underground
a creative essay by Kate

I stood on the platform staring up at an advertisement waiting for the train to arrive. The crowds were starting to disappear, so I turned to see if the train had come. At once, the whole platform was empty. Panicking, I shouted, "Mom!" but my voice just echoed back at me. I stood alone, shivering. I didn't know what to do. I did not know where I was and I had no money.

I started to walk into the main station when a huge crowd of people came trampling round the corner. I felt so small in such a big crowd. I sat down on a step and buried my face into my knees trying to think of what to do. After what seemed like ages, I heard a train come into the station. I stood up quickly looking up and down the cold, damp tunnel trying to figure out which platform was mine. I saw a couple of people hurrying down one side of it so I raced down the tunnel in the same direction and came to a halt. My train had left.

I dropped my head in disappointment. How would I get home now? The next train wouldn't arrive for another

"I raced down the tunnel in the same direction and came to a halt. My train had left."

hour. I glanced sideways to see if anyone else was waiting for a train, but the only person left was asleep on a bench. I suddenly saw a glimpse of silver on the floor beside the bench. I ran towards it and picked it up. It was a fifty pence piece. I zoomed towards the phone box and dialed my number. My dad answered and I told him everything and where I was. He told me not to worry and that he would collect me. All of my worries washed away.

Bullied
a creative essay by Georgina

A hot, wet, trickling tear rolled down my cheek as I sat in the dark corner of the playground throwing tiny pebbles onto the floor and sobbing into my arms. I felt so isolated and unwanted. I felt like I was screaming as loud as I could inside, but no one could hear me anymore. I had been buried so deep, in feeling, emotion, and hatred.

A shadow of pure evil came over to me. I closed my eyes and looked up, only to see their conniving and sadistic faces beaming down on me like hyenas preying on some helpless animal, stuck on the floor. I scrambled into

the corner getting myself even more trapped as they started their ritual of teasing and pushing, punching and calling names, until I burst into tears of misery.

Every day it would be the same again and again and I had no one to reach to, no one to tell. So I lived through this every day, day after day. Until one day when I was sitting in the back of the playground as usual, a towering shadow came over me. I expected the same as usual, shouting and swearing, but instead there was just a soft cooing voice.

SCHOOL DAYS: Georgina

Georgina is up every day at 6:30 in the morning so that she is ready to get a ride to school. She must be there at 8:00 in the morning twice a week for running club and for ballet, which she practices before classes start at 8:50. School does not end until nearly 5:00 p.m. Throughout the year, Georgina's classes include French, English, Mathematics, Biology, Chemistry and Physics, Geography, History, Religious Studies, Art, Drama, and Gym. In Gym class, the sports are Netball, Field Hockey, and Rounders (which is like baseball for girls). Georgina also does sculling (or rowing) on the River Thames in the summer.

Ideally, if Georgina could do anything she wanted in the whole, entire world, she would want it to involve fun and not hard work.

Did You Know?

- England is part of Great Britain, which also includes Scotland and Wales. Along with Northern Ireland, Great Britain is part of what is officially named the United Kingdom of Great Britain and Northern Ireland. The UK has been part of the European Union since 1973. London is its capital city.

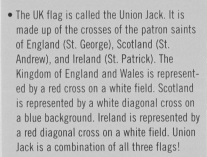

UK Flag

- The UK flag is called the Union Jack. It is made up of the crosses of the patron saints of England (St. George), Scotland (St. Andrew), and Ireland (St. Patrick). The Kingdom of England and Wales is represented by a red cross on a white field. Scotland is represented by a white diagonal cross on a blue background. Ireland is represented by a red diagonal cross on a white field. Union Jack is a combination of all three flags!

UK Currency

- In addition to being the Queen of England, Queen Elizabeth is Queen and Head of State of 15 other countries, which collectively make up the Commonwealth Realm. In the UK, Queen Elizabeth is head of the Executive, Judicial, and Legislative bodies of government, Commander-in-Chief of the armed forces, and Supreme Governor of the Church of England. But you won't see her donning any military gear or a judge's wig! Most of her authority is carried out by the Prime Minister and other officials in government.

England

North Atlantic Ocean

North Sea

Irish Sea

Manchester

Ireland

Stratford - upon-Avon

London

Stratford-upon-Avon is where Shakespeare lived

Georgina's and Kate's home city

Lynsey* Edinburgh, Scotland

Lynsey

Nationality: Scottish
Religion: Protestant
Languages: English, a little Spanish, and a little German
Brothers and Sisters: None
Hobbies: Chatting online; hanging with friends; dancing
Talents: Being friendly, dancing (well, I'm okay)
Favorite Sport: I like football, soccer, and hockey.
Favorite books: The Slippers that Sneezed by Gyles Brandreth; Jacqueline Wilson books; and Judy Blume books

Favorite food: Tuna fish and Pickled Onion Monster Munch, a type of crisp (potato chips)
Least Favorite Food: Eggs (any kind)
Whom do you most admire? I admire my parents because they have taught me nearly everything I know.
Favorite Possession: Hamish, my teddy bear
Do you help with chores at home? I sometimes set and clear the table, sometimes Hoover (vacuum), and sometimes clean my room (only when it is a real mess).
Do you have your own telephone or computer? I have my own cell phone and a mini laptop.
Do you use the Internet? Yes, I love messenger.de and www.google.com.
Where would you most want to travel? Egypt, so I can see a real pyramid.
What comes to mind when you think of the United States? Big burgers
...and France? Baguettes and funny hats
...and China? Chinese food
...and Kenya? Sun
What do you talk about with friends? BOYS!!!!!
What do you want to know about other girls your age? Their typical day

Pickled Onion Monster Munch

* Lynsey was born and grew up in Edinburgh, Scotland. When she was 12, she and her parents moved to Germany, where she now attends the International School of Dusseldorf.

About Me

Even though, I have only been alive for thirteen years, five months, four days, and exactly sixteen hours, I have had a very busy life. I was born in the Western General Hospital, Edinburgh, Scotland, on the 8th of December at 8 p.m. I was four days late. I lived in Scotland 12 years, then I came over to Germany!

When I visited the International School of Düsseldorf, I felt really different. Everyone was speaking in funny accents—American accents. After a few days of being at ISD, I started to speak the same. When I moved to Germany, apart from my family, I missed my BESTEST

EVER FRIEND, Jennifer so so so much! Jennifer and I had been best friends practically our whole lives. We're both into the same things and we were both quite sad when I had to leave. I miss my other friends too (you know who you are).

Ever since I've lived in Germany, I've become different (weird different). First of all having Margaret as your best friend makes you weird (just kidding, Margo!), but I seem to like weird things. I'm not talking about boys or anything, just things you generally like in life. Like…I like the word "teapot," and I like to call myself a "strawberry." My name being "Strawberry" first came about when I said that I felt like a strawberry at the bottom of a fruit bowl because I'm always the last to know things. Since then the name's just stuck. I also like the word "umbrella" and "curly." I think curly is a funny word because you have to curl your tongue so you can say it!

In my spare time, I like to go online and chat to my friends, I like to read and phone my friends and I also like to hang out with my friends. Maybe down at the park or just around my neighborhood. I love Jacqueline Wilson books. Especially Lola Rose and Best Friends!! They're great! I also like the Harry Potter books, but they sure do take a lot of reading! My favorite book of all time is The Slippers That Sneezed, by Gyles Brandreth. Alexander McCall Smith has written a series called the No. 1 Ladies Detective Agency. Those books are BRILLIANT!!! I love them! I only started to like reading last summer, but since then I have read many books. I like The Pigman by Paul Zindel. It was so funny in some parts that I was laughing out loud!

Every year I go on holiday abroad. This has happened ever since I was about three. I love going abroad but sometimes I get so freaked about thinking of going on a plane. When I'm on the plane it's fine, it's just the thinking of it. I have been to, Mallorca, Florida, Portugal, Spain, Rome, Paris, Fuertaventura, Rhodes, Turkey for one day, St. Anne's in north England, and I've also been to Scotland. This year my Mum, Dad, and I are touring Italy for two weeks. I would love to go to Egypt some day. I really want to see a pyramid!

Lots of exciting things have happened in my life, too. I once got a plectrum (guitar pick) from Steve Moore, the younger of the two guitarists in Deep Purple. When I went to their concert I was with my Mum, Dad, my German friend, Sandra, and her Dad, Marek. I stood right at the front beside the speakers with Sandra and Marek. At the end of the show, Steve Moore threw the plectrum at me but he didn't throw it far enough, so the security guard picked it up and put it in my hand! I was so happy. My Mum said "I've been going to music concerts for more than thirty years and I've never gotten anything, especially a plectrum from the guitarist!"

I am really happy with how my childhood has been. I have a great family—very loving and caring. And I have made great friends!

I love to dance in my bedroom and one day I would like to perform my dancing in front of people. I used to want to be a singer. I think my voice is okay…but I would prefer to be a dancer! I'm the type of person that can listen to a song two

"I like the word 'teapot,' and I like to call myself a 'strawberry.'"

> "I am a total shopaholic!!!! I love SHOPPING!!! I just can't get enough of it!"

or three times and pick up the chorus…I'm sure many people can do that, though!!

I am a total Shopaholic!!!! I love SHOPPING!!! I just can't get enough of it! I love getting new Sketchers!!! Oh, I also love bags!!! Handbags, backpacks, whatever!! I love bags!! At the moment I'm trying to talk my Mum and Dad into getting me a really cool Adidas bag. It is so cool…I just gotta have it! I think I might be getting it tomorrow. Well, my Mum said, "We can look at it tomorrow," which in my opinion means, "Let's go get it tomorrow!"

Some more little facts about me: some of my friends say I'm too nice, others say I worry too much, and others say I'm funny and just laugh at stuff I say or the way I act.

Well, that's really all about me and my life!! I would just like to finish by saying: I am very lucky and happy to have so many friends from around the world: I am so happy to be within an international environment and learning about other people's lives and their cultures. I am so grateful to my family. Without my Mum and Dad, I would not be where I am today. Well, I wouldn't be here at all, would I?!?! Thank you to everyone. My friends. My family. And everyone who has helped me through this part of my life…a long way still to go….

Meeting Lynsey
by Starla

Lynsey!!!!!!!!!

Lynsey from Scotland, now living in Germany, has a freckle the shape of a heart on her right shoulder and she is very nervous because it seems to be disappearing! When she writes, she has such strong ideas in her head that she uses a million exclamation points for emphasis, and when she uses the word "so," as in "I like it so much," she will put a million gazillion o's after the s. Oh yes, and she sometimes exaggerates. She also sometimes feels like a strawberry.

Lynsey was born and grew up in Edinburgh, Scotland, and moved to Germany with her parents when she was 12. Now she attends the Dusseldorf International School and really enjoys it. Of course, she also misses Scotland, and her family and friends there, but when she is home in Scotland she misses her friends in Germany! Lynsey's family lives in a yellow house with three bedrooms. Lynsey's bedroom is on the second floor of the house. Her bedroom walls are covered with posters of her favorite singers and actors. Her room also has slanted ceilings, so if she jumps, she sometimes hits her head…as she knows from experience.

You have probably gathered that Lynsey is unique. She is also a great friend. Although she has lots to say about everything, in school she is actually quite reserved. According to one of her teachers, Lynsey is creative, self-assured, not a follower, she thinks before she speaks her mind, and doesn't have to be the center of attention.

If Lynsey could explore space she would visit the nine planets in a fluffy purple rocket and plant a different flower or vegetable on each one: a Jupiter tulip, a Venus Rose, a Uranus Carrot, and a Pluto Geranium, etc…Oh yes, and Lynsey's nickname…is Lynzoid. Need I say more?

If I Could Be…

If I could explore outer space I would want to stay there for a week or so. I would want to see many different planets. I believe that there are living things/creatures on other planets. I mean, why would God make planet Earth so special and unique?? Why not make every planet have its own countries and living things? I'm not saying that the things on other planets are human beings, I'm just saying that there could be living things such as animals, bugs (etc) living, or inhabiting other planets. I do not, however, believe that the moon is made out of cheese like in Wallace and Gromit. I'm merely stating that astronauts, NASA, scientists and other space stations should find a way to go to another planet (say, Pluto or Venus) and see what they can find. Even a plant growing on another planet would be a sign of living life. It would be cool if scientists and space stations around the world discovered a way to make other planets holiday resorts for people from Earth (which is the only planet that I am sure has living life on it—100 percent sure of it). I'm not 100 percent sure why I decided to write about visiting outer space. I think I picked it because it was very out of the ordinary and I thought I could maybe use some of my "creative writing" (as my teachers call it) in this piece. I would love to meet an alien. I think it would be "out of this world" (pun not intended!) Imagine meeting an actual alien!

I love things like UFO's and stuff like that. I used to love it down at my old library, because they had a section with newspaper cuttings and it was all about sightings of UFO's and little men, or women, or maybe neither. What if people from other planets are not even male or female? Weird, but cool. Maybe I'm so into aliens because my cousin Wendy called me E.T. when I was born. She said I looked like E.T. and maybe it's just stuck in my mind. Wendy also gave me a nick-name: Lynzoid, which sounds very alien-ish.

When I visit Outer Space (I am now determined to do it), I am going to fly in a fluffy, purple rocket. The fluffiness on the outside of the rocket will keep me insulated inside. I don't know how, but it will. Then the furry walls on the inside will be comfy to lean against. The fluffy floors will be comfy to walk on, too. Purple is my favorite color so that's why I decided on the color. In my rocket, the gravity will be as it is on Earth so I won't need to wear the funny space suits. I can just wear jeans and a T-shirt—maybe a jumper too as I might get cold. I will have a space suit with me though. Well, I'll need to because once I step out of the rocket the gravity will be as it is in space. I will fly by myself because I could get into the Guinness Book of World Records for being the youngest girl to fly around outer space for a week on her own. I think I'm going to fly into outer space sometime next year.

On each planet I will stick a flag into the planet's surface. The flag will be a "Lynzoid" flag. It will have a dark purple background and then my "Lynzoid" signature in light purple. This flag will show that I have been there. Obviously!

Did You Know?

- Scotland is part of the United Kingdom of England, Wales, and Northern Ireland. Edinburgh is its capital city.

- English is the official language in Scotland (although Scots is also spoken in some parts of the country). But English spoken with a thick and heavy Scottish accent can be difficult to understand for other English speakers. There is even a website that has phonetic translations of Scottish accents. Check out the Scottish Translator at www.whoohoo.co.uk.

- Kilts, famous for their plaid patterns, were worn by Scottish "Highlanders" as early as the 10th or 11th centuries. Different patterns identify specific clans, families, or regiments.

Scottish Flag

Scottish Currency

Some words in Scots
Hello = Halò
Goodbye = Mar sin leat
Please = Toilich

Thank You = Tapadh leibh
You're welcome = 'S e ur beatha
Girl = Chaileag
How are you? = Ciamar a tha sibh?

Scotland

North Atlantic Ocean

North Sea

Glasgow

Edinburgh

Irish Sea

Ireland

Lynsey's home city

English Channel

Katie County Wicklow, Ireland

Katie

Nationality: Irish

Religion: Protestant (Church of Ireland)

Languages: English and Irish

Brothers and Sisters: I have four sisters and one brother.

Pets: I have a hamster named Houdini, a pony named Sam, and two dogs, Tiga and Ailbhe (pronounced "Alva").

Hobbies: Playing tennis; swimming; horseback riding; playing Camogie; Irish dancing; playing the tin whistle and the violin

Talents: Playing music and dancing; and I am good at getting along with people of all ages.

Favorite Sport: Camogie

Favorite Books: The Harry Potter books by J.K. Rowling; The BFG by Roald Dahl; and Northern Lights by Philip Pullman

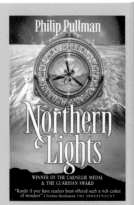

Two of Katie's favorite books.

Favorite Food: Shepard's pie, a dish made of minced meat and vegetables topped with mashed potatoes

Least Favorite Food: Fish, except for smoked salmon

Whom do you most admire? Christina Noble because of the work she is doing for orphans in Vietnam

Favorite Possession: Sam (my pony)

Do you help with chores at home? Yes, we all help out in the house and on the farm.

Do you have your own telephone or computer? No

Do you use the Internet? Not very often

Where would you most want to travel? Australia

What comes to mind when you think of the United States? The Big Apple!

…and France? Wine and cheese

…and China? Chinese food

…and Kenya? Brave people

What do you talk about with friends? Boys

What do you want to know about other girls your age? Are they friendly?

Katie's pony Sam (left) and her sister's pony.

Lost in the Wood

a creative essay by Katie

Katie with her pony Sam.

"I live on a farm in the Wicklow Mountains one thousand feet above sea level."

I live on a farm in the Wicklow Mountains one thousand feet above sea level. One day, my father and mother lost a sheep and they asked me to go and find it with my horse Sam and my dog Tiga. We set off with our packed lunch and journeyed to a wood nearby, but we did not go in because I was scared of that wood. There were creepy things inside it, scary trees, and it was all dark.

Suddenly I heard a bleating from inside the wood and I knew that it was the lost sheep. I gathered up all my courage and the three of us went inside the wood. We walked for ages, but there was no sign of the sheep. It was getting late so I got down from Sam, my horse, and we all had a rest. After about ten minutes, I got back up again and we turned to go back, but I couldn't remember which way we had come. I ran about in panic calling for help. I went back to the animals, but both Sam and Tiga looked blank.

I sat down and started to cry. After a while I got up and walked around. The trees pulled at my face and there were lots of weird noises and everything kept moving above (or so it seemed to me!). I sat down again. "Is somebody there?" a voice called. "Hello?" I called back. Out of the trees came a very pretty tall girl with long blond hair. She said her name was Georgia. "Are you lost?" she asked. I nodded. "Me too!" she cried.

We made shelter and a campfire. Then we sat in the shelter and shared my packed lunch and talked about our families and where we lived. In the end, we tried to go to sleep. We spent a sleepless night tossing and turning. An owl kept hooting and it sent shivers up my spine.

Eventually we must have gone to sleep because we woke up in the morning. We went in search of a river and found one near-by. Sam and Tiga had a long drink, and Georgia and I washed. My feet were cut and bleeding so I bathed them and then bandaged them with cloth. Soon we set off with Sam and Tiga. After we walked for a long time, we found our track home.

On our way home, we heard a bleating in the hedge. We stopped and I got off Sam and peered over the hedge. There was the lost sheep. The sheep walked lazily home in front of us, eating a bit of grass here and there. When we got home, Georgia phoned her parents and they collected her. Then I retreated to my bed. After all, I had had an action-packed 24 hours!

Katie and her sister ride in from the woods.

Meeting Katie by Starla

Katie

The day I meet Katie is not planned at all. It is a typical Irish rainy day, and my husband and I are sitting in an Irish Golf Club in County Wicklow warming ourselves in front of the fire. Just then, Captain Mike, Katie's father, a retired British army captain, walks in, and he is followed by two little girls.

"It's Katie," my husband says (he comes from Ireland and knows Katie's family well). We had planned to set up a meeting with Kate, but hadn't done it yet. Instead, fate worked its magic, and we are soon sitting together as Katie and her sister, Jessica, are digging into burgers and chips (French fries). Katie's mother is out of town for a few days and the girls are "roughing it" with their dad. All rules are suspended…chocolate cake for breakfast, no bedtime, burgers and chips for lunch! Well, not every rule—Katie's father is a former army captain after all—but there is mischief in the air.

Soon enough, we have been invited to hike up their hill and soak in the view. Katie adds that we can have tea, cakes, and ice cream after our walk. How could we refuse?

Katie lives in a house and farm complex on top of a hill—their hills—Wicklow Mountains. In Ireland, it is quite common for one's home to have a name rather than a street number, so we drive around the twisting roads looking for the name Kilcoagh. At last we come upon it, way up in the hills. The feeling in and around the house is otherworldly, or perhaps other-timely. Next to the house, there are several stables where you can

The gate at Kilcoagh.

find Captain Mike's workshop and Katie's pony, Sam. On the wall, outside the workshop, overlooking Sam's stable, is a clock dating from the 1600s. The clock keeps perfect time, thanks to Captain Mike's handiwork. Inside the house, nearly everything has been made by hand, including the wheel in Houdini the hamster's cage.

When we arrive, the rain has stopped and the girls prepare to take out their ponies. Katie and Jessica run into their rooms to put on their jodhpurs, riding hats, and coats. Their dogs, Ailbhe and Tiga, jump around happily, knowing that they are about to go out.

The girls take off down the trail with the dogs running alongside. We meander slowly, trying to capture the view of the green valley that is obscured by fog. The only audible sound is the soft thudding of the ponies' hoofs. Katie leads us along the twisting path that eventually ends at the opening of a dense wood. This is the forest featured in her creative essay, "Lost in the Wood," and it looks pretty spooky all right! A fast-running brook of fresh, cold water blocks our path to the wood. The ponies take a drink from the brook, and then it is time to head back. The girls are given orders to go straight back home and put on the tea. They gallop off as we stroll back to the house. The fog lifts and Ireland's green rolling fields unfold below us.

Tea, ice cream, cakes, and cookies all made from scratch, are spread out

Katie and her father in his classic car.

on the homemade kitchen table that was made-to-measure for the family. Although Katie and Jessica are the only siblings living at home at the moment, they have several older brothers and sisters with nicknames like Bear, Tango, Tissie, and Eki, who are never away from home for too long.

Because it is Sunday afternoon, Katie has to start preparing her things for school. The following day, she will return to Dublin, where she attends boarding school during the week. Katie sets up the ironing board in the kitchen and starts pressing her school clothes. She does this entirely on her own, without any prompting from her father. It seems there may be a bit of the army captain in Katie as well!

SCHOOL DAYS

Katie's new school in Dublin has over 700 students, both boys and girls, who come from all over the world. Most of the students live at the school like Katie, although there are only 22 border girls out of 115 students in Katie's year. The rest are boys. No wonder she and her friends talk so much about boys. They are surrounded by them! The girls all go to breakfast together after roll call at 7:45 each morning. After breakfast, they tidy their dorm and then head to chapel for a short reading or to sing hymns.

Katie has eight classes on most days, but only five classes on Wednesday and Saturday (she has school on Saturdays). Katie studies Irish, English, German, History, Geography, Science, Mathematics, Music, and she just started Spanish. Geography is her favorite class, and Irish is her easiest class since she studied at Ring, an Irish-speaking boarding school. Katie has little free time during the week because of all of her sports: Camogie and basketball practice twice a week, and games in each of these sports twice a week! She is starving by dinner time at 6:00 p.m., and joins the stampede to the dining hall.

From 7:00 until 9:00 in the evening, it is homework time, after which the boys and girls head to the social area for gossip. Katie has friends from all corners of Ireland.

The day is meant to end at 10:30 p.m., but the kids rarely quiet down until 11:30 p.m. (although they don't want to get caught making noise after lights out or it is early morning punishment!)

The kids wear school uniforms—a white shirt, necktie, dark blue V-neck sweater with the school emblem, and dark blue slacks. It is all very regimented at Katie's school, but there is also a lot of fun and adventure.

Katie in her school uniform.

Gaeltachts

Although this is Katie's first year of boarding school in Dublin, she has been a boarder before. Last year, she had a uniquely Irish experience at a boarding school called Ring in Country Waterford. Ring is a Gaeltacht, where Irish, rather than English, is the primary language. Many children gather from different corners of Ireland to spend some portion of their schooling in a Gaeltacht, in order to perfect their Irish and learn more about Irish culture and traditions. While English is the language most widely spoken in Ireland, Irish (or Gaelic) is actually Ireland's first language, according to the Irish Constitution. It is a melodic Celtic language similar to Scottish and Welsh, and not at all like English.

My Best Day

I was in Ring, an Irish-speaking boarding school. In Ireland there are only a few areas left where Irish is spoken all the time. In Ring, everything is done in Irish—sports, classes, meals, and even talking at nighttime in the dormitories. You only go there for one year; the last year of primary school. I wish I could go back there for one more year and especially wish I could live this day again.

It was three days before the end of the school year and a water fight was organized by some of the leaders in Ring. After school, everyone got into their swimming togs [bathing suits] and a T-shirt and, in my case, a pair of flip-flops. We all went out to the lawn in front of the school. There was a huge area, about the size of a tennis court covered in black plastic. All the leaders were pouring suds and water on to the plastic so that it would be really slippery. Every-one ran down and sat on the grass behind the plastic. There were four blue barrels (two at either end) full of water and loads of sponges.

Two teams stood at either end of the plastic and when the whistle was blown everyone grabbed a sponge (dripping wet) and ran onto the plastic and fired the sponge at some-one. Then ran back and grabbed another. While everyone was slipping and sliding and getting soaked, Olivia, the head leader, had

County Kerry in Ireland.

the fire hose out and was spraying us all.

When a whistle was blown, we were supposed to stop, but everyone kept going. It was blown about five times before we all actually stopped. Then everyone claimed their team had won, but really there is no winning, and it is all just fun! It all went round in circles so that everyone got at least three turns. At the end, we had to sit down while the manager picked ten boys and ten girls for a mixed run to end it all up. I was in that and it was great fun. Even though the weather in Ireland is not hot and we were all dripping wet with cold water, we weren't cold because we were having so much fun and moving around an awful lot.

Afterwards we all went inside dripping wet and went for showers. But there was a huge line, so my two best friends, Georgia and Rachel, and I went downstairs and ran through the college church and found some gorgeous showers that were really hot and nice.

That was the best fun I have ever had—that day in Ring—and I still remember every detail of it. It is different from a normal day because the whole school participated and the school is normally strict and sensible and would never do an outrageous thing like having a water fight.

If that had been a normal day, I would have been playing volleyball with just the girls on my team and another team. It was great fun because it is a memory of my last few days with my friends, most of whom I shall never see again.

If I Could Be...

I would like to go to outer space very much. I wouldn't like to be elected the leader of my country, to become a pop star, or to win a gold medal at the Olympics because I would rather not be famous. I don't think that I could handle the attention and I value my privacy a lot.

I would like to go to space because I am very interested in animals and I would like to see if there is any life there. People always say different things like there are such things as aliens or there aren't and I would like to see for myself.

Space is so huge and we only live in a tiny piece of it, and so it would be great to explore it. There could be new worlds with woods and seas for all I know. The sea on our earth itself is a totally different

A boy in Hurling gear.

"The sea on our earth itself is a totally different world within our world with mammals and fish and different, beautifully colored plants and corals."

world within our world with mammals and fish and different, beautifully colored plants and corals. There are also lovely assorted kinds of shellfish. I spend a lot of my summer holidays in Galway, on the west coast of Ireland, snorkeling and exploring the sea. I imagine that visiting outer space would be a little bit like snorkeling because you float automatically in the sea and I would love the similar floating sensation in space. Imagine the feeling of being lighter than air! While snorkeling

you have to breathe a different way (through a pipe called a snorkel, which goes from your mouth back to the surface of the water) and you have to learn to trust it. In space you have to breathe by using special equipment too.

I can't imagine the build up of excitement as I would strap myself in and hear the countdown to take-off. I think that it would be really exciting to wear different clothes and eat preserved food, like dried strawberries! I would have to live in a totally different way to what I am used to. I really can't imagine sleeping in space. I would just be too excited to go anywhere near sleeping.

I really have no idea about what I might find if I went to outer space, but I have a vision of finding a really amazing new plant. It might be 12 feet tall with purple stalks and leaves. The plant I envision moves around of its own accord. It flowers once a week. The flower is about the size of a grapefruit and orange and yellow in color. The flower devours rocks by the dozen and after about two hours it withers and dies until the next week.

I could find something totally different or maybe nothing at all, who knows? I can't find out until I go there.

CAMOGIE

Katie's favorite sport, Camogie, is uniquely Irish. Similar to field hockey, it is played exclusively by girls. Boys play a similar game called "Hurling." The object of Camogie is to get the ball through the opponent's goal posts using a stick similar to a hockey stick called a camàn (pronounced roughly, "come on"), and a ball called a sliotar (pronounced "shlitter"). The sliotar is about the size of a tennis ball, but it is solid and made of leather. The girls pass the sliotar from player to player by hitting it along the ground or overhead with the camàn. The game is played on a grass field and goals are scored by passing the ball below the horizontal bar between the posts (3 points) or over the horizontal bar (1 point).

IRISH DANCING

Irish dancing, one of Katie's hobbies, was featured in the popular Broadway shows Riverdance and Lord of the Dance. This style of dance is learned by almost every Irish person, both girls and boys. Each dance tells a story, either historical or mythological, and is danced in groups. The dances are characterized by quick foot movements, which tap out a drum-like rhythm on the dance-floor, while the dancers' arms and upper bodies remain stiff, except when used to further the story.

Courtesy Abhann Productions Limited

A Riverdance show poster.

There are different levels of dancers: Novice, Primary, Intermediate, and Open. The dancer must complete certain requirements to advance to the next level, such as performing well at the Feis competitions, where children, teenagers, and adults can all compete for titles and prizes.

The costumes of the Irish dancers reflect the country's history, copying the ancient styles of traditional peasant dress worn hundreds of years ago. Today, each of the different dance schools uses its own distinctive costumes. They are brightly colored and adorned with hand-embroidered Celtic designs based on the Book of Kells [a beautifully illustrated text from the year 800 AD, which includes four of the Christian Gospels]. The interlocking lines, which follow the pattern of Celtic-knotted crosses, represent the continuity of life, and other special symbols on the costumes are used to celebrate local folklore, religion, and cultural history.

A girl in her Irish step-dancing dress.

Katie's father, Katie, and her dog.

Did You Know?

- The Republic of Ireland ("Ireland") gained its independence from the United Kingdom in 1922 after 700 years of British rule.

- Northern Ireland is still part of the United Kingdom. For decades, it has been the setting of bitter dispute between Irish Republicans (who want Northern Ireland to join Ireland) and Unionists (who want to remain part of Britain).

Irish Flag

- Ireland has produced many of the world's greatest modern writers, including James Joyce, William Butler Yeats, Samuel Beckett, and Oscar Wilde. Several Irish writers are also Nobel Prize recipients, the most recent example being poet Seamus Heaney.

Irish Currency: The Euro

- Katie's family belongs to the Church of Ireland, which is a Protestant denomination. Today about 95 percent of the population in Ireland are Catholic, but people live peacefully without religious discrimination, and many Irish towns have both Catholic and Protestant churches. However, in Northern Ireland, (where about 50 percent of the population are Protestant) political and religious tensions have created separate religious communities between Catholic and Protestant worshippers.

- In 1973, the Republic of Ireland joined the European Union, a confederation of European countries, including countries such as the United Kingdom, Denmark, Poland, Czech Republic, Slovakia, and many more. Currently, there are more than 20 member countries in the European Union. Among these countries, several (Ireland included) have replaced their national currencies with the Euro.

- Referred to as the "Celtic Tiger," Ireland's economy is one of the world's fastest growing economies. The workforce in Ireland is young and well educated, and have succeeded in pushing the country to the forefront of the high technology industry. For example, Ireland is one of the leading exporters of software technology, which is a considerable change for a country that was once solely dependent on agriculture.

- The United Kingdom, Denmark, and Norway are the only countries in Europe that do not use the Euro.

Some words in Irish
Hello = Dia dhuit
Yes = Sea, tá
No = Ní hea, nil

Thank you = Go raibh maith agat
Goodbye = Slán agat/slán leat
Friend = Cara
Many welcomes = Céad míle fáilte

A castle in the Irish countryside.

Ireland

Atlantic Ocean

Where Katie goes to school

Irish Sea

Dublin

County Wicklow

Katie's hometown

Camille Lillebonne, France

Camille Marie ("Camille")

Nationality: French

Religion: Catholic

Languages: French, and I am studying English and German in school.

Brothers and Sisters: One sister and brother

Pets: None

Hobbies: Reading; listening to music; playing cards; and talking with my friends

Talents: I don't have any particular talents, but I love playing tennis.

Favorite Sport: Tennis and skiing

Favorite Books: The *Harry Potter* books by J.K. Rowling; *Willie Wonka and the Chocolate Factory* by Roald Dahl; *Bridget Jones' Diary* by Helen Fielding;

and a French book called *120 Minutes Pour Mourir* (*120 Minutes to Die*) by Michel Amelin

Favorite Food: A good chocolate cake

Least Favorite Food: Tongue

Camille with her tennis racket, her favorite possession.

Whom do you admire most ? Garou [French pop singer]

Favorite Possession: My tennis racket

Do you help with chores at home? Yes

Do you have your own telephone or computer? No

Do you use the Internet? Just for e-mail

Where would you most want to travel? To the Caribbean and to America

What comes to mind when you think of the United States? Bigness and obesity. (This is because I think about hamburgers and then fat people in America. I know that not all Americans are fat, but that is what I think of, as well as big skyscrapers and big cities like New York.) Also, I think of the White House and political power.

...and France? The Eiffel Tower

...and China? Rice

...and Kenya? Photo safaris and animals

What do you talk about with friends? We talk about our daily lives.

What do you want to know about other girls your age? What they do in their spare time

Camille's copy of Charlie and the Chocolate Factory in French.

About Me

translated from French

Camille with her family at home.

My life is not unusual in any particular way. I just have the life of a completely normal French girl. I was born in Sainte Addresse next to Le Havre, and when I was one year old, my family moved to Lillebonne— a small village of 10,000 people, located in Normandy about 2 hours from Paris, 45 minutes from Rouen, and just 30 minutes from Le Havre.

When I was two years old, I started kindergarten, but when I was three, I changed schools in order to attend one that was closer to our home and the pharmacy that my parents own. Oh yes! I forgot to mention that both of my parents are pharmacists. Coming back to my kindergarten, this is where I first met my best friends Justine, Anne-Sophie, Valentin, Timothée, and Clément.

Now I am 13 and am in the fourth year of collège [junior high school]. I have kept all of the same friends from kindergarten, but have also met others. And, my friend Valentin left this year for Louisiana in the United States. He has moved there for three years because his father is working there. We were (and still are) all very sad that he has moved. We had a huge going-away party for Valentin. There were 20 of us in the living room of my house. The theme for the boys was "Men in Black" and for the girls: mini-skirts and high heels!

I love playing tennis. Tennis is my favorite sport. I play about two hours a week and have even been in some regional tournaments. I also take one hour of modern dance a week and, until I had my Confirmation, I also studied one hour of Catechism each week.

I love my life with its ups and downs. And I adore my friends and family. But, there are many things left for me to do and experience, and lots and lots of time to live my life and many things to learn because at 13 one has learned very little about life.

Camille lives just two hours from Paris, home of the Eiffel Tower and the Arche de Triomphe.

Camille's Favorite Chocolate Cake:

(for 6 people)

200 grams (7 oz.) of chocolate

50 grams (¼ cup) of butter

4 eggs

400 grams (1 ¾ cups) of sugar

75 grams (⅔ cup) of flour

15-18 grams (1 tbs.) of milk

Melt 200 grams of chocolate in a little milk. Add 50 grams of butter and let cool. Beat 4 eggs and 400 grams of sugar. Add the chocolate mixture and 75 grams of flour. Cook for 30 minutes at low heat. (Approximately 150 °C)

Meeting Camille by Starla

Camille and her older sister, Benedicte, are standing outside to welcome me as I arrive at their home in Lillebonne, in the northern region of France called Normandy. Camille is wearing flared jeans, a maroon top, and chunky sports shoes. Her brown bobbed hair is parted in the middle and she bears a striking resemblance to a famous French movie actress, who stars in a hit French movie called *Amélie*. In fact, Camille looks typically French, both chic and natural with a certain *je ne sais quoi* style that only French people seem to have.

AUDREY TAUTOU   MATHIEU KASSOVITZ

Courtesy of Miramax Films

Le Fabuleux Destin d'*Amélie* Poulain

Un film de JEAN-PIERRE JEUNET

Movie poster featuring Audrey Tautou as Amélie Poulain.

I am with Camille's aunt, uncle, and cousin, and we have arrived for Sunday lunch. As Camille and Benedicte help their mother prepare the table, I try to nudge Camille into overcoming her modesty and admitting that she does have a talent. Not dancing? Not singing? Not tennis? Finally I ask Camille's mother to tell me what Camille's talent is. She immediately responds *la gaiété*, which means "being happy." That is the best introduction to Camille.

Camille is 13 years old and the youngest of three children. Benedicte and her brother Marc both live away from home now that they are in university, so Camille shares her home with her parents, Valentine and Philippe. Their house sits in the middle of a large green lawn that is abloom with flowering trees and bushes. Their town of Lillebonne is nestled between rolling green hills that are dotted with thatched, white cottages, and spotted cows. These cows produce the delicious dairy products for which Normandy is

known. The cool, wet air smells like the sea (we are very close to the Atlantic coast and to the English Channel, which separates England and France), and the gathering dark clouds threaten rain.

It is always a treat to be invited to Sunday lunch in France. We are having typically French foods, but mixing cuisines of Normandy and the Ardèche region of France, where Camille's mother is from. We start with a table full of seafood and *foie gras*. Then Camille's mother comes out of the kitchen with a steaming casserole containing Duck with Olives (*Canard aux olives*). This is followed by a cheese course, where we are presented with eight different varieties of cheese. Then we have dessert, an apple, pear, and raspberry crumble. The French take their food very seriously. During the cheese course and dessert, we look at family photo albums. There are pictures of Camille dressed up for a school performance, white-water rafting, swimming at the beach with her friends, and snowboarding on the snowy mountain.

Camille, her mother, and I take a stroll to Camille's school. It is now pouring rain, but there are plenty of raincoats and umbrellas to go around, as one would expect from a household in Normandy.

Camille on her snowboard.

SCHOOL DAYS

Camille attends a French public school just around the corner from her house. Classes start at 8:00 in the morning and last until 5:00 in the evening. The kids have eight classes every day and a whole hour for lunch. As Camille lives very close to the school, she usually walks home for lunch. Throughout the week, Camille takes French, Latin, English, German, History, Geography, Civics, Mathematics, Physics, Chemistry, Biology, Music, Art, and Gym class. In her Music class, Camille plays the flute and sings.

If I Could Be...

translated from French

I would most prefer to become a famous singer or actress, especially an actress (because I am not the greatest singer).

I would not want to explore the universe because one must feel really small relative to everything else when you are up in space. And then, when you think that you are more than a billion light-years away from your friends and family, far from everything, it must feel very lonely. I would not want to be elected the leader of my country because you must go into politics and I don't like politics at all. And, there would be so many things to do, I would never have time for myself.

I would love to win an Olympic gold medal because this is a great recognition of one's talents. But still, I would prefer to be a famous singer or actress because this has been my dream since I was little. This is the dream of all little girls. Young girls love to sing their favorite songs or dream of acting in films like their favorite actors and actresses.

It must be wonderful to be a role model for girls all over the world, to sign autographs, give concerts, be applauded by crowds, and, on top of that, to be well paid! It must also be wonderful to meet all of the other stars that you always wanted to meet.

But, it isn't all wonderful to be a star. There are also negative things like having people tell lies about you, and the paparazzi always searching for the latest "scoop," as they say. You can't take walks, or run errands in peace without people running after you for autographs and wanting to talk to you and things like that. But I assume you become accustomed to this.

But now I would like to ask a question to you who are reading this book: In your country do you feel the same way I do?

Did You Know?

- France is the oldest nation in Europe, founded in the 5th century. Paris is the capital, and French is the official language.

- Similar in size to the US state of Texas, France is the largest country in Europe.

- In France, people greet one another by kissing on the cheek, rather than shaking hands. This ritual, called *faire les bises*, can cause some confusion if you are not used to it. First, which cheek to present? There is no rule, but it is most commonly the right cheek first. Next, how many times to kiss? In Paris, one kiss on both sides is the norm. Outside of Paris, it is harder to judge with three to four kisses not uncommon. It is best to just keep your eyes open and let your French hosts be the guides.

French Flag

French Currency: The Euro

Normandy, France.

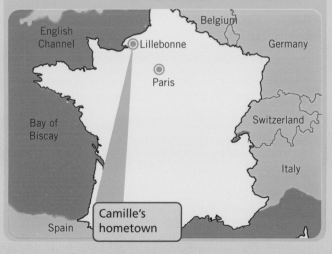

France

English Channel
Belgium
Germany
Lillebonne
Paris
Bay of Biscay
Switzerland
Italy
Spain
Camille's hometown

Some words in French

Yes = Oui
No = Non
Thank you = Merci

Hello = Bonjour
Goodbye = Au revoir, Adieu
Good morning = Bonjour
Good night = Bonne nuit

Franzi Kiel, Germany

Franziska Zoe ("Franzi")

Nationality: German

Religion: Christian

Languages: German, English, a little bit of French, and I am just starting to study Spanish in school this year.

Brothers and Sisters: One little brother

Hobbies: Dancing; singing; drama; reading; listening to music; playing tennis; drawing; and designing clothes, especially dresses.

Talents: Dancing

Favorite Sport: Dancing; tennis; and skiing

Favorite Books: Abby Lynn by Rainer M. Schroder; Tell Me I'm O.K., Really by Rosie Rushton; and Witchchild by Celia Rees

Favorite Food: Salads

Least Favorite Food: Brussels sprouts

Whom do you most admire? Some great dancers

Favorite Possession: A tattered pincushion named "Junior"

Do you help with chores at home? Sometimes in the garden (but I don't really love it!). I also tidy up my room but I think that is not very special.

Do you have your own telephone or computer? No

Do you use the Internet? Yes

Where would you most want to travel? Around the world to see different countries with different traditions

What comes to mind when you think of the United States? The Statue of Liberty and people from different countries

…and France? The holiday some years ago with my family in Bretagne; baguettes; and the Eiffel Tower

…and China? People who can smile even if they are angry

…and Kenya? Our last school project was about the Mau Mau rebellion.

What do you talk about with friends? School

What do you want to know about other girls your age? Their countries and traditions; hobbies; family; school; personality; favorite books; songs; food; etc…

Franzi's pincushion, "Junior!"

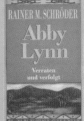

Franzi's favorite books: Abby Lynn; Witchchild; Tell Me I'm O.K., Really.

Franzi's dress designs.

If I Could Be...

translated from German

I would like to be a famous dancer and dance in musicals. Obviously, I would first have to finish school. But during the time at school, I would participate in dance contests. But fortunately, school does not last forever so after my graduation, I could go to Australia and get my training in different dancing styles at dance schools there: ballet, tap-dance, and modern dance. On top of that, I would probably have to take some acting classes. Once I had finished all my training, I would apply for different parts in musicals and I would have to try out for them during the castings. Maybe I would even get a part in my favorite musical: Cats! It would only be practice, practice, and practice! I would tour through Europe, America, Australia, China, and many other countries.

Franzi performing at the Kieler Woche.

But, at some point, I would suddenly get the idea to not only dance, but to also prepare a choreography. It would be great to come up with a choreography for a musical. I would probably try everything to make this idea come true. For days, I would do nothing but think of step combinations for dances; I would spend my nights writing down my ideas. At the end, I would have to, together with the director and the musical director, cast the dancers and singers. I would not only judge them by their skills, but also by their personality and their aura. To be able to express feelings, the aura is very important for a dancer.

After all parts had been given out, I would immediately start with the rehearsals. I would have to teach the dancers my choreography, and if they had suggestions on how to improve it, I would be ready to incorporate those ideas in the choreography. The musical would have to be a complete success. And again, I would tour through different countries, but this time as a choreographer, not a dancer.

Then suddenly the thought would appear inside my head to become a teacher at dance schools. It had been so much fun to teach other people my choreography and my ideas, so why should I then not be able to become a good teacher? I would first need some training myself, training to teach. So I would go to school again, this time to become a teacher in the fields of modern dance and

> "I would go to America, to a city by the sea where I would build my own dance school."

About Kiel

by Franzi, translated from German

Kiel is the capital of the state of Schleswig-Holstein and is located at the Baltic Sea, way up in Northern Germany. Once a year, there is the Kieler Woche. That is the biggest sailing show in the world. Gigantic ships drive through the Nord-Ostsee Kanal (a canal that links the North Sea and the Baltic Sea). Down by the sea, they put up sausage booths, and every evening, radio stations organize concerts. If you are lucky, you will even have nice weather.

Franzi (second from the left) and her family.

ballet. Afterwards, I would have to apply for a position as a teacher at different dance schools. There I would then teach young dancers. Later, I would get the training to become a teacher for tap-dance and acting, and then I would be allowed to teach in the four fields in which I had graduated myself.

But since I do not run out of ideas regarding dancing so easily, I would at some point decide to open my own dance school. This time, I would go to America, to a city by the sea, where I would slowly start to build my own dance school. First, it would be very small. I would only have a few teachers, a few piano-players, and very few students. But we would all make a great effort and give very good classes in the different dancing styles, acting, and singing. Little by little, I would even open up a little department for acrobatics. My students would get parts in musicals and more and more teachers would apply to teach at my school. The school would keep growing and would become famous. I would give classes in acting, ballet, tap-dance, and modern dance until I would be too old to dance. Then I would first turn back to the choreographies, and later, I would pass on the direction of my school to someone else. Finally, I would travel around the world to see my former students in their parts at the theater. I would also write my autobiography, which I would at some point publish as a book with photos from the time of my training.

To be a dancer would really be a great job for me. I need dancing like food and drink!

Meeting Franzi
by Starla

When I meet Franzi, she is dashing about gathering her costume for an afternoon dance recital...time is running out. She decides to ride her bicycle to the outdoor stage so as not to be late. This will be the second time that Franzi's dance troupe will perform at the Kieler Woche festival this year. A few days ago, they were the main attraction at the port's center stage. Kieler Woche is a big festival that features a boat race between the world's largest and most beautiful Tall Ships. All of Kiel is celebrating, and crowds of tourists are in town.

Franzi's mother and I soon leave to stake out our positions in front of the stage. The sun is shining although it is still chilly for June. People gather as a TV crew sets up and sound technicians test the volume of the music. The program begins with Franzi's group called The Trolls, who are modern dancers that combine hip-hop moves and jazz steps. The girls are all wearing matching outfits: beige-colored, suede-looking tops, snakeskin-patterned pants, black scarves around their waists, and black dancing shoes. They all have long hair that is pulled off their faces in French-braids. They perform three different dances to popular music and receive huge cheers.

After the show, we walk together along the harbor along with thousands of other people. There are so many activities going on around us it is hard to keep track: singers and dancers performing on the stages, bungee jumpers falling from cranes over the water, snowboarders maneuvering down a temporary ski-jump (complete with real snow), bicyclists on

Franzi needs dancing like food and drink!

tightropes, and food-stands galore. Franzi is hungry after her performance, so we all buy warm crepes and walk back to Franzi's home.

Much of Kiel's center, which was rebuilt after World War II, is very modern. In comparison, Franzi's house looks old and majestic, and of all its rooms, Franzi's is the loveliest as it opens onto a large deck overlooking the back garden. Franzi's bedroom is decorated with a plethora of knickknacks, postcards, photographs, seashells, figurines, small picture frames, books, and memorabilia neatly arranged on the dresser and shelves. Her mother tells me that the thought of this bedroom made the family's last move a little easier for Franzi (She has moved four times already). Now, in Kiel for nearly three years, Franzi seems to have settled in well. She is very active with her dance troupe and also recently started taking singing lessons with her best friend, Noushin.

SCHOOL DAYS

Franzi's school is nestled in a wooded area not far from er home. She leaves for school on her bicycle every morning at 7:20 and meets up with her friend, Nora, to ride to school together. Classes start at 7:55 and end at 1:05 or 1:55 depending on the day of the week.

In Germany, children have 13 years of compulsory education, so Franzi is gearing up for her final 4 years. This year, she is studying 11 subjects: English, French, Spanish, German, Mathematics, Physics, Chemistry, Biology, Geography, Gym, and Music. In two years, Franzi will also learn Latin. Her favorite subjects are English, Spanish, Chemistry, and Geography. She has between one and two hours of homework in the evenings.

After classes, Franzi and her friend, Nora, jump back onto their bicycles and ride back home for lunch. School in Germany is only for academics; there are no school-sponsored sports clubs or interest clubs to keep the kids after school. However, Franzi's school does double as Kiel's Music School, where Franzi takes singing and jazz dancing lessons. So, she gets back on her bicycle to return to school for these activities in the afternoons, Monday through Wednesday. She has also begun ballet again and has lessons at the local opera house once a week.

Did You Know?

- Germany was first a large kingdom that grew out of the Frankish Kingdom (now France), then a collection of many small states or duchies until the late 1800s. Otto von Bizmark, the Chancellor of Prussia, unified Germany in 1871.

German Flag

- After World War II, Germany split into two countries, West Germany and East Germany. The latter was brought under Soviet influence. Germany was still two countries when Franzi was born, and reunited after the fall of the Berlin Wall, which had separated East from West for more than two decades.

- Germany is a founding member of the European Union, which is made up of several countries in Europe. One of its main objectives is to achieve greater stability and strength through cooperation among its member states.

German Currency: The Euro

Some words in German
Hello = 'allo
Goodbye = Auf Wiedersehen
Yes = Ja
No = Nein
How are you? = Wie geht's?
Good morning = Guten Morgen
Good night = Gute Nacht

A view of Kiel.

Germany

North Sea
Kiel
Berlin
Netherlands
Belgium
Poland
Czech Republic
France
Austria

Franzi's home city

Karoliina Hollola, Finland

Laura Karoliina ("Karoliina")

Nationality: Finnish

Religion: Lutheran

Languages: Finnish, and I am studying English and Swedish at school.

Brothers and Sisters: I have two brothers, Miika and Ville.

Pets: None

Hobbies: Basketball; fishing; and reading

Talents: Acting and writing stories

Favorite Sport: Basketball

Favorite Books: Harry Potter and The Prisoner of Azkaban by J.K. Rowling; The Two Shall Meet by Marilyn Kaye; and The Diamond Throne by David Eddings

Favorite Food: Pizza

Least Favorite Food: Liver

Whom do you most admire? Princess Diana

Favorite Possession: My pillow

Do you help with chores at home? Yes, emptying the dishwasher and cleaning my room

Do you have your own telephone or computer? I have my own cell phone and I share a computer with my brothers.

Do you use the Internet? Yes

Where would you most want to travel? Australia

What comes to mind when you think of the United States? New York and cactuses along desert highways

...and France? Paris and the Eiffel Tower

...and China? Panda bears and an industrialized country

...and Kenya? Savannah

What do you talk about with friends? Boys

What do you want to know about other girls your age? About their lives; how and where they live; what kind of families they have; what are their hobbies; and do they have pets

One of Karoliina's favorite books.

Karoliina's brother and father in the computer room.

About Me
translated from Finnish

My name is Laura Karoliina, but I go by Karoliina. My family is made up of my mother, Sirpa, my father, Kaarlo, and my two older brothers, Miika and Ville. I am the youngest child in my family. My mother is a kindergarten teacher and works at a school near our home. My father is a marketing manager at Stala [an appliance corporation in Finland].

We live in Hollola, which has 20,000 people. Hollola is a neighboring town of Lahti, which is known for the

Nordic Ski World Championships and cross-country skiing. We live in a residential area in a yellow brick house. We have a sauna in our house, like in nearly all Finnish homes. I have my own room that was recently wallpapered. I like my room a lot. I spend a lot of time there when I'm alone. Sometimes I read books there for several hours at a time.

My hobbies include basketball, fishing, and reading. I have been playing basketball for about five years and I attend basketball practice four times a week. My basketball team is really great. Every player on our team has a personality of her own, and without even one of them, there would be something lacking from the team. In addition to playing basketball, our team spends a lot of time together. We have game nights when we play board games and talk.

My father taught me to fish, but my oldest brother also taught me some good tricks for catching fish. My favorite places to fish are a lake near my aunt's summer cottage and also a lake near my home.

I read a lot of fantasy and fiction books. Every few weeks, I go to the library to borrow new books.

The names of my best friends are Hanna, Kristiina, Isa, and Pauliina. They are really nice and we do all kinds of fun things together. In my free time, I go out with my friends or play with the computer, read books, and watch TV. I also go to the movies and camps with my friends. My last two camps were a horse-riding camp and an exercise camp.

The most important things in my life are home, family, health, and friends. I would like to succeed at school so that I can get a good job and be successful.

SCHOOL DAYS

I go to school in Lahti at the Kivimaa Upper-Level Comprehensive School. The distance to Kivimaa School from home is ten kilometers. I go there by bus. My class is Mathematics-oriented and there are 18 students in the class—6 girls and 12 boys. I have been studying English for four years and I will begin to study Swedish this year. At school, my favorite subjects are Mathematics, Finnish, and Home Economics.

The ski jump at Lahti.

WOMEN IN GOVERNMENT

In Finland, the government pays for daycare, and many children spend their days and nights (if necessary) in the centers while both of their parents work. Historically, women in Finland, like in much of northern Europe, have played an important role in society and government. Magnificent daycare centers are an example of the strong female influence in the country where women were first granted the right to hold elected office and vote in 1906, twelve years before English women and 14 years before American women. Since then, Finnish women have remained actively engaged in politics. Today, the president of Finland is a woman! It is not surprising that Karoliina's dream is to one day lead her country. In Finland, her dream just may come true.

The daycare where Karoliina's mother works.

Meeting Karoliina

by Starla

Karoliina lives farther north than any other girl in this book in a land called Suomi. That is Finland to you and me. Karoliina lives near the city of Lahti, which is just north of Finland's capital, Helsinki. Here, the sun barely sets in the summertime. Tall pine trees reflect in the clear, blue lakes, and the summer evenings grow warmer and warmer thanks to the ever-present sunlight. Winter is a different story, however. Sunlight is scarce and, boy, does it get cold. To beat the cold, the Finns invented saunas. As Karoliina said, nearly all Finnish households, including Karoliina's family, have saunas in their homes!

When I arrive in Lahti, Karoliina's father collects me at the bus station and gives me a quick tour of the town (stopping at one of Lahti's main tourist attractions, the ski jumps where the Nordic Ski Championships are held). It is a glorious, sunny day and we go to pick Karoliina up at school. We have been given strict instructions not to do anything that might embarrass her, like enter the school! But, of course we can't help ourselves and stealthily slip through the front doors. Classes are in session, so the colorfully decorated halls are quiet. Then, ten minutes before the school bell rings, Karoliina appears. She is tall, slim, and athletic, with light blond hair, blue eyes, and a peachy complexion. Dressed in flared jeans, a blue T-shirt, and sports jacket, she smiles at us. Some of her friends had seen us lurking around and tipped her off. Luckily, she doesn't mind.

With Karoliina, we continue our tour of the area with a stop at Sibelius Hall [named after the famous Finnish composer, Jean Sibelius]. Next, we visit the local library, which is packed with people. Finland has more public libraries—and people borrowing books from those libraries—than anywhere else in the world. In the children's section of the library, there are children's books in multiple foreign languages. There are also computers available for eight to twelve year olds, and I see that several children are logged onto the Internet. In fact, Finns are the most "connected" people in the world in terms of per person use of the

Internet and cellular phones. They certainly start early. Karoliina is already an expert with computers and computer games, and you should see how fast she types an SMS on her cell phone.

My great day with Karoliina.

Karoliina's yellow brick house is surrounded by a vast green lawn. It is located in a cul-de-sac, where her father has put up a basketball hoop so that Karoliina can practice. When Karoliina is not in school, her free time is devoted to her basketball team. Like in many other European countries, Karoliina's basketball team is not sponsored by her school, but is part of a community center, and the girls' families are very active in supporting the costs of the team. The girls themselves also host fundraising events to collect money for their tournaments around the country. Of course, it is always fun! Recently, Karoliina's team wrapped Christmas presents and sold cookies to raise money. All for a good cause!

My great day with Karoliina concludes with a spectacular outdoor dinner on the family's back terrace. Although, technically speaking, it is "evening," the sun shines like midday as we sit down to eat. We have Finnish meatballs cooked on the grill, potato casserole, and salad, accompanied by a special Finnish rye bread. During the dinner, no one speaks and I maintain a running dialogue to fill the awkward silence until coffee is served and the conversation resumes. I learn later that in Finland, it is not polite to talk while eating! The sun barely moves so we don't notice the passing time until I nearly miss my bus back to Helsinki.

Finland's capital, Helsinki, is the chief seaport and the largest city in the country.

If I Could Be...

translated from Finnish

I would like to be the leader of my country; in Finland, that would be the president. I could decide on matters concerning my country and could try to improve living conditions in Finland. Also, I could visit other countries on official visits. I would reconsider Finland's membership in the European Union. Finland would then be free to independently decide its own matters.

Finland is losing almost all of its independence, and, among other things, its money now that the Euro has replaced it. In a hundred years it might be that there are only six countries in the world where the six continents are and they will all have the same language and they'll fight wars or compete with each other.

I think foreigners should be able to come to Finland, but they should be given work permits right away. They should also learn the Finnish language.

There are also not enough skilled teachers in Finland probably because teachers' salaries are so low. I would raise teachers' salaries so that young people would also become interested in the teaching profession.

I would forbid cigarette smoking in public places, parks, and streets. Anyone over 16 years old could smoke, but tobacco products would still not be sold to those younger than 18. Those under 16 would be fined for smoking.

I would also develop the smaller towns so that everything would not be centered in the metropolitan areas. Small towns would have just as many opportunities for development. For example, all decision-makers are focused on large Southern cities. Finland has more beautiful places than just Helsinki. The Finnish Lake District has magnificent scenery and Lapland has gorgeous hills.

Santa Claus

Santa Claus is probably the most well-known Finn. He is said to live with his wife and their dozens of little helpers on the top of a mountain called Korvatunturi far North in Finnish Lapland.

Did You Know?

- Finland is bordered by Sweden, Norway, and Russia, and—across the Gulf of Finland—by Estonia.

- Helsinki is the capital city of Finland and both Finnish and Swedish are official languages in the country.

- Finland became an independent country in 1917. Before that, it was part of the Kingdom of Sweden (from the 13th century until 1809), and then part of imperial Russia from 1809 to 1917.

- Finland's land is mostly forest and lakes, where bears and elk roam. Reindeer make their home in Northern Lapland.

Finnish Flag

Finnish Currency: The Euro

Some words in Language
Hello = Hei
Goodbye = Näkemiin
Yes = Kyllä

No = Ei
Thank you = Kiitos
How are you? = Kuinka voit?
Friend = Ystävä

Finland

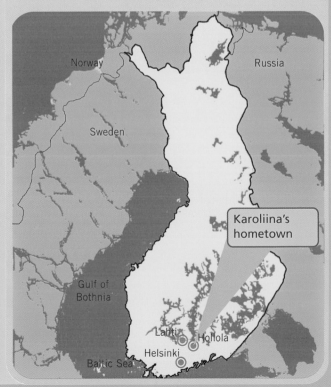

Norway

Russia

Sweden

Karoliina's hometown

Gulf of Bothnia

Lahti   Hollola

Helsinki

Baltic Sea

Karoline Nedre Eiker, Norway

Karoline Margrethe ("Karolina")

Nationality: My nationality is Norwegian.

Religion: Christian, but I have to say that I'm not sure if I believe in God. Sometimes I do and sometimes I don't.

Languages: My first language that I speak everyday is Norwegian. Besides Norwegian, I speak English.

Brothers and Sisters: I have an older sister Christina; a big brother, Alexander. Then there is me, Karoline Margrethe. After me is my little brother Kristoffer.

Pets: I have a rabbit. Her name is Sussi and she turned seven on Christmas Eve. She is brown and white. Then I have a cat named Dolly. She is four years old and all black and pretty.

Hobbies: I love dancing; nothing is better. Tuesday and Thursday, I dance ballet. Friday, I dance "street dance." It is a bit rough and we dance to pop music. I also spend time with my friends. When we are together, we talk and watch TV and have fun. In the summer, we go swimming. I also like to read, but not always.

Talents: My talents are dancing, handball, and track & field.

Favorite Sport: Track & field. I like to run and jump.

Favorite Books: My favorite books are The Diary of Anne Frank, Nancy Drew books, and Helen Keller. Anne Frank is a Jewish girl, who tells her true story during the war. Nancy Drew is exciting!

"Nancy Drew is exciting!"

You never know who the killer is! Helen Keller was a girl who was blind, but had a wonderful teacher, Anne Sullivan, who helped her a lot.

Favorite Food: Tacos. You put meat, cheese, salad, cucumber, or whatever you like on it, and put it in a taco shell and you eat it. Very good!

Least Favorite Food: Aspic, a gelée on fish, egg, or carrot. Maybe I'll like it when I am older.

Whom do you most admire? I am a big fan of twins, Ashley and Mary-Kate Olsen. I really admire them.

Favorite Possession: My bedroom is my favorite thing. It is yellow with white curtains. I feel good when I'm in my room. My other favorite thing is my ballet shoes.

Do you help with chores at home? Ever since I was little I loved to tidy up and clean. So, I clean when I want to and I do it voluntarily. But I don't really like to clean the kitchen or do the dishes.

Karoline prizes her ballet shoes!

Do you have your own telephone or computer? I don't have my own telephone, but I will soon get a cell phone. I don't have my own computer.

Do you use the Internet? We have the Internet at home so I use it a lot. I use it at school too.

Where would you most want to travel? USA, Spain, Brazil, Egypt, and Italy. My sister lived one year in Brazil, so it would be fun to see what that country is like.

What comes to mind when you think of the United States? California; San Francisco; and the Golden Gate Bridge

...and France? Paris and the Eiffel Tower

...and China? I think that they don't like to

Karoline with her pet rabbit, Sussi.

have girls, only boys.

...and Kenya? Lions and giraffes

What do you talk about with friends? We talk about everything. At the moment, we are talking about the Winter Prom and what we are going to wear. We often talk about teachers, other friends, our problems, and, of course, boys.

What would you most want to know about other girls your age? What I most want to know about other girls my age is maybe about their traditions.

My Best Day

This year the whole family went to a wedding in England. My mother's cousin Janecke from Norway, who lives in England, married a man from England named Gee.

We were there for six days and we had so much fun. We went to Brighton, where we went swimming in the English Channel. There were such big waves. In London, we used the Underground everyday. We stayed in Notting Hill and while we were staying there a carnival was taking place.

My grandparents went out in a sightseeing bus in London and really

Karoline's family.

enjoyed it. They liked the trip so much that they treated us to a trip on the sightseeing bus, too! Oooh, we saw everything: Big Ben, London Bridge, Tower Bridge, and Trafalgar Square. And then we took a boat trip on the River Thames. We had so much fun. We even went swimming in Hyde Park; it was so warm.

The wedding day was one of the best days in England. The day was so warm; it hadn't been that warm since 1934! We went to the Church and after that went to a hotel by the River Thames. This was in Richmond. We danced, ate, took a lot of pictures, and had fun. My family from my mother's side was there, too. Half of the party was from Norway and the other half was from England.

What I Most Want The World To Know

I would like the world to know that I am a girl who can believe in what I want, say what I want, and that I can have any opinions that I want. If I got married, I would have the same rights as my husband. I can get married with the one I want, and my parents will not make that decision. I am worth the same as boys are. Here, where I live, everybody has the same rights as me, whether you are a boy or a girl.

Meeting Karoline
by Starla

Oslo, the capital city of Norway, is preparing for a big celebration. It is the day before Norway's Constitution Day and the streets are closing on the parade route that runs through the city center. There is palpable excitement in the air as the Norwegians complete their last-minute shopping before the holiday. There is also a large number of young people (18 year olds?) running about the city dressed in either red or blue overalls, handing out business cards and generally acting silly. "What is going on?" I wonder as I board the train to Møjdalen, near Nedre Eiker, where Karoline lives.

Karoline is standing with her father next to their SUV as I step off the train. She is dressed in a turquoise-and-white striped sweater, blue jeans, and shoes with chunky soles. Quite tall for her age, Karoline has a cute, freckled face, and long, curly reddish-blond hair. She also wears braces, which she is quick to tell me she hates! She and her father speak English perfectly. Karoline also writes in English.

Karoline's house sits in a residential area surrounded by hills covered with fir trees. Inside the sunny home, Karoline's brothers and sisters appear one after another, first her brothers, Alexander and Robin, and then her sister, Christina. Much to my surprise, Christina appears wearing…the red overalls! Finally, I can get to the bottom of

Graduation Cards

this! Karoline explains that, not only is it the day before the Constitution Day, but it is graduation for Oslo's college students. The graduates in the college of liberal arts are all dressed in red, and those from the scientific college are dressed in blue.

They act silly (I knew that!) and hand out cards—not business cards, but graduation cards, which the children run around collecting. Karoline has been collecting these cards since she was little and has quite a stack.

Karoline has also been dancing since she was little—since the age of five, to be exact. She dances ballet on the tips of her toes (which, she admits, hurts a little bit), and does a kind of hip-hop dancing. She prefers ballet, even if her ballet teacher is very strict, because she gets to dress up in beautiful costumes. Not surprisingly, Karoline wants to be a dancer when she grows up, but not just any kind of dancer…a can-can dancer in Paris!

The Norwegian Constitution Day Parade.

In light of the celebrations in Norway, we are having a traditional Norwegian Constitution Day lunch at Karoline's home. The table is festively adorned with red-and-blue napkins and candles to match the Norwegian flag, and we are served a feast of cold and cured meats with sour cream, bread, and potato salad. We have lamb, ham, and reindeer! Reindeer meat, a delicacy here, and has a very nice taste. Sorry Rudolph!

SCHOOL DAYS

Karoline attends middle school for grades eight, nine, and ten at what is considered one of Norway's most beautiful schools. The children in Norway don't usually wear school uniforms, as is the case in Karoline's school.

School starts at 8:15 in the morning and ends at 1:45 in the afternoon. Karoline takes Norwegian, English, History, Sciences, Religious Instruction (where the children learn about all of the world's religions), Geography, Civics, and Gym. On Thursdays, there are three extra hours of language instruction in either English or German. At the end of each school day, the children can stay at the school until 3:30 to do their homework for the next day.

Bunad: Traditional Dress

A highlight of the Constitution Day celebration is that Norwegians all over the country wear their traditional dress.

When they are little, each Norwegian child gets their own special traditional dress, called bunad, the design of which is based on family traditions and where one's parents originated. Karoline is already busy thinking about the one that she will wear next spring.

The night before Constitution Day, Karoline's mother lays out the family's traditional clothes.

I was lucky enough to get to see Karoline in her bunad. As you can see, it is very colorful. Each component is symbolic, including the colors, the embroidery, the scarves, belts, and the matching silver jewelry. The spectacle of everyone dressed in these special clothes is quite impressive.

Karoline poses in a Norwegian forest wearing her traditional bunad.

Did You Know?

- Oslo is the capital city of the Kingdom of Norway and the official language is Norwegian. King Harald V and Queen Sonja are the Norwegian royals.

- In Norway, equality of men and women is a basic tenant of society. Women make up half of the Norwegian workforce.

- The Norwegians and Danes both share a Viking heritage. Norwegians are traditionally sea-faring people, and there have been many great Norwegian explorers. Leif Ericson, a Norwegian Viking sailor, is recognized as the first European to reach North America, approximately 500 years before Christopher Columbus, and Thor Heyerdahl made numerous ocean expeditions in reed boats, proving that there was sea travel between South America and Polynesia long before it was thought possible.

Norwegian Flag

Norwegian Currency

Some words in Norwegian	
Hello = Hallo	Thank you = Takk
Goodbye = Ha det	Good morning = God morgen
Yes = Ja	Good night = God kveld
No = Nei	How are you? = Hvordan står det til?
	Friend = Venn

Norway

Norwegian Sea

Sweden

Finland

Gulf of Bothnia

Oslo

Nedre Eiker

Karoline's hometown

Sara Sønderby, Denmark

Sara Aggerholm ("Sara")

Nationality: Danish

Religion: Our family is Protestant. We do not go to church or pray everyday, but I sometimes "talk" to God, asking him to do me a favor.

Languages: Danish; English; and a little German

Brothers and Sisters: I have a big sister Christel and a little brother Bjørn.

Pets: I have a big fat tomcat named Blackie, because he is completely black, except for his stomach and a tiny bit on his forelegs and the tip of his tail. I love him very much and would be very sad if he were to die.

Hobbies: I love to sing and I also read a lot.

Talents: I love to sing and people tell me that I am good at it. I am also good at school and get good grades.

Favorite Sport: I am not the sporty type, but if I am to watch, it would probably be handball.

Favorite Books: The *Harry Potter* books by J.K. Rowling; and two Danish books called (translated) *Children in the Dust* and *I Miss You, I Miss You*

Favorite Food: Pork cutlets in a dish

Least Favorite Food: Liver, no matter how prepared

Whom do you most admire? I admire my mother because she has her own opinions and she is not afraid to stand by them. She is strong-willed and not embarrassed to say what she wants.

Favorite Possession: My diary and my cat. I couldn't live without my diary. In there, I write all of my ups and downs and I get rid of my aggression. It is like having a boxing pillow for your feelings.

Do you help with chores at home? My sister and I used to have things like vacuuming and folding and putting away clothes. But now we must concentrate on our school subjects. Only my little brother and my parents who do things around the house (and my little brother does very little).

Do you have your own telephone or computer? Everyone in my family shares a computer.

Do you use the Internet? I use it for research for school projects, and to visit chat rooms and read comics online.

Where would you most want to travel? Greece

What comes to mind when you think of the United States? The television series "Beverly Hills 90210"

...and France? Monet and the Eiffel Tower

...and China? The Great Wall

...and Kenya? Giraffes

Sara with her cat, Blackie.

What do you talk about with friends? We talk about what parties, and things like that...everything between the earth and sky.

What do you want to know about other girls your age? Do they sometimes feel that everyone expects way too much from them; they expect you to get the best grades; always speak politely; earn your own money. I don't know how they expect so much from one person.

Really in Love

a creative essay by Sara, translated from Danish

In a little town, in a little house in the country lived a young girl with her family. They lived all together in more or less peace and tranquility. The girl kept up with her schoolwork and her friends and on the outside all seemed to be nice and neat and in order. But inside, inside the young girl felt something was wrong, very wrong.

Since she had had her first period about a half of a year ago everything seemed to have been turned upside down. New feelings and impressions came crashing down in a confusing manner. Her body had begun to change, her hips and breasts became bigger and awful, and unsightly pimples started to appear.

Changes also occurred in school. No longer was it the one who had the best and prettiest jump rope who was popular, but rather who was dressed in the latest fad, the most outrageous clothes. Everything happened way too fast and she couldn't keep up. Even her homework became more difficult and there was more of it.

And, while the girl could only look on, her friends began to change one by one. Her former best girlfriend became unbelievably self-centered and stuck up and after a while they were no longer best friends at all because all the girlfriend could talk about was herself. Whereas, the ones with whom she never socialized suddenly became her friends. Now they had something in common.

The girl had begun to write in a diary. For even though she trusted her friends one hundred percent, there was always something that she couldn't share with others. For example, a new boy had just started in their school. He was the hottest boy in school and almost all the girls had a crush on him, herself included. She felt as if she were going to faint each time she saw him pass by. She didn't know what to do.

One day there was a party. Then, there he was, practically next to her. She gathered all of her courage and, at last, went over to talk with him. After they had talked about absolutely everything, he leaned over and gave her a long passionate kiss. It wasn't the first time she had been kissed, but it was the first time she really felt anything. It was as if she disappeared into another world and she just wished that she could melt completely into him and just sit there forever. Now she knew what it meant to be in love, really in love.

> "Since she had had her first period... everything seemed to have been turned upside down."

Did You Know?

- Denmark has one of the most advanced social welfare systems in the world, and is known for its progressive and liberal politics. Danish people, friendly and open, are often called the Latins of Scandinavia. Copenhagen is the capital city, and Danish is the official language.

- Hans Christian Andersen, the author of children's fairy tales like The Ugly Duckling and The Emperor's New Clothes, was Danish.

- Denmark joined the European Union in 1973, but decided not to trade their currency, the Danish Krone, for the Euro.

Danish Flag

Denmark

Skaggerak

Sweden

Kattegat

Sara's hometown

North Sea

Sønderby

Copenhagen

Baltic Sea

Marta Florence, Italy

Marta Consuelo

Nationality: Italian

Religion: Catholic

Languages: Italian; English; and a little bit of French

Brothers and Sisters: I have an older sister named Francesca.

Pets: None

Hobbies: Reading and learning violin

Talents: Singing

Favorite Sport: Tennis

Favorite Books: The Changeling by Roger Zelazny; Harry Potter and the Chamber of Secrets by J.K. Rowling; and an Italian book called Andrea & Andrea by Domenica and Roberto Luciani

Favorite Food: Pizza

Least Favorite Food: Salad

Whom do you most admire? Politicians, because what they do is very difficult—trying to understand what people want and then translating that into facts

Favorite Possession: A small ring I wear on my toe

Do you help with chores at home? No

Do you have your own telephone or computer? No

Do you use the Internet? Yes. My favorite website is Virgilio.

Where would you most want to travel? To Ireland or Norway

What comes to mind when you think of the United States? Computers

...and France? Paris

...and China? Overpopulation

...and Kenya? Savannah

What do you talk about with friends? Books

What do you want to know about other girls your age? If they like reading

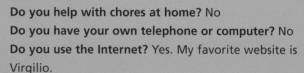

Marta's toe ring.

*Marta's copy of **Andrea & Andrea**.*

SCHOOL DAYS

In school, which runs from Monday to Saturday, Marta studies Italian, Geography, History, English, French, Art, Technology, Mathematics, Science, Music, and Gym. Among those subjects, her favorites are Art, Italian, English, History, and Mathematics.

My Best Day

translated from Italian

> "I felt kind of special to represent my family on this occasion."

My most beautiful day in the last two years was the anniversary party for the 100th birthday of my great-grandmother Consuelo. She was my father's grandmother. She was born on February 5, the same day as me, and therefore Consuelo is my second name.

I was in Bricherasio, a small town in the Piedmont region where my grandmother's family house is. I arrived in the train after a voyage of more than four hours. We had left really early in the morning together with my grandmother, Giulia, Mia, one of my father's cousins, and her daughter, Consuelo. Consuelo is my sister's age: turning 16 next year. During the trip, I talked, sang, and read. I also had lunch.

We arrived in Bricherasio the day before the party. It was the first time I had gone by myself. I felt kind of special to represent my family on this occasion. My mother had an exam the day after the party and, therefore, my mother and father stayed home. My sister Francesca did not want to go.

My grandmother's house is very big and old. Once it was a spinning mill. There is a huge garden that ends where the house of my great-grandmother, Consuelo, once lived and where my grandmother's brothers now live. It is a large villa with a beautiful garden.

From left to right: Marta's sister, mother, father, and Marta.

The morning of the party I woke up at 8:30, had breakfast, got dressed, and went to church by bicycle. The air was cold and so I was happy to arrive at church. My family members were there because we were celebrating mass for my great-grandmother. I'm not accustomed to going to church so I didn't pray during the mass. When mass ended, I took the bicycle and went back to the house. At the house, my aunt had meanwhile been preparing brunch. Just as I walked in, the pleasing warmth possessed me. I went to see how everything was being prepared and I was completely taken aback. It was amazing. The table was full of everything. Bacon, scrambled eggs, mozzarella, boiled eggs, tomatoes, cold cuts, honey and bread, and an infinity of delicious entrées. It was a picture-perfect brunch just like they describe in books.

Then I started eating. Meanwhile, my grandmother was taking photos to show the family in Florence. She was using a digital camera that she had bought during a recent trip to the United States, and of which she was very proud. If you wanted to, you could cancel the photos after taking them. The thing that struck me about the photos was that my granny managed to take photos of people in the strangest positions! In the meantime, other people were preparing pancakes.

After eating, Consuelo and I took photos of Federico, another of my father's cousins. Then we all went out into the garden and had Consuelo climb a tree so that we could take her photo. Next, Consuelo and Federico started jumping the hedges while I took photos.

The trip to the train station was fun, although nothing actually happened. Once at the station, we got the train. It was evening. I was happy to get home. As soon as we arrived, I fell asleep at my granny's house because it was midnight. This day was a very beautiful and important experience for me because I had never been part of a party that was so beautiful and so well organized.

Meeting Marta
by Starla

Marta in her room.

Marta is a lucky girl, in my opinion, for the simple fact that she lives in the beautiful Tuscan hill country outside of Florence, Italy. She lives in an authentic, old, sprawling, Italian colonial villa. No matter that she says it is a little uncomfortable because it is so old, or that she has to share a room—a messy one with posters of rock groups covering the walls— with her sister; there is nothing like a Tuscan villa.

On weekends, dressed in a mini-skirt or oversized jeans, and usually a black T-shirt, Marta goes into Florence with her friends. Florence is the home of Michelangelo's famous sculpture of David, the breathtaking Boboli Gardens, and the world-famous Duomo (an ornate cathedral) not to mention the Uffizi Gallery with it paintings by Botticelli. Marta and her friends bypass all of this and head to the local record stores to find the latest CDs, or better yet, classics by the Clash or Bruce Springsteen. Then, for cool, affordable

Marta's house in Florence.

clothes, they head to il mercato, Florence's fantastic outdoor market, all the while, talking away in their beautiful Italian.

Like many girls her age, Marta is one person with her friends: "very outgoing, funny, and a little sarcastic," and another to her teachers at school: "a mature and responsible girl who behaves like an angel, and is a very good student and always interested in learning new things." (Okay, I am paraphrasing slightly!)

Marta loves putting her inquisitive mind to work reading crime novels. As she reads Sherlock Holmes, or Agatha Christi, Marta enjoys trying to figure out "who done it." Marta also likes to contemplate "why." In fact, Marta's unique ambition is to become a criminal psychologist.

Marta has been exposed to a lot of culture. This is partly due to the fact that she lives in Europe, where children study several languages in school, and encounter people from other cultures all of the time, as a matter of course. She has traveled to South Africa, Sardinia (Italy) and Corsica (France), but her knowledge of world cultures expands beyond these trips. Marta has a great appreciation for how her life has been affected by different cultures, as you can see below.

What I Most Want The World To Know
translated from Italian

- I would like the Americans to know that I very much like the Internet.
- I would like the Swiss to know that I love their chocolate.
- I would like the French to know that I very much like their language.
- I would like the Spanish to know that I love their coasts and cities.
- I would like the English to know that I would like to study in their colleges.
- I would like the Canadians to know that I like their life-style.
- I would like the Japanese to know that I really like their cartoons.
- I would like the Indians to know that I love their traditional cooking.
- I would like the Australians to know that I would love to visit.

Left: The Coliseum; right: a river view of Florence.

If I Could Be...

translated from Italian

I would like to become a criminal psychologist because it interests me to know how the criminal mind functions. For example, I want to know what they think they will gain through committing a murder, how they organize it, and what type of people they are? I would like, in this way, to collaborate with the police to help solve crimes by seeking to single out characteristics of the personalities of the possible suspects, or outlining the methodology of a possible assassin; find clues in common between crimes that seem different. This passion for criminal psychology has come to me after reading mysteries, because when reading these books, you discover various personalities and how to reason out the crime.

Did You Know?

- Italy was once the center of the Roman Empire, one of the world's largest empires ever. At its height in the 200s, the Roman Empire stretched from England in the North to Libya and Egypt in the South and to Turkey and beyond in the West.

- Vatican City, home of the Pope and center of the Roman Catholic religion, is an independent sovereign entity with its own police force, postage stamps, and mint.

- The first pizza was made by a baker in Naples, Italy named Raffeale Esposito. His creation was so popular that he was requested to make a pizza for King Umberto and Queen Margherita of Italy in 1889. This pizza had only tomato sauce, cheese, and basil, and was named the Margherita pizza.

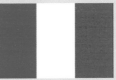

Italian Flag

Italian Currency: The Euro

Some words in Italian
Yes = Sì
No = No
Thank you = Grazie

You're welcome = Prego
Hello = Ciao
Goodbye = Arrivederci or Ciao
How are you? = Come sta?

Italy

Switzerland
Austria
Hungary
Slovenia
Marta's home city
Bosnia Herzegovina
Croatia
Florence
Adriatic Sea
Corsica
Rome
Tyrrhenian Sea
Mediterranean Sea
Tunisia

Cristina Llavaneres, Spain

Cristina

Nationality: Spanish
Religion: Catholic
Languages: Catalan; Castilian; and English
Brothers and Sisters: I have one younger sister.
Pets: Yes, a rabbit and a parakeet.
Hobbies: Drawing and horseback riding
Talents: Handicrafts and golf
Favorite Sport: Tae Kwon Do

Favorite Books: *Treasure Island* by Robert Louis Stevenson and *Que farem? Que Direm?* (*What Shall We Do? What Shall We Say?*) by Pep Coll
Favorite Food: Fried rice with tomato and topped with an egg
Least Favorite Food? Vegetables
Whom do you most admire? My mother
Favorite Possession: My computer
Do you help with chores in your home? I make my bed and set the table.
Do you have your own telephone or computer? Yes, I have my own computer.
Do you use the Internet? Yes. My favorite website is el Messenger.
Where would you most want to travel? Distant, unknown countries
What comes to mind when you think of the United States? The American flag
...and France? The Eiffel Tower
...and China? Many people and contamination
...and Kenya? Safari
What do you talk about with friends? Music
What do you want to know about other girls your age? What they like and their hobbies...

One of Cristina's favorite books.

Cristina and her family.

My Best Day
translated from Catalan

The best day that I have had in the last two years was last summer in the Dominican Republic. In the two weeks that I was there, I had visited a lot of places; I had visited different islands where I had done different activities, like taking a boat tour and going to the bottom of the sea, and there you could pick up and look at some enormous starfish. I had never seen starfish in their natural habitat and I had certainly never seen such big ones. I had also visited a typical ranch from there, with typical Dominican food and coffee, which is really nice. That was where I had my first coffee, which was very smooth. All the days I was there were wonderful, but the one I liked best and will never forget was the day I am going to tell you about.

It was a bright morning, the sun was shining, my mum got my sister and me up. That day we were going to an animal park called "Manati Park." When the bus arrived, we got on and set off. The journey was a bit hectic as the bus was not very comfortable, but that was the last thing on my mind. What I was really thinking about was arriving and being able to swim with the dolphins. When we arrived at "Manati Park," we were very happy. The moment was getting nearer and nearer.

When we went in, someone put a snake on us and took our photos. We couldn't swim with the dolphins until ten o'clock, so we went to look at different shows.

When it was time, we went to the swimming pool where the dolphins were. We were put in groups of six or seven people and were made to wash our hands and feet with really strange water.

When I was in the swimming pool and I saw those enormous creatures, I was amazed. My sister is very brave and held onto the fin above the head and the dolphin started to swim. We spent a while with them in the pool. People were scared and didn't touch them, but my sister and I made the most of it and touched them, as this was a once-in-a-lifetime opportunity.

Afterwards, we were asked to line up and one by one the dolphins held out their fins for us to hold onto and took us to the other end of the pool where, with one on each side, they gave you a kiss on the cheek. When we got out, the first thing we did was kiss and hug our mum and dad to thank them.

That was an unforgettable day in my life.

What I Most Want The World To Know
translated from Catalan

I must thank my parents for everything they have done for me. Even though I do not often show it, as I am at a bad age, the only thing I can say is that I LOVE THEM!

Did You Know?

- More than five different languages are spoken in Spain today, and Castilian (otherwise known as Spanish) is the official language. Other languages—such as Catalan, Occitan, Galician, and Basque—are regional. Catalan is spoken by 17 percent of the population and is similar to the Occitan language, which is spoken primarily in southern France and used by about one-fourth of the French population. Galician and Portuguese are similar to each other, and are spoken by people on the western fringe of Spain. Basque (Euskera) is spoken in northern Spain, in the Basque Country. It is the only pre-Roman language spoken in Spain.

Spanish Flag

Spain

France
Galician
Basque
Occitan
Spanish
Llavaneres
Portugal
Madrid
Catalan

Cristina's hometown

About the Author

Starla Griffin is originally from the state of Indiana in the USA. She is a lawyer by training and is currently Managing Director for EMTA, Europe, a trade association that represents investors in Emerging Markets.

Throughout her studies and professional career, Starla has spent a great deal of time traveling the world, and watching it change before her eyes. During her undergraduate studies at Emory University in Atlanta, Georgia, she spent a year studying in Paris, France. Upon graduation, she was hired as an English teacher by the Japanese Ministry of Education and spent a year in Hitachi, Japan. Back in the United States, Starla entered law school in Washington, DC, only to go abroad again after receiving a Rotary InternationalScholarship, which she used to spend a year studying law at the University of Bologna in Italy. Starla received her Juris Doctor, cum laude, from Georgetown University Law Center in Washington, DC in 1993.

"Here are just a few of the hundreds of tickets and souvenirs from my travels. Many of them are self-explanatory postcards, stamps and stickers from Russia, Japan, Australia, Norway, England, Finland, Kenya and China. Upper left is the taxi cab instruction for going to the Grand Theater in Shanghai -- "Grand Theatre" is written in English and Chinese so the cab driver can read it. (Make sure you always get one of these from your hotel concierge if you are in China!) Center is my ticket for the gondola ride to the top of the Great Wall (Scary!) and lower right is my ticket for the Forbidden City!"

As a practicing lawyer, Starla focused on international issues, working for clients in Latin America and Europe. For her job, she was based first in New York, then Paris and Rome. Starla joined EMTA in 1996 and began to travel to Poland and Russia and other countries inside the former Soviet Union. It was these experiences that really brought home to her just how much the world had changed, and sparked her curiosity about how the younger generation was responding to these changes. Starla spent the last several years working on the Girl, 13 project, while living in Paris, France with her husband.

Starla speaks English, French, and Italian fluently and understands some Spanish, Danish, and Russian. She currently lives in London, England with her Irish husband, Peter, and her Italian greyhound, Luna.

SIBELIUSTALO

请送我到 Grand theatre

上海大剧院中剧场

i Rd.

AUSTRALIA

RENAISSANCE.
MOSCOW HOTEL
MOSCOW, RUSSIA

BUSINESS 076
BOARDING PASS
搭乗券

お名前 Name of passenger
HENRICHSCOHEN/STARLA   MRS

出発地 From   目的地 To
TOKYO-NRT JAPAN BEIJING CHINA
便名 Flight   クラス Class   搭乗日 Date
NH 0905   C   30APR
搭乗口 Gate 搭乗時刻 BoardingTime 座席 Seat
B75   1005   11K
                  NO.

北海

北京师慕田峪长城
缆车服务有限公司
地方税务局监

HELIGE HELSEVESEN   DET OFFENTLIGE HELSEVESEN
7.00   NORGE   7.00   NORGE

成人双程票
伍拾元 ¥50.00

京地税 2001 同
005299

CITY
BIDDEN
噌送 噌送 噌送

Girl, 13 Reading List

120 Minutes Pour Mourir (*120 Minutes to Die*) by Michel Amelin

5000 Stories about the Ancient World

Abby Lynn by Rainer M. Schröder

Abhorsen by Garth Nix (Book 3 of the *Abhorsen* trilogy)

The Adventures of Huckleberry Finn and *The Adventures of Tom Sawyer* by Mark Twain

The Alchemist by Paulo Coelho

All-American Girl by Meg Cabot

The Amber Spyglass by Philip Pullman (Book 3 of *His Dark Materials* trilogy)

Ancient Egypt

And the Two Shall Meet by Marilyn Kaye

Andrea & Andrea by Domenica and Roberto Luciani

Are You There God? It's Me, Margaret by Judy Blume

Artemis Fowl by Eoin Colfer

Bad Girls by Jacqueline Wilson

Best Friends by Jacqueline Wilson

The BFG by Roald Dahl

The Bible with Pictures for Little Eyes by Kenneth N. Taylor

Boy Meets Girl by Meg Cabot

Bridget Jones' Diary by Helen Fielding

Calikusu (The Autobiography of a Turkish Girl) by Resat Nuri Güntekin

Card Captor Sakura (Japanese comic books series) by CLAMP [an all-women team of animators]

Cartas a un Gnomo (*Letters to a Gnome*) by Margarita Maine

The Changeling by Roger Zelazny

Chi-Bi Marubo

Children of the Dust by Louise Lawrence

Confessions of Georgia Nicolson series by Louise Rennison

Corazón (The Heart) by Edmundo De Amicis

The Copycat Killer by Miyuki Miyabe

The Days of Being Naughty by Huang Beijia

The Diamond Throne by David Eddings

The Diary of Anne Frank by Anne Frank

Double Act by Jacqueline Wilson

The Dragon is Sleeping by Miyuki Miyabe

Dreamland by Sarah Dessen

El Pequeño Principe (*The Little Prince*) by Antoine de Saint Exupéry

Evgeny Onegin by Aleksandr Pushkin

Fairy Tales of the Brothers Grimm by the Grimm brothers

The Famous Five series by Enid Blyton

Freckle Juice by Judy Blume

The Giving Tree by Shel Silverstein

Gossip Girl series by Cecily von Ziegesar

Hamlet by William Shakespeare

The Happy Prince and Other Tales by Oscar Wilde

Harry Potter and the Chamber of Secrets

Harry Potter and the Goblet of Fire

Harry Potter and the Order of the Phoenix

Harry Potter and the Prisoner of Azkaban

Harry Potter and the Sorcerer's Stone by J.K. Rowling

The Headless Horseman (*The Legend of Sleepy Hollow*) by Washington Irving

Helen Keller by Margaret Davidson

Helen Keller: A Life by Dorothy Herrmann

The Hobbit by J.R.R. Tolkien

I am the Flag-raiser Today by Qin Wenjun

I am Not Esther by Fleur Beale

I Miss You, I Miss You by Peter Pohl and Kinna Geith

I Want to be a Good Child by Huang Beijia

Island of the Blue Dolphins by Scott O'Dell

Jane Eyre by Charlotte Brontë

Jonathan Livingston Seagull by Richard Bach

Julius Caesar by William Shakespeare

La Edad de Oro (*The Year of Gold*) by José Martí

The Last Jungle on Earth by Randhir Khare

Lassie books

Les Miserables by Victor Hugo

The Lights Go On Again by Kit Pearson

(Book 3 of the *Guests of War* trilogy)

Life of Pi by Yann Martel

Lirael by Garth Nix (Book 2 of the Abhorsen trilogy)

Little Angels in the Forest

Little Women by Louisa May Alcott

Lola Rose by Jacqueline Wilson

Looking at the Moon by Kit Pearson (Book 2 of the *Guests of War* trilogy)

Lord Arthur Savile's Crime and Other Stories by Oscar Wilde

The Lord of the Rings trilogy by J.R.R. Tolkien

The Magician in Hell by Yogin Yokkaido

Many Waters by Madeleine L'Engle

Martilar (Seagulls)

Matilda by Roald Dahl

Mcuri by Mikhail Lermontov

A Midsummer Night's Dream by William Shakespeare

Moby Dick by Herman Melville

Mr. Canta and the Healer of Souls

Much Ado About Nothing by William Shakespeare

The Nancy Drew mysteries by Carolyn Keene

The Neverending Story by Michael Ende

The No. 1 Ladies Detective Agency series by Alexander McCall Smith

The Northern Lights (or The Golden Compass) by Philip Pullman (Book 1 of *His Dark Materials* trilogy)

Now and Forever by Danielle Steele

Number the Stars by Lois Lowry

Out and About by Shirley Hughes

Oxford Guide to English Grammar by John Eastwood

Peter Pan by J.M. Burrie

The Phantom Tollbooth by Norton Juster

The Picture of Dorian Gray by Oscar Wilde

The Pigman by Paul Zindel

Pippi Longstocking by Astrid Lindgren

Que Farem? Que Direm? (*What Shall We*

Say? What Shall We Do?) by Pep Coll
Romeo and Juliet
by William Shakespeare
Sabriel by Garth Nix (Book 1 of the
Abhorsen trilogy)
Second Helpings by Megan McCafferty
The Secret Heart by David Almond
The Secret Seven series by Enid Blyton
Silent to the Bone by E.L. Konigsburg
Sisi series by Marie Luisevan Ingenheim
Sixth Grade Secrets by Louis Sachar
The Sky is Falling by Kit Pearson (Book 1
of the *Guests of War* trilogy)

The Slippers that Sneezed
by Gyles Brandreth
The Sonnets by William Shakespeare
The Subtle Knife by Philip Pullman (Book 2
of *His Dark Materials* trilogy)
Summer Sisters
Tales of a Fourth Grade Nothing
by Judy Blume
Tell Me I'm OK, Really by Rosie Rushton
This Lullaby by Sarah Dessen
The Tiggie Tompson Show by Tessa Duder
To Kill a Mockingbird by Harper Lee
Treasure Island by Robert Louis Stevenson

Tree of Desire by Victor Kusmenko
Troy by Adele Geras
Uplynul_as_Detsk_ch Heir (*When I was
Little*) by Sonja Peterova
Vechera Na Khutore Bliz Dikan'ki
(*Evenings on a Farm near Dikanka*)
by Nikolay Gogol
Where the Red Fern Grows by Wilson Rawls
Willie Wonka and the Chocolate Factory
by Roald Dahl
Winnie the Pooh by A.A. Milne
Witch Child by Celia Rees

Girl, 13 Favorite Websites

Rachel from Canada recommends Addicting Games, a website full of fun flash Internet games. *www.addictinggames.com* She also uses her local library's website—*www.vpl.ca*. Here she can get help on homework, search for books, and learn more about events. Check to see if your local library has its own website. Rachel also loves using the Internet, especially looking up info on Google, a search engine where you can find facts on almost anything! *www.google.com*

Lynsey from Scotland loves Google too! She also likes to chat with her friends on *messenger.de*.

Rachel from South Africa loves Bubblegum, which includes games, prizes, animation, mini-movies, downloads, and even coloring books. *www.bubblegumclub.com*

Dolly Magazine's, an Australian teen magazine, is, of course, **Alex's favorite**. It features celebrity interviews, fashion, and beauty tips. *dolly.ninemsn.com.au/dolly/*

Kirsten from the USA has fun on ABC Family Worldwide—ABC TV's online site showcasing latest info on shows, celebrities, and movies. *abcfamily.go.com*

Lavanya from India likes playing online Flash games on *www.orisinal.com*

Manuela from Colombia is always checking for new email on MSN Hotmail, a very popular email service, which also includes the latest news and juicy gossip. *www.hotmail.com*

Nathalie from Brazil chats with her friends on ICQ, an instant messenger service where you can also plays games and shop online. *www.icq.com*. She also likes Kazaa—a peer-to-peer sharing site featuring previews of latest movies, music videos, and songs. *www.kazaa.com*

Both **Brianna from the USA** and **Kate from the UK** love caring for their virtual pets and playing games on *Neopets.com*—a virtual pet site, which also offers trading auctions, greetings, messaging, and much much more.

Dieu from Vietnam loves Shoujo in Italia, a website that includes info on fabulous animation characters. *www.shoujoinitalia.net*

Miska gets all the latest news on her favorite website—TV Markiza, which features news, sports, and much more. *www.markiza.sk*

Marta from Italy has fun on Virgilio, an Italian website featuring celebrities, games, news, and downloads. *www.virgilio.it*

Katasi recommends Yahoo.com, a very cool website that includes email, shopping, games, and much more. *www.yahoo.com*

Cristina from Spain chats with her friends on Yahoo Messenger (Spanish)—Yahoo's instant messenger service in Spanish. *es.messenger.yahoo.com*

Meera from UAE loves checking out quotes of all kinds on *www.firehotquotes.com*

Girl, 13 Fun Facts

If Girl, 13 came down to statistics, what would we learn?
Well, here is a quick glance of some of our fun results after polling all 43 girls!

Number of girls who speak more than one language: 27

Number of girls who like to collect comic books: 2

Harry Potter fans: 18

Cat owners: 12 Dog owners: 16

Girls with more than 2 siblings: 6 Girls that are only-children: 7

Number of girls who talk about BOYS with their friends: 12

Number of girls who wore jeans when I met them: 11

Number of girls who attend all-girls schools: 6

Number of girls who wear uniforms to school: 13

Number of girls who the Oxford English Dictionary is a favorite possession: 1

Number of girls who go to school on Saturdays: 5

Number of girls whose hobby is graffiti art: 1

Number of girls who like to draw or paint: 10

Mathematicians: 7

Number of girls whose least favorite food is liver, in any shape or form: 4

Number of girls who swam with dolphins: 2

Number of names that are derivatives of Kate: 5

Number of girls who think of the safari when they think of Kenya: 7

Number of girls who want to travel to Greece: 2

Number of girls who think of the Eiffel Tower when they think of France: 18

Number of girls who think of the Great Wall of China when they think of China: 11

Future Olympic medalists: 4

Future country leaders: 6

Future astronauts: 5

Future pop or movie stars: 12

Number of girls whose favorite food is pizza: 5

Numbers of girls who use computers: 33

Number of girls with pin cushion named Junior: 1

Pet cows: 1   Pet calves: 1

Photo albums as favorite possessions: 2

Numbers of girls who like writing: 10

Amateur sleuths: 1

Number of girls who like to sing: 13

Piano players: 5

Gold medals from the Ontario Winter Games: 1

Amateur clothes designers: 1

Number of girls who love their cuddly toys: 7

Number of girls who wrote about their first kiss: 1

Number of girls who have their own cell phones: 12

Accordion players: 1

Badminton stars: 3

Number of girls who think of the FBI when they think of the US: 1

Number of girls who take Tae Kwon Do: 2

Basketball players: 5

Pets named Houdini: 2

Ballerinas: 4

Parrots: 3

Snail farms: 1

Pet Turtles: 1

Pet Names

Here are some of the very cute pet names found in Girl, 13.

Aandhi (dog)
Ailbhe—pronounced "Alva"(dog)
Beema (dog)
Bellyflop (fish)
Bijli (dog)
Blackie (cat)
Bubbles (fish)
Carmen (dog)
Casey (dog)
Cleopatra (dog)
Dany (dog)
Decomo (cat)
Devaki (cow)
Djeco (hamster)
Dolly (cat)
Elsie (cat)
Galaxy (dog)
Goldie (goldfish)
Guangguang (parrot)
Gus (dog)
Harry (dog)
Houdine (hamster)
Houdini (cat)
Jack (dog)
Jatraprasad (calf)
Kajol (dog)
Larry (parrot)
Mathilda (cat)
Maximus (dog)
Mitzi (cat)
Nini (parrot)
Patch (cat)
Percy (parrot)
Rinta (dog)
Romeo and Juliet (parakeets)
Roxy (dog)
Sabrina (fish)
Sam (pony)
Skye (dog)
Snuggles (cat)
Splash (fish)
Sussi (rabbit)
Tiantian (parrot)
Tingo (gerbil)
Tiga (dog)
Tiger (cat)
Titus (dog)
Toofaan (dog)

Acknowledgements

By its very nature, *Girl, 13* is not the kind of book that one develops in isolation. In fact, the book exists today thanks to the help of many, many people. Of course, credit is due primarily to the effort of the girls who participated so enthusiastically, and I would like to acknowledge all of these participants and send a heartfelt thank you to all of them. Thank you *Girl, 13* contributors! I would also like to thank all of the girls' parents, whose support for the project, and faith in my ability to see it through, was a tremendous motivator.

The book also would not have been completed without the help and support of my husband, Peter, who traveled with me to meet girls, put up with my absence when I was traveling on my own, and read draft after draft of the chapters with unwavering interest once I returned.

I would also like to thank my family for their support, suggestions, editing, and other assistance that they provided me over the course of the project: Thanks Mom and Hugo, Dad and Judy, Marlise, Karna, Karen, Margie (for all of the girls you helped me find in Finland, Egypt, Vietnam, and Brazil!), Kenneth and Anne in Denmark, and Peter and Mary Griffin in Ireland.

Throughout the course of the *Girl, 13* project, many friends, colleagues, and even people I met by chance assisted in the search for contributors. Many of these friends (they are all friends now) went beyond just putting me in touch with their niece, goddaughter, cousin, friend's daughter, or whoever the lucky girl turned out to be; they also helped me with transla-tions, and with the grueling task of organizing my trips and providing me with additional information whenever I asked. I am thinking in particular of Alena Cernejova in Slovakia, Xiaoqing Ding, Suni Liu, and Coleen Yang in China, Daniela Tchoroleeva (and her family) in Bulgaria, Saroop Bansil in Kenya, Denis Bazlov in Russia, Beverley Nambozo and Charles Mwebeiha in Uganda, Jan and Phil Reid in Australia, Mrs. Aiko Furukoshi in Japan, David Craig in Paris, Anya in Ukraine, who helped me find Dasha, and Susannah and Pierre Bisson in France.

I would also like to single out those of you who helped me to find and communicate with contributors in hard-to-reach regions of the world. Thanks so much for all of your help Gabriel Villar and Merida Lopez in Cuba, Merwan Lomri for Algeria, and Yulia Yugay for Kazakhstan.

Then there are all of you who, even though you may not have known me very well, stuck your necks out and recruited a friend or relative to share in my venture. Without your help, the book would never be what it is today. So thanks very much to Mauricio and Fabiana Zonis for Argentina, Pia Ximenez Rodriguez and Maria Consuelo Rodriguez for Colombia and Scotland, Samantha and Hamish Findlater for Australia, Sifelani Thalepo for Botswana, Myriam Gewerc for Brazil, Renée Theriault, Richard Boivin, and Su T. Fitterman for Canada, Mandy and Julian Mant for England and Spain, Mike and Pooh Bolton for Ireland, Iris Dana, Aviva Werner, and Ariel Teitel for Israel, Alla Lee for Kazakhstan, Maria Virkki for Finland,

Brendolyn McKenna for Louisiana, Ken and Kari Fleuriet, Randy and Gerry Fleuriet, and Jose Luis Cavazos for Mexico, Carlo Daneo for Italy, Tri Dinh for Vietnam, Prosper Hillairet for New York (and all of your helpful suggestions along the way), Campbell Walker and Charlotte Gibbs for New Zealand, Unni Friedheim for Norway, Maria del Pilar and Alain De Vries for Spain and Peru, Hector Sequero and St. George's International School in Malaga also for Spain, Maria Sara Jijon and Alice Kriz for South Africa, Chris Pittinger for Abu Dhabi, UAE, Selda and Mark Coyne for Turkey, Gordana Ilic for Yugoslavia, and the Rotary Club of New Orleans for bringing Franzi from Germany into the book.

A special thanks goes to my other translators not already mentioned who did not charge me for their work. Thank you Ricky Wong for the Japanese, Joachim Knoll for the German, Claudia Bortolani for the Italian, and Bety Zimon for the Spanish.

And thank you for your assistance along the way James Bohan, Nanou Leleu Knobil, Barry Lyons, L.J. Goldstein, and Conor Byrne, your many great ideas Samantha Bennahum and Niamh Byrne, and for the photos Ludmila Reznick and Adam Bronstone.

It would also have been impossible to complete the book if I had not been able to take time from my job. Thank you very much Michael Chamberlin and my colleagues at EMTA for letting me go and for taking me back again. For your support at various key moments, I would also like to thank Henry Weisberg, Barbara Grossman, Barry and Gerri O'Callaghan, my Russian teacher and friend, Nadia Gordiani, my friends Virginie Kharouby and Susannah Davies, and my cousin Michael Kahn, who introduced me to George Greenfield, my agent. And thank you Beth Martin Quittman, who happened to walk into Hylas on that fateful day in Irvington.

I would also like to send a big thank you to the Hylas team: Sean Moore, Karen Prince, Gus Yoo, Gail Greiner, Rachel Maloney, Hannah Choi, Shamona Stokes, Angda Goel, Sarah Postle, and Joaquín Ramon Herrera for your continuing faith in the project, and for your enthusiasm, dedication, and creativity. You have made *Girl, 13* into a beautiful book and I am very grateful to you all!

My one regret is that every girl who participated could not be in the final draft of the book. Regrettably, I had difficulty staying in touch with some of the girls and their contacts, which made their continuing participation in the project impossible. Then, the editors had to make the difficult determination of who would be included in the final list of contributors for the book based primarily on length and geographic representation. As it was, we struggled with space to include who we did. My special thanks and recognition go to all of the other girls who participated, and in particular to Fella, Louisa, Afrin, Ana Clara, Rayane, Arabella, Kristina, Kelebogile, Zena, Ariadne, Sonali, Meenani, Anuradha, Minami, Maria Ines, and Zorana.

Thanks so much to everyone once again! You have all made *Girl, 13* a reality and I will never forget your kindness and support!

Cheers!
Starla

Selected Bibliography

Starla's Note: Want to know more about China or India? Taking a trip to Canada or Ireland? Researching a paper on Ancient Egypt?

Because there are so many reasons why you might want to know more about the countries featured in Girl, 13, we thought we would share with you some of our fun book and web findings. Use these to dig up more cool facts about countries abroad and amaze your friends and families! The website list is quite extensive, so put on your surfing gear (net surfing, that is) and take a virtual trip around the world!

East Europe + Russia

Bulgaria
Websites:
- Wonderland Bulgaria, "Bulgarian Folk Music," Omda Limited, http://www.omda.bg
- Mother Earth Travel, "History of Bulgaria," Mother Earth Travel, http://www.motherearthtravel.com/bulgaria/history.htm
- Bulgaria.com, "History of Bulgaria," http://www.bulgaria.com
- Facts on File, History Database Center, "Bulgars," Facts On File, Incorporated, http://www.factsonfile.com

Slovakia
Books:
- Whipple, Tim D., ed. After the Velvet Revolution: Václav Havel and the New Leaders of Czechoslovakia Speak Out. Freedom House, 1991.
- Lacika, Jan. Visiting Slovakia: Bratislava. DaJama Publications, 2000.

Websites:
- Slovakia.org: The Guide to the Slovak Republic, http://www.slovakia.org
- WorldRover, "Slovak Republic," http://www.worldrover.com/history
- Long Hair Lovers, "Sissi's Magnificent Mane," http://www.longhairlovers.com/sissi.html
- Slovak Tourist Board, "Bratislava: Highlights, Bratislava's New Bridge" http://www.sacr.sk/files/bratislava.pdf

Ukraine
Books:
- Ludlow, Hope. The Soviet Union and Eastern Europe. Scholastic Book Services, 1973.

Websites:
- Information Resource about Ukraine, "Legend of the Founding of Kiev 482 AD," InfoUkes Incorporated, http://www.infoukes.com
- Brama: Gateway Ukraine, "History of Ukraine," Brama, Incorporated, http://www.brama.com/ukraine/history
- Learnpsyanky.com, "The Basic Steps," http://www.learnpysanky.com
- Kiev City Guide: The Capital of Ukraine, http://www.uazone.net/Kiev.html
- Chevrona Ruta Cruise Company, "Lavra," http://www.ruta-cruise.com/en/cruise/option.html

Russia
Books:
- Taplin, Mark. Open Lands: Travels through Russia's Once Forbidden Places. Steerforth Press, 1997.
- Service, Robert. A History of 20th Century Russia. Harvard University Press, 1997.

- Chamberlain, Leslie. Volga, Volga: A Journey Down Russia's Great River. Picador, 1995.

Websites:

- The Russian-American Chamber of Commerce, http://www.russianamericanchamber.org
- DiscoverySchool.com, http://school.discovery.com
- Word IQ: Dictionary & Encyclopedia, http://www.wordiq.com
- Mindspring.com, "Russian Names," EarthLink,Incorporated, http://www.mindspring.com/~garyduanecox/russnames.htm

Asia + Oceania

China

Websites:

- Federation of American Scientists, "China's Space Activities: The Information Office of the State Council of the People's Republic of China, November 22, 2000," Federation of American Scientists, http://www.fas.org
- Beijing Summer Olympic Games, http://www.beijing2008china.com
- Time Magazine, "'A Generation of Little Emperors,' by Lori Reese, September 27, 1999," Time Incorporated, http://www.time.com/time/asia/magazine/99/0927/children_palace.html
- Time Asia, "Sun Yat-Sen," Time Incorporated, http://www.time.com/time/asia/asia/magazine/1999/990823/sun_yat_sen1.html
- Cable News Network, "'Labor Class: Maoist Legacy for China's Schools,' by Rose Tang, March 9, 2001," Time Warner, http://www.cnn.com/2001/WORLD/asiapcf/east/03/08/china.school.labor/
- ACWeb: Connecting ACSians Globally, "The Historical Origin and Cultural Significance of Chinese Chess," http://www.acs.sch.edu.sg
- Condensed China: Chinese History for Beginners, http://asterius.com/china
- Washington State University, "Ch'ing China: The Opium Wars," http://www.wsu.edu:8080/~dee/CHING/OPIUM.HTM
- Discovery.com, Discovery Channel, "China: People and Places," and "Great Wall of China," http://school.discovery.com
- EduNETConnet: Learning Categories, "Chinese Festivals and Culture," http://www.edunetconnect.com/categories/originals/chinafest/chinesef.html
- Go Taikonauts, "Why Taikonaut?" www.geocities.com/CapeCanaveral/Launchpad/1921/taikonaut.htm
- Chinese Culture Center of San Francisco, "Zodiac Page," http://www.c-c-c.org/chineseculture/zodiac/zodiac.html

Vietnam

Websites:

- VietMedia: Vietnamese Culture, "Cultural Differences," http://www.vietmedia.com/culture/?L=culturaldifferences3.html
- The American Experience, WGBH, "Vietnam Online Timeline," PBS Online, http://www.pbs.org/wgbh/amex/vietnam/time/timeline2.html
- Modern History Sourcebook, "Vietnam Declaration of Independence, 1945," Fordham University, http://www.fordham.edu/halsall/mod/1945vietnam.html
- Vietnamese Language, "Vietnamese Culture," http://vietcatholic.net/culture/language.htm
- Asia-Discovery.com, "History of Vietnam," http://www.asia-discovery.com/Vietnam/history.htm

India

Books:

- Isenberg, Irwin. The Indian Subcontinent. Scholastic Book Services, 1972.

Websites:

- King's College History Department, Women's History's Resource Site, "Indira Gandhi," King's College, http://www.kings.edu/womens_history/igandhi.html
- Britannia: America's Gateway to the British Isles, "Victoria: British Monarchs," http://www.britannia.com/history/monarchs/mon58.html
- WorldRover, "India's History," http://www.worldrover.com/history/india_history.html

- Embassy of India, The High Commission of India in Singapore, http://www.embassyofindia.com
- Geographia.com, "An Introduction to India," http://www.geographia.com/india

Kazakhstan
Websites:
- World and I Online Magazine, "In Transit: Traditional and Soviet Influence in Kazakhstan," http://worldandi.misto.cz
- The Government of Kazakhstan, http://www.president.kz
- Kazakhstan Information, http://www.kazakinfo.com

South Korea
Websites:
- Daejeon Metropolitan City, South Korea, "City Tour," http://www.metro.daejeon.kr/english/tourguide/
- One World: Cities Online, "Cities of the World: The Most Populated Cities in the World," One World: Nations Online, http://www.nationsonline.org/oneworld/bigcities.htm

Japan
Books:
- De Mente, Boye. Passport's Japan Almanac. Passport Books, 1987.

Websites:
- Embassy of Japan, "Spotlight: Education," http://www.embjapan.dk/Spotlight2/education.htm
- TOPICS Online Magazine for Learners of English, "Authentic Ceremonies for Children in Japan," http://www.topics-mag.com/internatl/holidays/japan/3-5-7children.htm
- Origami, the art of paper folding, "Origami Gallery," http://www.origami.com

New Zealand
Websites:
- Destination-NZ.com, Qantas, "Online Guide to Traveling in New Zealand," www.destination-nz.com
- New Zealand's Department of Conservation, www.doc.govt.nz
- Netball: New Zealand, TV NZ Interactive, http://www.netballnz.co.nz/

Australia
Websites:
- Australian Rules in Football, http://www.coachwyatt.com/ausfootball.html
- City of Melbourne, http://www.melbourne.vic.gov.au
- Aborigines, http://users.orac.net.au/~mhumphry/aborigin.html

Africa + the Middle East

Uganda
Websites:
- WorldRover, "History of Uganda," http://www.worldrover.com/history/uganda_history.html
- 1UP Travel: Uganda, "Uganda History and Culture," http://www.1uptravel.com/international/africa/uganda/history-culture.html
- GORP.com: Adventure Travel and Outdoor Recreation, "Lake Victoria,"

http://gorp.away.com/gorp/location/africa/kenya/ke_lkvic.htm
- Encyclopedia Americana, "Uganda: The People," Scholastic Library Publishing, Inc., http://go.grolier.com/gol

Kenya

Websites:

- The Internet Living Swahili Dictionary, "Swahili Pronunciation Guide," Yale University, http://www.cis.yale.edu/ swahili/sound/pronunce.htm
- Arham Group, "About Jainism," http://www.arham.com/abt_jain_index.htm
- Maasai Association, "Maasai People," http://www.maasai-infoline.org/
- GORP.com: Adventure Travel and Outdoor Recreation, "Maasai Mara National Reserve," http://gorp.away.com/gorp/location/africa/kenya/ke_masai.htm
- Wikipedia: The Free Encyclopedia, "The Equator," http://en.wikipedia.org/wiki/Equator
- About.com, "Geography: The Equators, Hemispheres, Tropic of Cancer, and Tropic of Capricorn," About, Inc. A PRIMEDIA Company, http://geography.about.com/library/misc/blequator.htm
- Lands and People Online, "Kenya (Kenya Mountain)," Scholastic Library Publishing, Inc., http://go.grolier.com/gol

South Africa

Websites:

- South Africa.info, "South Africa Alive with Possiblity: The Official Gateway," http://www.southafrica.info
- Zar.co.za, "Fun Facts and Trivia on South Africa and its People," http://zar.co.za/trivia.htm
- World Factbook, "South Africa," CIA, http://www.cia.gov/cia/publications/factbook/geos.sf.html
- Stats Online, "Statistics South Africa," http://www.statssa.gov.za
- The Information Gateway to South Africa, South African Tourism, "Rainbow Nation," http://www.southafrica.net/index.cfm?sitepageID=13562
- Infoplease.com, "Afrikaans," Pearson Education, http://www.infoplease.com/ce6/society/A0802680.html

Egypt

Websites:

- St.Augustine.com, "'The Nile: Without the world's longest river there can be no Egypt,' by Donna Abu-Nasr of the Associated Press, September 9, 2001" http://www.staugustine.com/stories/090901/act_0909010001.shtml
- Religion of Islam, "Introduction to Islam," http://www.iad.org
- The Temple of Pharaoh Maatkare Hatshepsut Daughter of Amun Ra, "Women in Ancient Egypt," http://www.maatkare.com
- Arabic German Consulting, "Egypt: History," http://www.arab.de/arabinfo/egypthis.htm
- FYI: From Rome to Mecca, "Odyssey in Egypt," http://www.website1.com/odyssey/week5/FYI.html
- Ancient Egypt: An Introduction, "Egypt and the Rising Persian Empire," http://www.terraflex.co.il/ad/egypt/the_rising_persian_empire.htm
- Internet Modern History Sourcebook, "Modern Egyptian History: The Earl of Cromer: Why Britain Acquired Egypt in 1882," Fordham University, http://www.fordham.edu/halsall/mod/1908cromer.html

KENYA 80/-

Phoeniconaias minor

Lesser Flamingo
Heroe Mdogo

COURVOISIER

Israel

Websites:

- PageWise, Incorporated, "What is a Kibbutz and Moshav in Israel?" http://nvnv.essortment.com/whatiskibbutz_rghm.htm
- Country Studies US, "Israel: Kibbutz and Moshav," US Library of Congress, http://countrystudies.us/israel/57.htm
- Judaism 101, "Bar Mitzvah, Bat Mitzvah, and Confirmation," http://www.jewfaq.org/barmitz.htm
- Lion Pac, "Facts about Israel," Columbia/Barnard Hillel, http://sky.prohosting.com/lionpac/funfacts.shtml
- Extreme Science, "Why is it called the Dead Sea?" Extreme Science, http://www.extremescience.com/DeadSea.htm

Abu Dhabi – United Arab Emirates

Websites:

- IslamForToday.com, "'The Origins of the Sunni/Shia Split in Islam,' by Hussein Abdulwaheed Amin," IslamForToday.com, http://www.islamfortoday.com/shia.htm
- United Arab Emirates, Emirates.org, http://www.emirates.org
- United Arab Emirates: A Country Study, "United Arab Emirates," US Library of Congress, http://lcweb2.loc.gov/frd/cs/aetoc.html
- The Emirate of Abu Dhabi, "Abu Dhabi," http://www.uae.org.ae/general/abudhabi.htm

Turkey

Websites:

- British Geological Survey, "17 August 1999 Izmit, Turkey Earthquake," http://www.earthquakes.bgs.ac.uk
- History of England, "The Ottoman Empire," http://www.historyofengland.net/ottoman.html
- United Nations Children's Fund, www.unicef.org
- LexicOrient, Encyclopedia of the Orient, "Izmit," LexicOrient.com, http://i-cias.com/e.o/izmit.htm
- US Geological Survey: Earthquakes Hazard Program, Northern California, "Izmit, Turkey, Introduction and Damage Survey," http://quake.wr.usgs.gov/research/geology/turkey/
- BBC News Europe, "The Quakes that Shook Turkey: A Special Report," BBC, news.bbc.co.uk/1/hi/world/europe/422773.stm

North America + the Caribbean

U.S.A. – New York

Books:

- Burns, Ric, James Sanders and Lisa Ades. New York: An Illustrated History. Alfred A. Knopf, 1999.

Websites:

- The Museum of the City of New York, "Why is New York Called the Big Apple?" Museum of the City of New York, http://www.mcny.org/Research/answers.htm

U.S.A. – Indiana

Websites:

- EnjoyIndiana.com, Indiana Office of Tourism Development, http://www.enjoyindiana.com

U.S.A. – Louisiana

Websites:

- Gateway: New Orleans, "Louisiana: Some Flat Facts" and "Louisiana Purchase," http://www.gatewayno.com/history/louisiana.html
- "A History of New Orleans," by Donnald McNabb and Lee Madere, Jr., http://www.madere.com/history.html
- Twilight Bridge, "Mardi Gras," Twilightbridge.com, http://www.twilightbridge.com/hobbies/festivals/mardigras/history.htm
- Mardi Gras New Orleans.com, http://www.mardigrasneworleans.com

Canada

Websites:

- Government of Canada, canada.gc.ca/main_e.html
- Canoe, "Swimming: Mike Mintenko," Canoe.ca,

http://www.canoe.ca/2000GamesBiosA2M/mintenko.html
- Pan Pacific Masters Games Gold Coast, http://www.mastersgames.com.au/
- City of Vancouver, British Government, http://www.city.vancouver.bc.ca/
- City of Ottawa, http://www.ottawa.ca/
- Edelman, The Canadian Chamber of Commerce in Korea, "Building an Image for Foreign Countries and Companies in Korea," Edelman, http://www.edelman.com/people_and_perspectives/insights/CCCK_pickard2.ppt

Mexico
Websites:
- Talking about Mexico: Mexico for Kids, http://elbalero.gob.mx/kids/about/html/home.html
- The World of Frida Kahlo, http://members.aol.com/fridanet/kahlo.htm
- Tae Kwon Do, http://www.tkd.net/tkdnetwork/taekwondo.html
- International Tae Kwon-Do Association (International Headquarters), http://www.itatkd.com
- Black Belt World, "Master Jun Lee's Tae Kwon-Do," Black Belt World, Inc., http://www.blackbeltworld.com

Cuba
Books:
- Bethell, Leslie, ed. Cuba: A Short History. Cambridge University Press, 1993.
Websites:
- Official Website to Cuba, Cuba.com, http://www.cuba.com
- Havana Journal, "'Tracing Cuba's Tarnished Golden Age,' by Colin Barradough, Globe and Mail, March 10, 2004," Havana Journal, Incorporated, http://havanajournal.com/culture_comments/P1484_0_3_0/
- Fact Monster, Information Please, http://www.factmonster.com

South America

Colombia
Websites:
- Shakira Live off the Record, Epic Records, http://www.shakira.com
- LucidCafé Interactive Café and Information Resource, "Colombian Coffee," http://www.lucidcafe.com/bycounty.html
- Colombia Tourism, "Cumbia," Colegio Nueva Granada, http://gvc03c29.virtualclassroom.org/Music/colombianmusic/Cumbia.htm
- Ritmo Latina Canada, "Cumbia History," http://www.ritmolatino.ca/cumbia.html

Argentina
Books:
- Bernhardson, Wayne and Maria Massalo. Lonely Planet Argentina, Paraguay, and Uruguay. Lonely Planet, 1992.
Websites:
- Evita Peron Historical Research Foundation, http://www.evitaperon.org
- Patagonia, Argentina, http://www.patagonia-argentina.com
- No Borders, "Yerba Mate: For Better Health," No Borders Net Services, http://www.noborders.net/mate/health.html
- Global Policy Forum, "'Despair in Once-Proud Argentina After Economic Collapse, Deep Poverty Makes Dignity a Casualty,' by Anthony Faiola, Washington Post, August 6, 2002," Global Policy Forum, http://www.globalpolicy.org/socecon/develop/2002/0806argentina.htm
- Hallmark Press Room, "Quinceañera," Hallmark.com. http://pressroom.hallmark.com/quinceanera.html

Brazil
Websites:
- Rio de Janiero, "Introduction," interKnowledge, Corp., http://www.geographia.com/brazil/rio/index.htm
- PBS Home Programs, "Journey into Amazonia," PBS Online,

http://www.pbs.org/journeyintoamazonia/enter.html
- h2g2, "The Amazon Rainforest," BBC, http://www.bbc.co.uk/dna/h2g2/A925913
- Ipanema.com, "Carnival in Rio de Janeiro," http://www.ipanema.com/carnival/parade.htm

Europe

England
Websites:

- US-1 References, "Differences in UK and US Versions of Harry Potter Books," Department of Translation Studies, University of Tampere, Finland, http://www.uta.fi/FAST/US1/REF/potter.html
- Enchanted Learning, "United Kingdom's Flag: Union Jack," EnchantedLearning.com, http://www.enchanted learning.com/europe/britain/flag.shtml
- About.com, "British Flag (The Union Jack)," About.com, Inc., a PRIMEDIA Company, http://gouk.about.com/cs/royalty/a/unionjack.htm

Scotland
Websites:

- whoohoo.com, "Scottish Translator," CK Net Limited, http://www.whoohoo.co.uk/scottish-translator.asp
- The Gumbo Pages, "Our Beloved Haggis: The National Dish of Scotland," http://www.gumbopages.com/food/scottish/haggis.html.
- Celtic Net, "History of the Kilt in Scotland," Majestic Website, http://www.majestictech.com/the-celticnet/kilthistory.html

Ireland
Websites:

- Ireland On-Line, "History of Ireland," Esat Telecommunications Ltd., http://ireland.iol.ie
- Ireland's Eye.com, "The History of Irish Dance," Irelandseye.com, http://www.irelandseye.com/dance.html
- The Irish Times, "The Rules of Camogie," Ireland.com, http://ireland.com/sports

France
Websites:

- Internet French Property, "'Kissing in France,' by Sara Lesage, The Telegraph, February 24, 2004," Internet French Property, http://forums.french-property.com/showthread.php?t=532
- Wikipedia: The Free Encyclopedia, "Battle of Normandy," http://en.wikipedia.org/wiki/Operation_Overlord

Germany
Websites:

- Wikipedia: The Free Encyclopedia, "History of Germany," http://en.wikipedia.org/wiki/History_of_Germany
- Country Reports, "History of Germany," Emulate Me, http://www.countryreports.org/history/germhist.htm
- European Union at a Glance, http://www.europa.eu.int/abc/index_en.htm
- World Facts, "Kiel," http://worldfacts.us/Germany-Kiel.htm

Finland
Websites:

- Inter-Parliamentary Union, "Women's Suffrage, A World

Chronology of the Recognition of Women's Rights to Vote and Stand for Election," http://www.ipu.org
- International Reports.net, "'NATO Debate Tinged by Cold War Undertones,' The Washington Times, April 23. 1999," "'Sauna: More Than Just a Tradition,' by V.S. Choslowsky, The Washington Times, April 23, 1999," "'Women in Politics: Pushing the Limits of Tradition,' The Washington Times, April 23, 1999," http://www.internationalspecialreports.com/
- Nordic Council, "Between Solidarity and Neutrality: The Nordic Countries and the Cold War, 1945-1991," http://www.norden.org
- Virtual Finland, Ministry for Foreign Affairs of Finland, http://virtual.finland.fi

Norway
Websites:
- Lysator Academic Computer Society, "Norwegian History," http://www.lysator.liu.se/nordic/scn/faq63.html
- Ministry of Foreign Affairs of Norway, "The History of Norway" and "Norwegian Foreign Policy in the 20th Century," ODIN, http://odin.dep.no/odin/engelsk/norway/history, http://odin.dep.no/odin/engelsk/norway/foreign

Denmark
Websites:
- Infoplease.com, "Olympics 2004: Team Handball," Pearson Education, http://www.infoplease.com/spot/ol-teamhandball.html

Italy
Books:
- Hatchwell, Emily. Insight Guide: Italy. Langenscheidt Publishers, 2002.
Websites:
- Historical Text Archive, "Lectures in Medieval History: The Roman Empire at its Height," The Historical Text Archive, http://historicaltextarchive.com/ books.php?op=viewbook&bookid=64&cid=1
- Brainy Encyclopedia, "Italian Unification," http://www.brainyencyclopedia.com/encyclopedia/i/it/ italian_unification_1.html
- About.com, "The Roman Coliseum" and "Vatican," About.com, Inc., a PRIMEDIA Company, http://goitaly.about.com/cs/rome/p/coliseum.htm, http://goitaly.about.com/cs/rome/a/vatican.htm
- PageWise, Incorporated, "The History of Pizza," http://id.essortment.com/historyofpizza_rmgf.htm

Spain
Books:
- Williams, Roger. Eyewitness Travel Guides: Barcelona & Catalonia. Dorling Kindersley Publishing, 2003.
- Wintle, Justin. The Rough Guide History of Spain. Penguin Books, 2003.
- Buysschaert, Martine and Alberto Rossetti, and Edizioni Futuro. Spagna: Barcellona e le regioni orientali. 1989.
Websites:
- "Languages in Spain," Marta Ribas, http://www.june29.com/HLP/lang/Catalan/webcat3.html
- "Languages spoken in Spain," http://www.sispain.org/ english/language/language/index.html

Other General Sources

Books:
- Almond, Mark Almond, Jeremy Black, Felipe Fernández-Armesto, Rasmund McKitterick, Geoffrey Parker, Chris Scarre, and Richard Vinen. The Times: History of Europe. HarperCollins Publishers, 2001.
Websites:
- Diversity Resources, Inc., "Life Cycle Events in Different Cultures (extract from Multicultural Celebrations)," http://www.diversityresources.com
- MSN Encarta: Online Encyclopedia and Dictionary, http://www.encarta.com, was consulted for all other information not noted above.
- Language translations were found on Athropolis.com, http://www.athropolis.com/hello2.htm

Use these pages to make your own *Girl, 13* entry—all about you! You can add your submission onto our website at http://girl13.hylaspublishing.com

Place your portrait here

Nationality:

Religion:

Languages:

Brothers and Sisters:

Pets:

Hobbies:

Talents:

Favorite Sport:

Favorite Books:

Favorite Food:

Least Favorite Food:

Whom do you most admire?

Favorite Possession:

Do you help with chores at home?

Do you have your own telephone or computer?

Do you use the Internet?

Where would you most want to travel?

What comes to mind when you think of the United States?

…and France?

…and China?

…and Kenya?

What do you talk about with friends?

What do you want to know about other girls your age?

About Me

My Best Day

_____

_____

_____

_____

_____

_____

_____

_____

_____

_____

_____

_____

_____

_____

_____

_____

_____

_____

If I Could Be...

How to Submit to Girl, 13

Now that you have learned what life is like for Katia, Dasha, Philomena, Brianna, and the other girls in *Girl, 13*, it is now your chance to share your life stories with us, and the rest of the world, of course! Please send in your submissions to me, Starla Griffin, and to the editors at Hylas at http://girl13.hylaspublishing.com. You can also contact us at girl13@hylaspublishing.com. Who knows? You may find yourself in the next print edition as well!

On the *Girl, 13* website, not only can you upload your very own journal, but you also will have the opportunity to read the journals of other girls from around the world. And if that's not enough, check out the very cool *Girl, 13* messageboard, where you can post messages for all the original *Girl, 13* contributors to read as well as any new contributors. Another first for your generation! The first evolving and interactive website *virtually* written by girls your age! (Please note: If you are chosen for the next print edition of *Girl, 13*, your parents will be required to sign parental consent forms.)

Rachel
Canada

Erica
Canada

Kirsten
USA

Katie
Ireland

Laurel
USA

Kate
England

Lynsey
Scotland

Sara
Denmark

Karoli
Norwa

Georgina
England

Brianna
USA

Cristina
Spain

Marta
Italy

Kati
Bulga

Camille
France

Lilia
Mexico

Merida
Cuba

Katasi
Uganda

Louise
Uganda

Manuela
Colombia

Natalie
Brazil

Rachel
South Africa

Sofia
Argentina

Ilke
South Africa